Economic Growth, Biodiversity Conservation, and the Formation of Human Capital in a Developing Country

Göttinger Studien zur Entwicklungsökonomik
Göttingen Studies in Development Economics
Herausgegeben von/Edited by Hermann Sautter

Band 13

PETER LANG
Frankfurt am Main · Berlin · Bern · Bruxelles · New York · Oxford · Wien

Ludger J. Löning

Economic Growth, Biodiversity Conservation, and the Formation of Human Capital in a Developing Country

The Case of Guatemala

PETER LANG
Europäischer Verlag der Wissenschaften

Bibliografische Information Der Deutschen Bibliothek
Die Deutsche Bibliothek verzeichnet diese Publikation in der Deutschen Nationalbibliografie; detaillierte bibliografische Daten sind im Internet über <http://dnb.ddb.de> abrufbar.

Zugl.: Göttingen, Univ., Diss., 2004

Printed with kindly support by the Spinnhütte GmbH
and the Ibero-America-Institut for Economic Research
at the University of Göttingen.

D 7
ISSN 1439-3395
ISBN 3-631-52607-5
US-ISBN 0-8204-7309-X

www.peterlang.de

In Dankbarkeit, für meine Eltern

Contents

Acknowledgments

Writing this thesis has been unusually pleasant. My gratitude for the opportunity to experience the generosity and hospitality of the people of Guatemala and its countryside, during three research visits, is deep but beyond words. That this study could not have been written without the help and support of many people is obvious. Some of them are mentioned in footnotes throughout this text, but some deserve special acknowledgment here.

My thesis advisor, Professor Hermann Sautter, supervised the often seemingly insurmountable task of putting some of my thoughts onto paper. His encouragement, thorough reading of pre-papers and generous flexibility to help me meet the time schedule, were essential for the accomplishment of this study. Equally, I am indebted to Professor Manfred Zeller, especially for the discussion on a previous paper about deforestation. I also would like to thank the German Research Association, which financed this study and the interdisciplinary Research Graduate Program on Biodiversity Conservation at the University of Goettingen. Of my colleagues from the Ibero-America Institute for Economic Research, I am particularly indebted to Isabel Günther, Dierk Herzer, Jahir Lombana and Sebastian Vollmer, but also to Julia Johannsen from the Institute for Rural Development, and Michael Markussen from the Geographical Institute.

Guatemaltecos to whom I am indebted include Miguel von Hoegen for inviting me to the *Instituto de Investigaciones Económicas y Sociales* at Rafael Landívar University, Ingrid Morjan de la Vega and her family for helping me to organize my research visits and to get an insider view of the Central American culture, Jorge Lavarreda from the *Centro de Investigaciones Económicas Nacionales* for his interest and support, Odgen Rodas and the *Plan de Acción Forestal* for discussions and access to their Library, and Silvia Villatoro from *Banco de Guatemala* for her exceptional detective work at finding statistics. Finally, this thesis would not have been possible without Eduardo Somensatto and María Concepción Castro from the World Bank Resident Mission, as well as Juan Alberto Fuentes from the United Nations Development Programme.

I want to thank them all.

Table of Contents

Illustrations

Text Tables

Part One

Part Two

Text Figures

Part One

Text Boxes

Overview and Summary

A former head of the UN peace verification mission (MINUGUA) has qualified the prevailing social imbalances and ethnic divisions in Guatemala as being as ghastly as in the final stages of South Africa's apartheid regime.[1] An overwhelming part of the population in Guatemala is thought to have Mayan origin, most living in poverty and at the margins of modern society. In addition to the enormous social distress, the country has the second lowest level of formal education in the Latin American hemisphere. After a civil war lasting three-decades, the per capita growth performance of Central America's largest economy is mediocre. The economy is still predominantly agricultural, with more than $^1/_2$ of the country's labor force engaged in farming and forestry. Guatemala's richness in biodiverse forest resources was consecutively exploited during the course of its history. Currently, habitat destruction in Central America is higher than elsewhere in the world, and the annual deforestation rate in Guatemala is even higher than, for example, the rate for Brazil. Do these issues have something in common?

For the developing world, Auty (2001) argues that recent research reveals growing evidence that there may be a link between these items. Yet the literature does not allow drawing simple mono-causal explanations. The relationships stressed here are indeed puzzling phenomena. How and to what extend economic growth, human capital endowment, and the exploitation of biodiverse forests — or other natural resources — are linked to each other is not well explored. Similarly, Stedmann-Edwards (1998) finds many contradictions in this regard. However, only by understanding the factors that promote income generation, enhance social development, and drive people to make decisions to conserve their environment allows reasonable policy interventions to be proposed. The aim of this study is to fill *some* of these gaps and reinforce arguments from an empirical point of view. Sad to say, the Guatemalan case offers nearly a textbook example for exploring the chosen questions, in spite of not easily accessible data. Given the small size of the open economy and considering its heavy social contrasts, much appears to be clearer here than in other settings.

It should be made transparent from the beginning that due to the complexity of the issues involved, only *selected* avenues among these relationships can be documented. A focus of the present study lies on the role of human capital, i.e. formal education. Broadly speaking, there are two queries that can serve as a rough guidance throughout the study. First, the underlying question is whether human capital formation has the potential to promote economic growth and, at the same time, can slow down habitat loss. In documenting the correlation between economic growth, schooling and habitat conservation, the aim here is to point out

1 See Merrem (2001).

an interesting policy lever. Clearly, there is a substantial number of additional factors that must be taken into account as well. Second, if schooling proves to be significant, not only does the question arise about which level of education is important, but also of how to increase the access and quality of schooling in the complex setting of a developing country.

More specifically, the study consists of 3 independent parts. These parts follow individual research questions, use particular methodologies and come to distinct results. Although they are loosely connected, they should be read *separately* from another.

Part One investigates the impact of human capital on economic growth through the application of time series analysis and an extended growth accounting exercise. Apart from the elaboration of a data set and the application of an error-correction methodology, the contribution is twofold. First, very little analysis exists that analyzes the role of human capital on growth over a long time period and for an *individual* country. This study here presents such an analysis. Second, surprisingly rare in macro analysis, the study focuses on the contribution of different *levels* of education to growth.

To address the question of the role of education on growth, Part One is organized as follows. The first chapters briefly explore Guatemala's growth patterns over time and discuss the measurement of human capital to growth. After the construction of the relevant data, the following chapters display the results and test for robustness. The final chapter accounts for the sources of growth. The main findings indicate that both primary and secondary education appear to be a key factor for growth. In fact, human capital accumulation appears to explain more than 50 percent of the country's past growth trajectory. Interestingly, the macro evidence on the returns to education here is in line with micro studies. Part One also finds that the civil war and a resulting negative investment climate heavily affected the economy, and that complementary factors to human capital policies play a great role.

Part Two reveals that rural underdevelopment and low educational endowment are correlated with Guatemala's past agricultural growth polices. These policies, in turn, not only have hampered human capital accumulation and constrain long-term growth prospects, they also constitute a major origin for the causal structure of today's deforestation processes. To summarize a bit, Part Two is a general inquiry into the causes of deforestation and emphasizes the role of education. Given the *scant evidence* on the correlation between schooling and habitat loss, the detailed documentation and empirical analysis of this kind of relationship is a major innovation of the study. To address these questions, Part Two is divided into three main chapters: a conceptual analysis, a qualitative assessment of deforestation patterns in Guatemala, and an empirical analysis.

The conceptual analysis suggests that, in principle, the effects of schooling on habitat loss can be ambiguous. However, the empirical analysis reveals a more straightforward outcome. The empirics are based on three distinct analyses, compromising regional data, national household data and rather unique survey data from Guatemala's main agricultural frontier region: the Petén. Given its diversity in terms of endemic species, the analysis of this region allows a clearer look at the relationships between schooling, biodiversity loss, and other factors. The overall findings suggest that deforestation in Guatemala appears to be profitable and generally does *not* seem to follow subsistence-driven patterns. This questions a great deal of the current conservation policies. By contrast, basic primary schooling and, as a consequence, the higher probability of working in the non-farm sector have a strong potential to reduce habitat loss. However, many other factors are equally important. In particular, the effect of schooling and certain types of non-farm employment may be increased via the investment in complementary measures, such as infrastructure facilities in terms of sanitation and electricity.

Part Three is finally concerned with the question of how a developing country can increase the access to and the quality of rural education. By contracting directly with local communities, and learning from successful experiences in other countries, Guatemala has recently employed a unique model of educational decentralization. This part is divided into three main chapters and builds on the previous analysis whose findings suggest that primary education is of particular concern.

The first chapter shows that after the transition to democratic rule and the formal ending of the civil war, somewhat surprisingly, Guatemala has made progress in expanding rural primary education. Although a lot remains to be done, the country offers an interesting case showing that it is possible to draw on small innovations. The second chapter explains the institutional structure of the program. Based on results from evaluation studies and a rough empirical analysis on school survey data, the final chapter assesses the impact of the community-managed schools. Overall, the program has been remarkably successful in expanding educational opportunities and may have generated positive externalities at the local level. However, the available data also shows that the quality of the program remains a concern and that community-managed schools are not the panacea to improve access and quality of schooling. Other issues, apparently beyond the scope of the school organization form, also play a great role, such as school infrastructure, availability of books and bilingual teacher training.

Before proceeding, a few comments are needed on the scope and limitations of this study. First, it does not address the issue of all the potentially conflicting and complex interactions between economic growth, poverty reduction, and the conservation of biodiverse forest resource. There is clearly a considerable amount of tradeoffs that should be considered in *future research*. For example, somewhat simplistically, it may be reasonable to argue that over the long run, poverty declines with rising per capita incomes. If deforestation declines with rising income, it would follow that overall economic growth, particular in the rural areas, would act to reduce forest clearance and perhaps reduce rural resource degradation generally. However, rising per capita income may also generate a higher demand for agricultural products, provide resources for capital intensive projects in rural areas and allow subsidies for agriculture. These issues are *not* analyzed here.

Second, concentrating on the contribution of human capital to economic outcomes does not imply that other factors are less relevant and that schooling constitutes a remedy for solving all the oppressing problems of the country. In fact, the study explicitly attempts to analyze some of the fundamental determinants of growth and habitat conservation by placing emphasis on complementary issues.

Finally, it should be stressed that Guatemala constitutes a most challenging case for research. Throughout its history, as evidenced by UNDP (2002), there has been an impressive 'culture' of ignorance regarding the quality of scientific research as well as the collection of statistical data. In this vein, a considerable amount of the information for this study has been collected from disperse sources. In addition, some of the information comes from interviews, consultant's reports as well as the participation in workshops, conferences and field visits in various occasions during 2001-2003. Despite of a great deal of direct local assistance, helpful discussions on two earlier working papers, and the opportunity to learn from distinguished people, the author requests the reader to remain aware of potential uncertainties in a case study like this.

Part One
Human Capital, Productivity and Economic Growth in Guatemala: A Time Series and Extended Growth Accounting Analysis

The following study addresses the question of Guatemala's long-run determinants of growth. As documented by Easterly (2001) and others, economic growth can be viewed as a very powerful ingredient for expanding opportunities for poor people. Growth depends on innumerable factors, including the accumulation of human capital. By contrast, as documented by UNDP (2000) and others, Guatemala's history is marred by the exclusion of an overwhelming part of its people from polices that promote human capital accumulation and allow for income generation outside agriculture. Per capita growth in Guatemala was only 1.3 percent over the past five decades. Under these circumstances, it is no wonder that, among various antecedents, the low performance of the economy in the context of an appalling inequality in the distribution of wealth, is widely regarded as the principal cause for the outbreak of the three-decade lasting civil war.

The signing of the Peace Accord in 1996 finally ended a conflict, which was very destructive to social and economic development. To remedy this situation, the *Acuerdos de Paz* (1998) outlined a broad socio-economic development agenda that contains many quantitative targets. One target is to achieve 6 percent real economic growth. Other targets of the agenda are predicated on the assumption that the country indeed attains such high growth rates. In this vein, it is important to find out about the quantitative role of human capital and other factors aiming to promote growth.

> *"El crecimiento económico acelerado del país es necesario para la generación de empleos y su desarrollo social. El desarrollo social del país es, a su vez, indispensable para su crecimiento económico y una mejor inserción en la economía mundial. Al respecto, la elevación del nivel de vida, la salud de sus habitantes y la educación y capacitación constituyen las premisas para acceder al desarrollo sustentable en Guatemala."*
>
> Peace Accords, 1996

I. Introduction

This study examines the contribution of human capital to economic growth in Guatemala over the past 50 years.[2] The interest is twofold. First, for the country itself there are very few studies that thoroughly analyze past growth patterns, and there are no studies that empirically appraise the direct impact of education on growth. In general, evidence on human capital and growth comes almost entirely from cross-country analysis. Single-country studies, however, may be more illuminating since they overcome the heterogeneity problem and take into account the unique historical information for each country. Indeed, the original motivation of studying economic growth focuses on the time-series dynamics of macroeconomic variables. Moreover, the cross-section focus may be inadequate if returns to education or the quality of education differ substantially across countries.

Second, this study focuses on the contribution of different levels of education to growth. This is an important aspect regarding the problems associated with measuring *average* years of schooling. Looking at education in a disaggregated way also proves more fruitful to the policy-maker since it indicates how resources should be divided between different education levels. Finally, the empirical analysis is based on an error-correction methodology, deals with endogeneity, and explores several data construction and robustness issues. All this may be relevant for future case studies as well.

This study, probably for the first time, constructs a reliable data set that accounts for the determinants of long-run growth in Guatemala. In terms of data

---

2 I especially want to thank Silvia Villatoro (*Banco de Guatemala*) for her assistance in compiling part of the data. I have benefited from interviews and discussions with Christian Dreger (Halle Institute for Economic Research), Felipe Jaramillo and Andy Mason (World Bank), Stephan Klasen, Dierk Herzer, Michael Grimm and Julian Weisbrod (University of Goettingen), as well as Paul Schreyer (OECD) and Oda Schmalwasser (German Federal Statistical Office). Eduardo Somensatto and María Concepción Castro (World Bank), Armando Morales (IMF), Estuardo Morán (*Banco de Guatemala*) as well as Pamela Escobar and Juan Alberto Fuentes (UNDP) equally deserve many thanks.

availability, the country constitutes a most precarious case. Despite these caveats, however, satisfactory and coherent time series data were obtained. The results based on a production function augmented for human capital reveal that a better-educated labor force has a significant positive impact on long-run growth. Consistent with cross-country evidence, primary and secondary education appear to be most important for productivity growth, followed by tertiary schooling. These findings are in agreement with the micro evidence for Guatemala. Interestingly, the results also suggest that the effect of education in both micro and macro regressions is of similar magnitude.

This holds while changing the conditioning set of the variables, for example by considering trade openness. An interesting result is that *primary* schooling seems to be particularly affected by policies that promote competitiveness. This does *not* suggest, however, that other schooling levels are unimportant. Rather it seems that in Guatemala, during the past decades, a sufficient coverage *and* quality of primary education were the minimum requirement to adopt foreign technologies. Overall, the econometric results have been found robust, even after controlling for endogeneity as well as for alternative data sources.

Finally, a modified growth-accounting framework is presented which takes into account quality changes of physical capital and differentiates by the level of education. It shows that the human capital variables explain more than 50 percent of output growth. Of these, secondary schooling was the main determinant of growth. Due to an environment of social and political conflict, however, productivity growth was slightly negative over the past decades. In addition, given the increase of average education and a decay of the quality-adjusted physical capital at the same time, there is evidence of a missing complementarity between the country's skills and its technology base. Ultimately, the empirical findings point towards the importance of an institutional and political environment conducive to growth.

This study is organized into eight chapters. The following chapter briefly assesses patterns of growth and some of the reasons that led to a low endowment of human capital. Chapter 3 discusses how to measure the contribution of human capital to growth over time. Furthermore, it provides an overview of relevant empirical findings. Chapter 4 is concerned with data compilation. Chapter 5 introduces the empirical methodology and presents the main results, disaggregated by education level. Chapter 6 tests the robustness of the results. The regressions include several variables that help to explain the country's growth performance, for example measures for the quality of capital, trade, and military expenditures. Finally, based on the empirical estimates, chapter 7 accounts for the sources of growth. Chapter 8 concludes.

II. Patterns of Growth in Guatemala

To understand Guatemala's growth patterns, and hence the role of education, its turbulent political and social history must be taken into account. Average annual growth rates were about 3.9 percent between 1951 and 2002. According to Bailén (2001) this is in line with the neighbor countries.[3] Due to rapid population growth, however, *per capita* growth in Guatemala has averaged only about 1.3 percent per year. A continuation of this growth rate implies that the average Guatemalan would need approximately 53 years to double his real income.

Box 1. Guatemala: Growth with Low Productivity and Poor Social Development

Relatively few studies focus on Guatemala's growth experience over a long time period. One of the most comprehensive assessments is a voluminous study by Gómez and Ordoñez (1991). They focus on structural adjustment issues for the early 1990s, but their conclusions are still of interest. In particular, they claim that productivity in Guatemala was low because of manifold structural problems, including a deficient financial intermediation system and 'resistance' to technological change. That is, Guatemala's international competitiveness was traditionally based on a low-skilled labor force with consequently poor social development and little incentives for firms to increase productivity. In addition, a culture of rent-seeking among entrepreneurs as well as public institutional and financial weakness prevented significant change.

Historically, growth was not particularly pro-poor, i.e. favoring the rural or agricultural economy where the poor live. The elite domination and ethnic division failed to promote social and institutional development. Instead, growth in Guatemala's was accompanied by the exclusion of large parts of the society from wealth, and, as a consequence, accompanied by underlying social conflict. Poverty rates and inequality indicators are among the highest in the Latin American region. According to the World Bank (2003a) about 56 percent of Guatemala's population live in poverty in 2000.

Guatemala's recent growth experience can be divided into three broad episodes. Figure 1 visualizes annual GDP growth from 1951-2003, where selected

3 For example, growth has been lower than in Costa Rica (4.7 percent) but higher than in Honduras (3.7 percent), El Salvador (3.2 percent) and Nicaragua (2.1 percent).

parallel historical events are given from Luján (2000).[4] Table 1 presents the average output growth rates of primary, industry and service sectors for the period 1951-2003. In addition, there are three sub-periods. The growth rates of the primary sectors in Guatemala, which employ the majority of the rural and poor people, lagged behind other sectors for the *entire* time period. By contrast, in particular for the last decades, the growing sectors where those of electricity, communications and banking. Until approximately 1975, Guatemala appears to have had a reasonable growth performance, followed by a remarkable slowdown for the later periods. However, this requires closer examination.

Figure 1. Guatemala: Economic Growth, Social Conflict and Politics, 1951-2003 (growth rates in percent)

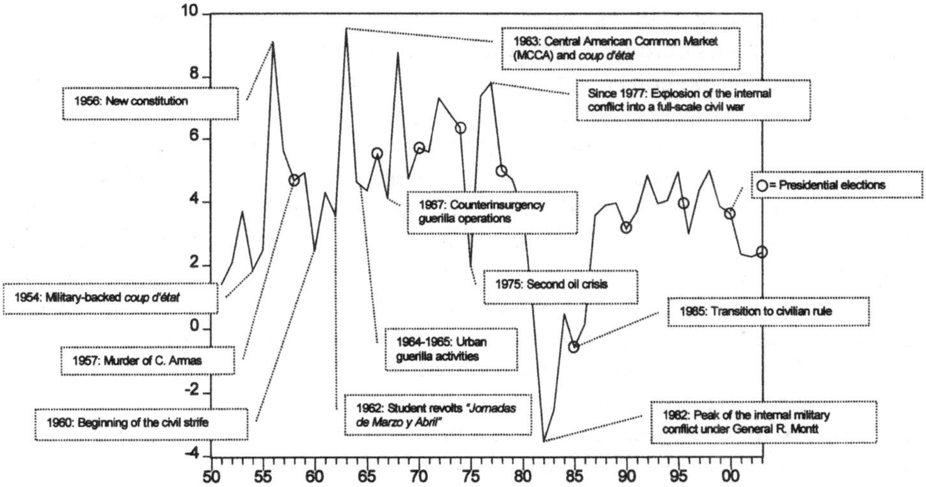

Source: Author's elaboration based on data from Banco de Guatemala. Data for 2002 (2003) is preliminary (estimated). Historical events are taken from Luján (2000).

La 'edad de oro', 1951-1975. During the first period Guatemala maintained reasonable growth rates. Ever since the 1954 coup, military governments were repeatedly in power, sometimes through fraudulent elections, sometimes by *coup d'états*. In terms of its growth performance, this era is sometimes referred to as the 'golden period' but the denomination is *very* misleading. This is because the

4 The correlations do not necessarily imply causality. Moreover, in many Latin American countries growth rates during the decades of the 1950s and 1960s were quite volatile as well.

structural imbalances of the economy remained unchanged and ultimately gave rise to the explosion of civil strife. Annual growth was highly volatile — a fact most likely associated with the dependence on agricultural export growth as well as political events. For example, in 1956 a new constitution was drawn up and in 1963 Guatemala was preparing to enter into the Central American Common Market (MCCA).[5] At first sight, Figure 1 suggests that the civil war's guerilla activities — starting around 1960 — appeared to have an impact only on short-run growth. However, the later growth accounting exercise suggests that, indeed, the trend growth of total factor productivity (TFP) was negatively affected by the civil strife from the beginning.

Box 2. Social Conflict and Guatemala's Growth Collapse

A key study for understanding the Guatemalan growth collapse after 1975 is Rodrik (1999). His core idea is that the effect of the external shocks on growth are increased within the context of 'social conflict' and weak institutions for 'conflict management.' The term social conflict refers to the depth of social inequality and ethic fragmentation. Conflict management refers to democratic institutions, an effective judiciary and a non-corrupt bureaucracy. All of these adjudicate distributional competition within a framework of rules and accepted procedures. However, as in the case of Guatemala, the economic costs of shocks can be magnified by the associated distributional conflicts. These are triggered because social divisions run deep and governmental as well as democratic institutions are weak. Consequently, the productivity of resource utilization can be diminished in a number of ways. For example, by delaying adjustments in fiscal policies and key relative prices, including the real exchange rate and real wages. In addition, these adjustments may generate uncertainty in the economic environment and paralyze the economy for years. Cross-country econometric evidence supports this hypothesis. Rodrik finds that countries experiencing the sharpest drops after 1975 were those with divided societies and weak institutions. This seems indeed to be the case for Guatemala, and is an important finding not only in retrospect but also for the future.

External shocks and the civil war, 1975-1985. A second period starts shortly after the deterioration of the terms of trade and the international oil crisis. In 1976 a major earthquake affected Guatemala. After 1977, social tension culminated in a full-scale civil war that reached genocidal proportions in the early 1980s.

5 An excellent review of the rise and fall of the Central American integration process for 1950-1999 can be found in de La Ossa (2000).

Consequently, growth declined dramatically. Apart from causing immense human sorrow, these events destroyed human life and physical capital. They also imposed high costs for long-run growth.

Recuperation and stagnation, 1985-2002. A third episode of growth begins approximately in 1985 when democracy was restored, albeit with civilian governments patronized by the generals. Although growth rates recovered, they have ever since followed a more or less stagnant pattern. A cornerstone in economic and social development in history was the signing of the Agreement of a 'Firm and Lasting Peace' in December 1996, the formal end to the civil war. Since the signing of the UN-sponsored Peace Accords, Guatemala has made progress by increasing investments in infrastructure and human capital. It has also made some efforts to improve public financial management, and in the area of tax revenues. However, UNDP (2003a) finds that the implementation of the Peace Accords has been uneven. Moreover, in particular during the past decades, Guatemala seems to be affected by electoral cycles. This issue has been investigated by López-Cálix (2002) who indeed finds weak empirical evidence supporting this hypothesis.

Table 1. Guatemala: Sectoral Output Growth, 1951-2003 (in percent) [a/]

Sector	1951-03	1951-75	1976-85	1986-03
Primary	*3.2*	*4.2*	*1.6*	*2.7*
Agriculture, forestry, livestock and fishing	3.1	4.2	1.5	2.6
Mining and quarrying	8.1	3.3	16.9	9.5
Industry	*4.3*	*5.6*	*2.8*	*3.2*
Manufacturing	4.0	5.9	2.4	2.2
Construction	4.0	3.9	5.4	3.9
Gas, electricity and water	8.4	9.7	6.0	8.2
Services	*4.2*	*5.0*	*2.5*	*3.9*
Wholesale and trade	3.8	5.0	1.3	3.3
Transport, storage and communications	6.2	7.5	3.4	5.9
Banking	6.9	8.3	6.1	5.3
Public administration and defense	4.6	4.5	5.6	4.5
Other services	3.4	4.2	2.4	2.9
Total GDP growth	*3.9*	*4.9*	*2.3*	*3.5*

Source: Author's calculations based on data from *Banco de Guatemala.*

a/ Information for 2002 (2003) is preliminary (estimated).

Finally, GDP growth has declined continually since 1999. The processes behind this decline are not exactly understood. It is uncertain whether this represents a decrease in Guatemala's trend growth or a prolonged cyclical downturn. However, it is not unreasonable to argue that this decline is partly associated with high levels of violence, kidnappings (including the central bank governor) and social unrest. In addition, Guatemala scores poorly on most governance indicators, particularly those for corruption, the rule of law and the justice system, and political stability. The culmination of these factors ultimately seems to damage the climate for growth and investment.[6]

Somewhat paradoxical, over the past decades, Guatemala has experienced relative macroeconomic stability. Guatemala has a rather low level of external indebtedness, inflation has been held back, and after a process of (uncompleted) structural reforms the economy is now fairly open and with low levels of protection. Thus, contrary to other Latin American countries, macroeconomic mismanagement may presumably not be regarded as the main factor to understand Guatemala's modest performance in terms of per capita growth. Rather, other issues undermine Guatemala's long-run growth patterns.[7] In addition to the factors already mentioned, one is low human capital endowment.

The current human capital base is essentially a product of past agricultural growth and eminently anti-distributional policies. The World Bank (2003a) and UNDP (2002) document that insufficient cheap labor, in particular for coffee, was the main barrier for the expansion of export crops during earlier periods. Hence, in order to create a low-wage labor force, the campesino and indigenous society was excluded from education. The plantation economy that resulted provided little incentives to accumulate human capital. Historically, the low level of schooling is also an outcome of a discriminatory education system. For the attentive observer, these issues are still felt today.

---

6 Hypotheses for the recent growth slowdown can be found in World Bank (2003b). These include restrictive macroeconomic policies, unfavorable external developments, the ending of the economic model relying on traditional agro-exports, and several political factors. As of June 2000, Guatemala is listed as non-cooperative country in the OECD-backed 'Financial Action Task Force on Money Laundering.' Equally, fearing high levels of corruption and fraud, for example, the German Chamber of Commerce does not recommend investment in Guatemala.

7 During a very brief episode in the early 1990s, inflation increased and fiscal discipline eroded. More recently, the World Bank (2003b) presents arguments suggesting that short-run growth *may* be related to the cyclical stance of fiscal and monetary policies.

Table 2. Guatemala, Central and Latin America: Comparison of Human Capital Indicators, 1998-2002

Indicator	Guatemala	Nicaragua	Honduras	El Salvador	Costa Rica	Mexico	Latin America
Public spending on education (in percent of GDP) (average 1998-2000) c/ d/	1.7	5.0	4.0	2.3	5.7	4.4	N.D.
Average years of schooling (2000) b/	4.8	6.3	5.3	5.1	6.7	7.9	7.3
Net primary school enrollment (in percent) (2000-2001) c/	84	81	88	81	91	103	97
Net secondary school enrollment (in percent) (2000-2001) c/	26	36	N.D.	39	49	60	64
Adult illiteracy (in percent of total population) (2002) a/	30.1	32.9	23.8	20.3	4.2	8.3	10.5
Infant mortality (per 1000 births) (2001) a/	43	36	31	33	9	24	28
Life expectancy at birth (years) (2002) a/	65.5	68.7	66.1	70.1	77.6	73.6	70.7

Source: a/ World Bank (2003c). b/ Cohen and Soto (2001). c/ UNDP (2003b). d/ Notice that Guatemala's public spending in education has increased recently. UNDP (2003a) reports a figure of 2.6 percent in 2002. N.D. = no data available.

Table 2 shows that the country still performs poorly for indicators of education and health, and ranks highest among states in the region for child malnutrition, despite some improvements over time.[8] In addition, Guatemala spends less on education than any other country in the region. Based on household survey data comparing the education level of age cohorts, the Inter-American Development

8 Anderson (2001) provides a brief synopsis of recent developments in the education sector. The recent improvement of the education sector will be focussed in the 3rd part of this study.

Bank (2001) finds that the educational gap between Guatemala and other Latin American countries is widening.

Historically, it may be that a certain degree of development and growth in Guatemala was attainable with a skilled elite and a large amount of unskilled workers. Since the economy has diversified over time and is now less dependent on agriculture than before (Segovia and Lardé 2002), the past exclusionary education policies may present an obstacle for future growth. On the micro level, there is evidence suggesting that insufficient human capital constitutes a constraint for production. For example, a firm survey by *Grupo de Servicios de Información* (1999) indicates that for all firms the quality of skills ranks as the second most important constraint. For small firms, important for employment and income generation, the quality of skills is the main production constraint.

III. Measuring the Contribution of Education to Growth

The accumulation of human capital through education has long been acknowledged to be an important factor in the development process of a nation. Education is thought to be beneficial because it decreases inequality, improves the quality of life, and in particular it is a factor in rising the income level and facilitating economic growth. This chapter will concentrate on the latter effect and summarize some evidence on the relationship between education and growth.

A. Augmented Solow Model and Endogenous Growth

The existing literature contains a number of distinct conceptual rationales for the inclusion of human capital in models of economic growth. According to Sianesi and van Reenen (2003), the two main macro approaches are the augmented Solow model and the new growth theories.

1. Augmented Solow Model

One way to estimate the impact of education on growth is to adapt the Solow (1956) model. The augmented version extends the basic framework to allow human capital as an extra input to enter the production function. In particular Mankiw et al. (1992) show that traditional growth theory can accommodate human capital and provide a reasonable approximation for empirical analysis. At the economy-wide level, it may also take into account human capital externalities. Still, one of the key insights is that the factor accumulation affects the *level* of income, but per se is insufficient to achieve long-run *growth*. Long-run growth depends rather on growth in technological progress. Human capital accumulation may therefore have only a short-term impact on the rate of growth.

However, rates of accumulation are expected to have explanatory power for growth rates during the transition to an eventual equilibrium growth path. In particular, considering the case of Guatemala — presumably far away from a balanced growth process — consideration of transition could open up the possibility of assessing the macroeconomic role of education for economic growth within this framework. In addition, since the 'short run' in the context of growth theory is often thought of in terms of decades, these effects can be worthwhile policy objectives. Up to now, for the reasons clarified below, this approach has remained the workhorse of applied empirical research. The model is fairly flexible and allows for alternative specifications that can be adjusted to best match the available data.

2. Endogenous Growth Approach

Expanding these ideas, new growth theories emphasize the endogenous determination of technological progress, which is determined within the model.

Thus, long-run growth can be affected by government policies instead of being driven by exogenous technological change. With respect to human capital, the endogenous growth approach argues that there should be an *additional* effect over and above the static effect on the level of output. Models that explain long-run growth by focussing on technological progress and research and development, such as Romer (1990a) and Grossman and Helpman (1991), argue that domestic technological progress results from the search for innovations. The discovery of an innovation, undertaken by profit-maximizing individuals, raises productivity and is ultimately the source of long-run growth. This kind of model attributes growth to the existing *stock* of human capital. A second category is the model of Lucas (1988). It broadens the concept of capital and suggests that human capital *accumulation* may be an engine of growth itself, due to spillover effects that negate diminishing returns in production.

In particular, with respect to developing countries, one way of characterizing the role of human capital is the consideration of technology transfer from innovating countries. Already Nelson and Phelps (1966) suggested that education facilitates the adoption and implementation of new technologies, which are continuously invented. For example, countries with lagging technological capacity may be most able to catch-up if they have a large stock of human capital. In this case, the level of human capital effects growth by facilitating improvements in productivity. Also Lucas (1990) conjectures that physical capital does not flow from rich to poor countries because of a relatively low stock of complementary human capital.

In a rather influential study, Benhabib and Spiegel (1994) propose an empirical growth model in which human capital externalities can be considered in subsequent advances in education and in new physical capital via technology import. Their results indeed suggest that human capital impacts growth through two mechanisms. On the one side, human capital seems to influence the rate of domestically produced innovation, as proposed in the endogenous growth model of Romer (1990a). On the other side, in the spirit of Nelson and Phelps (1966), they claim that the human capital stock effects the speed of adoption of technology from abroad. More recently, in a generalized version of their model of technology diffusion — that allows for a nonlinear specification of total factor productivity growth — Benhabib and Spiegel (2003) find that a minimum initial human capital level is necessary to exhibit catch-up in productivity relative to the leader nation.

However, Pritchett (2001) agues convincingly that the finding of *only* a level effect on growth is rather puzzling. First, in the framework of endogenous growth, spillover effects of knowledge should be *in addition* to rather *instead* of the production effects of human capital. In other words, finding only spillover effects may be inconsistent with the micro evidence on the returns to education. Second, as will be stressed in more detail in the next section, Jones (1995) criticism of endogenous growth models applies here. That is, growth rates cannot be made a function of non-stationary parameters unless cointegration between the variables is accepted.

B. Some Implications for Empirical Testing

Distinguishing between the role of education as a factor of production, and as a factor that facilitates technology absorption and the production of knowledge, is significant. Any policy measure which raises the level of human capital may only have a one-and-for-all effect in the first framework, but will increase the growth rate of the economy for ever in the second one. In such cases, the estimated increase in productivity is not simply a phenomenon in the transitional period since an increase in the flow of education leads to a gradual increase in human capital stock. Implicit is the claim that by increasing the level of education the rate of economic growth will increase over time. Empirically, however, there is no consensus over which is the appropriate approach.

1. Observational Equivalence

A main problem for empirical testing at the macro level emerges from observational equivalence. This means that, despite a number of different ways of hypothesizing how human capital can affect growth, empirical analysis can yield similar predictions regarding the relationship between some human capital variables and some variables of income growth. In other words, apart from data uncertainty, the empirical research seeking to test these alternatives has been hampered by the use of relatively similar econometric specifications. Insofar, macro regressions do not readily allow testing one theory against another. Rather they tend to emphasize an expanded set of variables as suggested by the literature. Consequently, Romer (1990b) argues that the role of an endogenous growth framework is not to generate testable predictions, but rather to guide the process of data analysis.

2. The Jones Critique

A second criticism, especially relevant for the present study, is the seminal contribution of Jones (1995). Testing endogenous growth models in the context of time series implies establishing a relationship between a variable that is usually stationary — without drift — such as income growth, and a variable which is usually non-stationary, such as years of schooling. In other words, his results fundamentally call into question the implicit prediction of many endogenous growth models suggesting output growth should exhibit large permanent increases.

Time series data over a very long time period for the United States and other OECD countries reveal that the growth rates of GDP per capita in these countries exhibit little persistent changes, and can be characterized by more or less constant mean.

This observation imposes a testable prediction. According to endogenous growth models permanent changes in certain policy variables, such as schooling, or the number of scientists and engineers engaged in research and development, should have *permanent* effects on the rate of economic growth. Empirically, however, neither in the United States nor in other OECD countries does economic growth seem to exhibit such an effect. Incidentally, albeit for different reasons than in the OECD countries, these stationarity properties seem to be equally true for schooling and income growth in the Guatemalan data, as demonstrated in the Augmented Dickey-Fuller (ADF) tests in Appendix One.

C. More Evidence on Education and Growth

Empirical studies usually take the form of regression analysis and typically look at many more explanatory variables than human capital. A large number of papers have found one or more variables that correlate with growth. In fact, their number is very large and the question arises which combinations of these variables are actually robust. In the context of the present study, some of these findings will be outlined next.

1. Weak Correlations

While there is strong theoretical support for a key role of human capital in growth, Sala-i-Martin (2002), Easterly (2001) and in particularly Pritchett (2001) argue that the empirical relationship between education and growth is weak.[9] However, more specifically, Temple (2001) points out that fragile correlations in cross-country data may be due to measurement error and influential exceptions. Also, some kinds of relationships are more robust that others. For example, what is less clear and weak is the relationship of educational *growth rates* on output growth, the role of different education levels, and differences in effects of female and male education on growth. By contrast, some measures of health seem to be positively correlated with growth. In addition to human capital, many other factors have been found to be important for growth. Following Barro (2001), these include

9 Pritchett (2001) uses measures of the *growth* rate of human capital and finds a *negative* impact on output growth. Easterly (2001) argues that human capital accumulation is not a panacea. He emphasizes indirect ways that explain technological progress and factor accumulation by looking at the features of economies that facilitate them, such as government policies and structural issues.

institutions, such as free markets, secure property rights and the rule of law. Similarly, more open economies and countries with lower initial inequality appear to experience higher growth.

2. Conditional Convergence

One much debated prediction of neoclassical growth models is that of convergence. Poor countries should grow relatively faster than rich countries if countries are similar with respect to their structural parameters for preferences and technology. The cross-country studies by Mankiw et al. (1992), Barro and Sala-i-Martin (1995) and Barro (2001) find some evidence of convergence, albeit in a modified form. More specifically, among other things, convergence is found conditional upon a country's initial human capital stock. Therefore, a poor country on average may grow faster, but only if the poor country's human capital stock is above the amount initially expected at the level of per capita income.

3. Reverse Causality

Most of the evidence of some sort of relationship between education and growth is based on statistical *correlations*. From these correlations, it has been generally inferred that higher levels of education cause higher growth. One critique of these findings comes from Bils and Klenow (2000) who suggest reverse causation. Based on a calibrated micro-foundation model, they claim that faster growth induces people to stay longer in school. In other words, the channel from schooling to growth that is assumed to dominate in many models cannot explain all the observed correlation between education and growth. However, the reverse channel provides some explanation. Therefore, in an econometric framework, schooling should be treated as an endogenous input with respect to income. This implies making use of econometric methods for dealing with this problem.

4. Few Individual Case Studies

Recent research has mainly relied on cross-country regression analysis. However, the original motivation of studying economic growth focuses on the time-series dynamics of macroeconomic variables. In addition, the cross-section focus may be inadequate if rates of return to education or the quality of education differ substantially across countries. Unfortunately, with respect to human capital, there are very few studies that analyze a single country over a certain time period.

The exception is a study from Jenkins (1995) using time series data from 1971-1992 for the United Kingdom. Still, the limited size of her time series sample makes it difficult to draw firm conclusions that can be generalized. Also Pissarides (2000) summarizes single case studies for India, Egypt, Tanzania and Chile. Part of an OECD project, these studies were to provide a more thorough test of the relation between human capital and growth in a single country context. For the case of India, the study less plagued with methodological or data problems, the regressions show a significant contribution of human capital on industrial output growth. The estimate suggests that an increase in the average number of years of schooling by 1 year should raise output by about 30 percent.

5. *Magnitude of the Education Effect*

In the augmented Solow model, the role of education can be inferred from estimates of the regression coefficients. However, with reference to the empirical research reviewed in Sianesi and Van Reenen (2003), there is no agreement on its magnitude. In principle, there would be positive empirical evidence in favor of a macroeconomic productivity effect of education if the elasticity of human capital resembles the share of human capital in factor income. As a measure of reference, one can calculate the share of human capital in labor income from back-of-the-envelope calculations.

For example, Mankiw et al. (1992) consider the minimum wage as the return to labor with no education. Historically, the minimum wage has been between 30 to 50 percent of average wage income in the United States. On this account, it would follow that the return to education equals about 50 to 70 percent in labor income, which is about 70 percent of total factor income. Obviously, the problem with this kind of calculation is that in developing countries the minimum wage is less enforced and less likely applicable.[10] Pritchett (2001) therefore uses an estimation based on the distribution of wages. Either of these calculations suggest that the human capital coefficient should be at least $^1/_3$.

6. *Effects of Education Levels*

Somewhat surprisingly, relatively few studies at the macro level address the question of level-specific education effects. The view that schooling does not have the same impact on economic growth at different education levels is based on the labor economics literature. Psacharopoulos and Patrinos (2002) provide a comprehensive review on the rates of return to education. International evidence suggests that returns vary according to the education level. Lower income countries tend to have higher returns to schooling. If education has economic externalities —

10 In Guatemala, the legal minimum wage currently amounts to approximately 3-5 U.S. dollars per day (UNDP 2003a). While the legal minimum wages are relatively high with respect to average wages, about $^1/_2$ of workers in Guatemala earn less than the legal minimum wage. This is because of weak enforcement and the fact that self-employed workers are not subject to the minimum wage regulation.

such as expanding well-being and the technological possibilities of the economy — the true benefits of education may be better captured by the study of different education levels on economic growth. This is because the computation of rates of returns based on microdata can only measure the effects of education through individual's wages. However, this might not hold in macro analysis.

Within an endogenous growth framework one can also derive a distinct role for each education level. The intuition here is that primary education provides individuals with basic cognitive skills that enhance productivity in the production of final goods, but only post-primary education facilitates the absorption of new technologies, and enables individuals to contribute to the production of knowledge. Empirically, in the framework of the augmented Solow model, treating each education level as a separate input into production can quantify the role of primary, secondary and tertiary schooling. While the standard approach in the literature is to consider an aggregate measure of human capital, there are some exceptions that will be briefly reviewed now.

Barro and Sala-i-Martin (1995) regress the growth rate of GDP per capita for a large sample of countries on initial income and a set of control variables. Four measures of educational attainment are always present. These are average years of male secondary and higher schooling as well as average years of female secondary and higher schooling. The male education variables have a jointly significant impact on growth. The female variables enter sometimes with a negative sign. One possible interpretation, advocated by Barro, is that females are discriminated in the formal labor markets. Another explanation for this rather 'puzzling' finding could be simply due to collinearity of the education variables.[11] Other regressions include average years of female and male primary education. None of these variables are found to be significant. Barro (2001) has continued to investigate the relations between education and growth using the same methodology. An important finding here is that school *quality* is much more important to growth than its *quantity*. Overall, the studies do not make very clear the effect of education levels on growth given the negative contribution of secondary female schooling, and the insignificant result for primary education.

---

11 Klasen (2002) argues that the education variables are generally correlated. Empirically, this makes it difficult to identify individual effects of female and male education. However, the negative effect for female secondary education disappears once regional dummy variables are incorporated into econometric models. This finding may be due to East Asia's large initial gender gaps in the 1960s, and the combination of low economic growth and comparatively lower gender gaps in Latin America.

Another paper that investigates the link between education levels and growth is Petrakis and Stamatakis (2002). In a cross-country regression with a relatively small sample size they consider three groups of countries: advanced, developed and less developed. The empirical results suggest that the link of education and growth varies with respect to a country's level of development. Primary education is more important in less developed countries, while higher education seems dominant in advanced countries. In fact, there is some similarity with Gemmel (1996) who also distinguishes between primary, secondary and tertiary schooling for these three groups of countries. He argues that the effects of human capital on growth are most apparent at the primary and secondary levels in developing countries, but at the tertiary level for OECD countries. Unfortunately, the findings in both studies do not allow one to assess with certainty the role of secondary education. In fact, it sometimes enters with a negative sign.

Finally, based on a framework similar to Benhabib and Spiegel, Papageorgiou (2003) is also concerned to empirically determine the contribution of primary and post-primary education on growth. In a cross-country regression he finds that primary education contributes mainly to the production of final output, whereas post-primary education contributes to the adoption and innovation of technology. When the data is divided into subsamples, the results are less encouraging. However, the implicit claim is that for the poorest countries human capital acts mainly as input into final production and, to a lesser extent, as a facilitator for innovation. The relative contribution of human capital to innovation seems to increase with country wealth. Overall this is an interesting study. Nevertheless, the analysis ignores the Jones (1995) critique, and the conclusions are ultimately derived from a priori assumptions.

D. Summing-Up

Empirical results often do not allow for a clear-cut measurement of the macroeconomic role of education on growth, and theory seems to be much ahead of empirics. Cross-country evidence suggests that the relative importance of education level varies by the degree of a country's development. Results that come close to a priori expectation of the magnitude of human capital on growth seem to share three properties. First, a specification of the underlying regression that is based on a production function. Second, in particular regarding human capital, empirical data of reasonable quality. And finally, a functional form of the regression equation that tends to reduce econometric problems.

Attempts to measure empirically the impact of education on growth can be divided into two broad categories. The augmented Solow model originates the first class, while the second group is inspired by an endogenous growth approach. However, this is rather a conceptual framework for thinking about growth, which can be useful in the analysis of data, but does not generate a set of easily testable equations nor sharp quantitative predictions. In the light of observational equivalence and given the problems associated with testing endogenous growth models in a time series context, the following analysis will be based on a production function augmented for human capital. Nevertheless, some attention will be given to variables that proxy for trade openness and technological innovation, and their joint impact on education.

IV. Data Compilation in a Post-Conflict Country

Guatemala is definitely deficient in easily accessible data. Thus, to identify the macroeconomic impact of education on economic growth, a primary task is to overcome information constraints. It is important to note that a significant fraction of the economic activity in Guatemala can be found in the informal sectors. Since this lack of documentation does not influence all factors equally, there remains a potential bias that cannot always be traced.

However, satisfactory and coherent results can be obtained. A sizable amount of information, although not easily accessible, can be compiled from disperse or bulky individual files. Even for local experts, this is a challenging task. The lack of a consistent compilation of data to allow a serious analysis of growth patterns hampers inter-temporal comparisons and, more generally, research of development patterns for the country. Given these constraints, so far, there is very limited empirical research on virtually any macroeconomic topic in Guatemala.

The following paragraphs describe the data needed for the analysis that follows. These are measures for the human and physical capital stock and the labor force, and quality indices for human and physical capital. Information other than that reported in this chapter is listed in Appendix one. The time series are mainly from *Banco de Guatemala*, and, in the case of educational statistics, from the Ministry of Education and the United Nations Educational, Scientific and Cultural Organization.

A. Human Capital Stock

The human capital stock of Guatemala is defined by average years of schooling evident in the labor force.[12] In line with most empirical analyses, this study assumes that years of schooling provides a reasonable approximation of the human capital stock, although it should be briefly stressed that the indicator is incomplete for several reasons.

(1) Education as proxy variable. Human capital is multifaceted and includes a complex set of human attributes. As a consequence, the genuine level of human capital is hard to measure in quantitative form. At best, average years of schooling can be regarded as a proxy for the component of the human capital stock obtained in schools. Therefore, in a later robustness test, life expectancy at birth will be

12 The use of labor force instead of total population data is due to problems regarding the Guatemalan population data for the 1980s. By contrast, the labor force proxy used here is assumed to take into account some of the effects of the civil war, i.e. migration and displacement.

included in the regressions. Life expectancy is commonly viewed as a companion indicator to educational capital that captures the effect of health.

(2) Quality changes. Average years of schooling measurements do not take into account quality changes within the education system. Quality changes may complicate comparison of schooling effects on growth over time as well as making comparisons with other countries difficult. CIEN (2002) and the World Bank (1995c) argue that the quality of the education system in Guatemala is rather low. Unfortunately, in terms of data availability, it proves impossible to include quality changes of education in this study.

(3) Aggregation bias. Average years of schooling raise human capital by an equal amount regardless of whether a person is enrolled in a primary, secondary or tertiary school. This is an important point because by defining human capital by average years of schooling, one implicitly gives the same weight to any year of schooling acquired by a person. This completely disregards the findings of the microeconomic literature on wage differentials. For example, Psacharopoulos and Patrinos (2002) suggests that the rates of return to education could be decreasing with the acquisition of additional schooling. Therefore, in order to capture the impact of education on growth better, a more complete picture will be presented by analyzing the role of primary, secondary and tertiary schooling.

After making some modifications to account for the statistical circumstances in Guatemala, the following procedure for constructing estimates of the human capital stock is used, based on the attainment census method advocated by Barro and Lee (2001). The use of a perpetual inventory method that employs census and survey information on educational attainment as benchmark figure can be seen as a major advantage over previous methodologies. The benchmarks are taken from various national censuses and surveys, see Table 3. Guatemalan statistics report distributional attainment stratified by age and sex in five cases: no formal education, first cycle of primary, second cycle of primary, first cycle of secondary, second cycle of primary and tertiary education. The data has been summarized into 4 broad categories, that is, no school, some primary, some secondary and some tertiary education.

The procedure starts to construct current flows of adult population, which are added to the initial benchmark stocks of the labor force (taken for 1950 from the Barro and Lee 2001 data set). The formulas for the three levels of schooling for the labor force aged 15 and over are as follows:

$$(1) \qquad HN_{0,t} = HN_{0,t-1} \cdot (1 - \delta_t) + L15_t \cdot (1 - PRI_{t-1})$$

(2) $HN_{1,t} = HN_{1,t-1} \cdot (1 - \delta_t) + L15_t \cdot (PRI_{t-1} - SEC_t)$

(3) $HN_{2,t} = HN_{2,t-1} \cdot (1 - \delta_t) + L15_t \cdot SEC_t - L20_t \cdot TER_t$

(4) $HN_{3,t} = HN_{3,t-1} \cdot (1 - \delta_t) + L20_t \cdot TER_t$

where

HN_j = number of the economically active population for whom j is the highest level of schooling attained (j=0 for no school, j=1 for primary, j=2 for secondary and j=3 for higher education)
PRI = enrollment ratio for primary education
SEC = enrollment ratio for secondary education
TER = enrollment ratio for tertiary education
L = number of the economically active population
L15 = number of persons aged 15
L20 = number of persons aged 20
$\delta_{h,t}$ = mortality rate of the human capital stock.

The mortality rate for the economically active population aged 15 and over is estimated from:

(5) $$\delta_{h,t} \approx \frac{L_{t-1} - (L_t - L15_t)}{L_{t-1}}$$

and assumes that the mortality rate is independent of the level of schooling attained, which is not entirely correct. The term L_t–$L15_t$ describes the number of survivals from the previous period, which are subtracted from L_{t-1} in order to estimate the total number of missing persons. Equation (5) as such describes the proportion of the labor force which did not survive from the previous period. The formulas can be rearranged to create the final equations that were used to generate the attainment ratios, hr_j, for the four broad levels of schooling for the economically active population aged 15 and over:

(6) $$hr_{0,t} = \frac{HN_{0,t}}{L_t} = hr_{0,t-1} \cdot \left(1 - \frac{L15_t}{L_t}\right) + \frac{L15_t}{L_t} \cdot (1 - PRI_{t-1})$$

(7) $$hr_{1,t} = \frac{HN_{1,t}}{L_t} = hr_{1,t-1} \cdot \left(1 - \frac{L15_t}{L_t}\right) + \frac{L15_t}{L_t} \cdot (PRI_{t-1} - SEC_t)$$

(8) $$hr_{2,t} = \frac{HN_{2,t}}{L_t} = hr_{2,t-1} \cdot \left(1 - \frac{L15_t}{L_t}\right) + \frac{L15_t}{L_t} \cdot SEC_t - \frac{L20_t}{L_t} \cdot TER_t$$

(9) $$hr_{3,t} = \frac{HN_{3,t}}{L_t} = hr_{3,t-1} \cdot \left(1 - \frac{L15_t}{L_t}\right) + \frac{L20_t}{L_t} \cdot TER_t$$

The procedure requires school enrollment ratios that are crucial for exact calculations, but the proper accounting for Guatemala is not easy. Even though net enrollment ratios would be more precise for estimating the accumulation of human capital, gross enrollment ratios are used, as only this data is available. As reported in Appendix One, the ratios are taken from various yearbooks of the Guatemalan Ministry of Education (MINEDUC) for the 1990s, the United Nations Educational, Scientific and Cultural Organization (UNESCO) for earlier periods, and other sources available for Guatemala. The data for primary, secondary and tertiary enrollment ratios have been found consistent over time. Interpolation techniques were used to fill gaps in the data, but the use of this approach was kept to a minimum. The tertiary enrollment time series were more difficult to compile and required greater use of interpolated estimates.

Table 3. Guatemala: Education Level of Labor Force, 1950-2002 (in percent) [a/]

Year	Source	No school	Some Primary	Some Secondary	Some Tertiary
1950	SEGEPLAN (1978)	72.3	24.9	2.3	0.5
1964	SEGEPLAN (1978)	60.7	33.4	4.7	1.2
1973	SEGEPLAN (1978)	51.7	40.8	6.1	1.4
1981	CENSO (1981)	(37.7)	(48.7)	(10.9)	(2.7)
1989	ENS (1989)	38.9	47.7	11.4	2.1
1994	CENSO (1994)	35.4	47.8	14.1	2.7
1998	ENIGFAM (1998)	(30.8)	(50.3)	15.9	3.1
2000	ENCOVI (2000)	28.9	48.6	16.5	6.0
2002	ENEI 1 (04-05/2002)	26.9	49.3	19.3	4.5
2002	ENEI 2 (08-09/2002)	24.7	50.8	19.3	5.2
2002	ENEI 3 (10-11/2002)	25.0	48.7	21.0	5.3

Source: Compiled from census and survey data, ENCOVI and ENEI figures are from UNDP Guatemala. a/ Brackets indicate uncertain figures. Discrepancies are due to rounding.

In general, the estimated attainment data compares favorably with the census and survey information. The less accurate fit for 1981 is here believed to be due to large measurement errors or the possible manipulation of the census, which took place during the peak of the armed conflict in Guatemala. Consequently, this discrepancy was not smoothed over. Equally, data for 1998 differs slightly from the estimate. This is due to the fact that the survey largely oversamples the urban population of the economy in that year. Given the simplicity of the assumptions of the underlying model, however, the overall results have been found quite satisfactory.

In any case, simply employing gross enrollment ratios would overestimate the accumulation of human capital. Gross enrollment ratios are defined as the ratio of total enrollment in the respective schooling level to the population of the age group that is expected to be enrolled at that level. Thus, gross enrollment ratios can exceed 1 and therefore exaggerate the true amount of enrollment when students repeat, which is often the case in Guatemala.[13] In response to this problem and in order to benchmark the estimated educational attainment data with census and survey information, the gross enrollment ratios have been adjusted by a depreciation factor for the respective education level, as reported in Loening (2002).

Finally, the formula to construct the measure for the human capital stock combines the estimated attainment data with the information on the duration of each schooling level. It is given as:

$$h_t = \sum_{j=1}^{3} hr_{j,t} \cdot d_{j,t} \qquad (10)$$

where h_t stands for the average years of schooling, hr_j is the estimated attainment ratio of the labor force and d_j is the average number of years of education received in the respective schooling level j. Average education values have been calculated from the *Encuesta Nacional Socio-Demográfica* (ENS) from 1989 and are assumed to have remained constant over time. This may result in a slight overestimate of the human capital stock for the period prior to 1989 and underestimate the average years of schooling for later periods. However, data from more recent household surveys suggest that this assumption may not be a large source of error.

How do these calculations compare to other sources? The correlation coefficients between the estimated average years of schooling here and those provided by Cohen and Soto (2002), Barro and Lee (2001), and Nehru et al. (1995), using different techniques and data sources, all exceed 0.95 in the case of Guatemala. Figure 2 compares the results. The time series shown by the solid line harmonizes to a large extent with alternative estimates at different points of time.

13 The use of net enrollment ratios is hampered by large data gaps. Also, net enrollment ratios introduce large measurement errors if there are under- or over-aged children starting at each level of education, see Barro and Lee (2001). In Guatemala students who start late constitute a significant fraction of total enrollment — in particular for primary schooling.

Unlike the Barro and Lee data set, there is no implausible jump for 1980. The Cohen and Soto (2002) estimate provides the closest approximation. Additionally, not shown by Figure 2, the average years of schooling estimates here come close to values obtained from census and survey data. For example, Psacharopoulos and Arriagada (1986) report that mean education in the labor force was in the order of 1.7 for 1964. Edwards (2002) reports a value of 4.3 years for 2000.[14]

Figure 2. Guatemala: Average Years of Schooling in Labor Force, 1950-2002

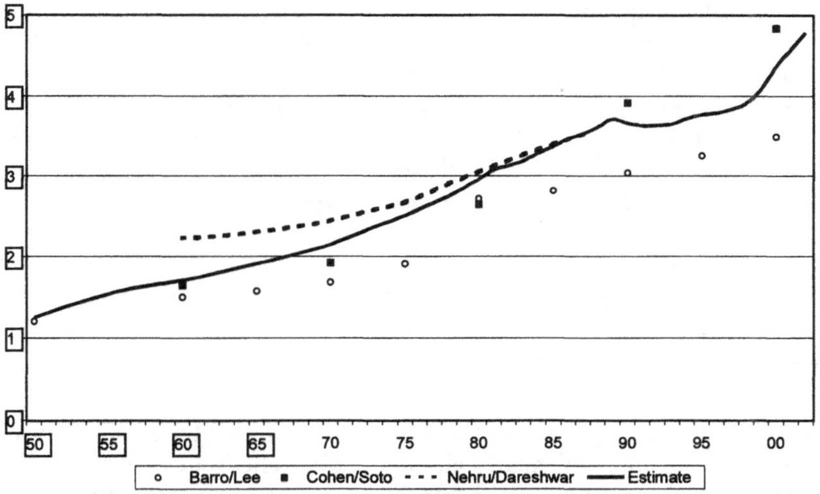

Source: Author's calculations, as well as Barro and Lee (2001), Cohen and Soto (2001), and Nehru et al. (1995) education data.

A closer look at Figure 2 yields two important descriptive outcomes. First, the data suggests that mean education evident in the labor force slightly declined during the early 1990s. This outcome is associated with the disastrous effect of the civil war on the country's human capital base. Those disadvantaged cohorts from the 1980s entered later into the labor force. Second, there has been substantial increase in the average years of schooling within the economically active population since 1998. This can be attributed to improvements within the education system and increased attention to education after the signing of the 1996 Peace Accords.

14 According to the estimate here, average years of schooling was in the order of 1.86 years in 1964 and 4.63 in 2000. See Appendix One.

Even so, as it can be appreciated from Figure 2, this increased attention to education only has compensated for the loss of educational capital caused by civil strife. Consequently, recent educational progress does not represent a major improvement regarding the long-run growth of the country's human capital base. In this context, it is worth recalling that educational attainment in Guatemala remains lowest compared to other Latin American countries.

B. Labor Force

The measure of labor quantity here is the economically active population. For Guatemala there are several estimates. The National Statistic Institute (INE) provides calculations different from those of the Ministry of Work, both of which date back to 1980. Based on census and survey data, estimates for selected years have also been provided by the United Nations Development Programme (UNDP) for Guatemala. The labor force is usually defined as the working and job-seeking population, but the different calculations do not always reveal what underlies the specific assumptions and age definitions used for calculations. To develop a consistent time series of the economically active population, the International Labor Organisation (ILO) has used information on age specific labor force participation rates and population statistics. Unfortunately, for the reasons clarified below, these estimates are unreliable.

(1) Data discrepancies. First, there is no agreement either on the level or on the growth rates of the labor force. Virtually all data is different from each other. For example, UNDP (2003a) reports a total labor force estimate of about 2.84 million for 1989, as compared to 2.54 million from INE or 2.95 million from ILO. Second, as typical for estimates in other countries, labor force data should show some cyclical fluctuations as labor responds to higher output growth. Official estimates for Guatemala, however, are remarkably free of *any* fluctuations and follow a monotonous trend. This suggests reliance on population statistics or use of interpolation techniques.

(2) Omission of the civil strife. Most importantly, these estimates do not take into account migration flows and the consequences of the civil war on the economically active population. Especially the last point devalues official estimates. According to the Commission for Historical Clarification (1999), the internal military conflict left an estimated 200,000 civilians dead and another 1 million displaced, for a total population of about 10 million. Such an immense impact of the civil strife should be reflected somewhere in the statistics □ but it is not.

In the absence of reliable information about the economically active population from these sources, labor is here proxied by the number of private contributors to the Guatemalan Social Security System (IGSS). The reliance on the number of private contributors to the Social Security System in order to account adequately for the economically active population is also adopted in an IMF study for the case of El Salvador by Morales (1998), and for Guatemala by Prera (1999). The numbers representing the labor force are calculated by assuming that the social security contributors account for approximately 25 percent of the total labor force. The participation rate has a negligible impact on the later calculations and is based on a historical mean value.[15]

Figure 3. Guatemala: Labor Force, 1950-2002 (millions of workers)

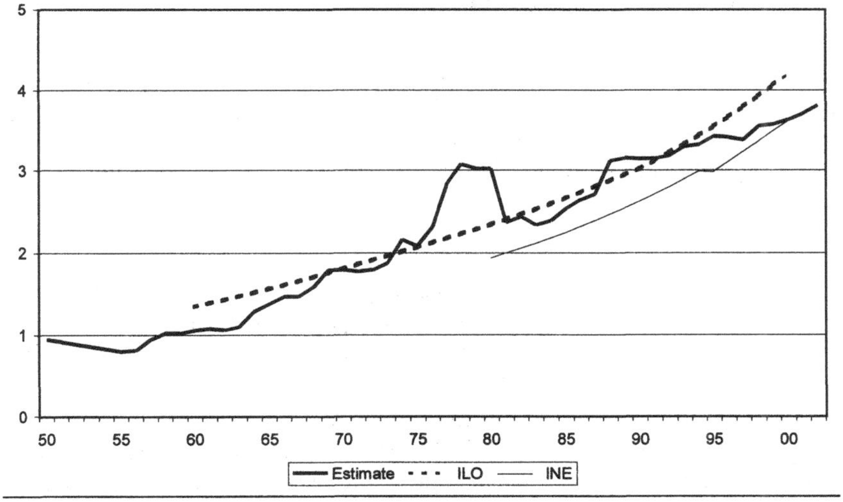

Source: Author's calculations based on *Banco de Guatemala* (2003), INE and ILO data.

Although a broad approach may limit the precision of calculations, the regressions in chapter 5 and 6 show that the variable has a high explanatory power on growth. Moreover, as can be seen from Figure 3, the estimated values give a more reasonable picture than the data from official sources. Notice that the *level* of the economically active population, but not its growth rate, is basically in line with ILO or INE calculations. In 1980s, when the civil war had already taken genocide

15 UNDP (2003a) reports a participation rate of 24.5 percent (2002). Based on INE data, as reported by Global Info Group (1999), this compares to 27.6 percent (1995), 29.9 percent (1990) and 28.2 percent (1985).

proportions, the labor force dropped dramatically by about 660,000.[16] For recent years, the estimate for the economically active population derived from IGSS statistics comes close to INE data.

C. Physical Capital Stock

Internationally, the Perpetual Inventory Method (PIM) is a common way to estimate capital stock, but there are uncertainties associated with the calculation. In general, due to the lack of information about the initial capital stock, questionable validity of assumptions about the rate of depreciation, and lack of information about the utilization of capital, estimates should be taken with care. With these reservations in mind, the PIM was used to construct the physical capital stock for Guatemala. The following paragraphs present two distinct calculations, one with aggregated and another with disaggregated investment data.

1. Estimate with Aggregated Investment Data

The physical capital stock that is used throughout the subsequent analyses is computed using the PIM with aggregated investment data. The procedure argues that the stock of capital is the accumulation of the stream of past investments:

$$K_t = K_{t-1} \cdot (1 - \delta_K) + I_t \qquad (11)$$

where K is the capital stock, I gross fixed capital formation, δ_K the annual depreciation rate of the capital stock, and t an index for time. The initial value of the capital-output ratio for 1950 is taken from the Nehru and Dhareshwar (1993) data set.[17] Information about gross fixed capital formation was provided directly by the Economic Research Department of the *Banco de Guatemala*. The data is compiled using the somewhat dated 1953 UN System of National Accounts, which is currently under revision.[18] In line with other studies for Latin America, such as Loayza et al. (2002) and Morales (1998), the overall depreciation rate is assumed at

16 It should be emphasized that the reliance on IGSS data may understate the drop of the economically active population during the 1980s. This is because the working population in the informal and rural sectors — typically not captured by the social security system — was particularly affected by violence and displacement policies.

17 The potential error of the estimate of initial capital stock diminishes over time due to depreciation. Based on international data, Nehru and Dhareshwar (1993) offer an estimate of the capital stock for Guatemala that was taken as a benchmark.

18 UNDP (2002) provides a brief summary of the associated empirical consequences and causes that prevented an actualization of the Guatemalan National Accounts.

5 percent. This is still a rather high estimate when compared with more commonly used thumb values.

However, regarding the armed conflict, which has lasted for 36 years, and several periods of high violence in Guatemala, it was found useful to adopt a high depreciation rate in order to account for both capital *destruction* and *distraction* from productive use. For example, the latter may have resulted in unprofitable military spending, several forms of non-productive investments, or temporary spare capital because of infrastructure deficiencies. As to be shown in the following chapter, the results of the regression analyses are not sensitive to moderate adjustments in the depreciation rate. In terms of data availability over a long time period, and given the robustness to alternative assumptions about depreciation, the capital stock series with aggregated investment data is adopted in the later regression analyses.

2. Estimate with Disaggregated Investment Data.

Based on the PIM, Morán and Valle (2002) present a second approach for Guatemala. In their model the capital stock is estimated for eight broad asset groups for 1971-2000. However, presumably because of too high depreciation rates for public and private construction, they seem to underestimate the genuine level of the capital stock.[19] Following their methodology but applying different depreciation rates and taking into account the initial benchmark estimate from Nehru and Dareshwar (1993), a second capital stock series has been calculated with disaggregated investment data for the period 1970-2002.

The initial values are obtained from a pre-estimate starting in 1950. The data gaps for the sectoral composition of the eight assets groups prior to 1970 are filled in by extrapolation techniques. These values, however, do *not* enter in the later regression or growth accounting exercise. They only provide reasonable initial values for the disaggregated capital stock. Table 4 presents the assumed average life service lines for each of these assets groups. The average service life for a given class of asset is considered to be identical for all kinds of economic activities. The service lives are arrived at by considering the nature of these asset groups, consulting experts, and a careful review of the average service lives used by other countries, as reported in OECD (2001b).

---

19 In addition, the following results of the quality index for the physical capital stock differ. This may be due to the possibility of an oversight in the logarithmic transformation by Morán and Valle (2002), as was pointed out in a personal communication with Estuardo Morán, *Banco de Guatemala*, October 15, 2003.

Table 4. Guatemala: Asset Classes and Average Service Lives

Asset Class	Average Service Life (Years)	
	Private Sector	Public Sector
Construction	50	50
Machinery and Equipment	...	15
Imported Capital Goods	15	...
Domestically Produced Capital Goods	10	...
Cultivated Assets and Major Improvements to Land	6	...
Other Assets	10	...

Source: Based on OECD (2001b) and expert consultation.

Based on average service life estimates, geometric depreciation rates are applied. With geometric depreciation, the market value in constant prices is assumed to decline at a constant rate within each period. The implicit depreciation factor for each asset group is set at a value that ensures that the initial value will have been reduced to 10 percent of the original value by the time it reaches the end of its expected service life. The main drawback of geometric depreciation is that it will never exhaust the full value of an asset. That is, the depreciated value of the asset falls asymptotically, approaching, but never reaching, zero. While the infinity problem is somewhat troublesome, geometric depreciation has the practical advantage of being suited better for benchmark estimates, such as in the present study.

D. Quality Indices of Capital and Labor

Based on the previous calculations, quality indices can be elaborated. The quality index of the labor force will only be used in the later growth accounting exercise since it already reflects improvements in human capital. However, the estimate for the quality of capital enters into the regressions. The following paragraphs are concerned with the construction of the indices for the quality of capital and labor, respectively, and a brief comparison over both indices for 1970-2002. The capital and labor quality indices yield interesting outcomes.

1. Quality of Capital

One can calculate a quality index of capital by using the disaggregated capital stock data. The estimate follows the methodology advocated by Laurits et al.

(1980) and Roldós (1997). For the case of Guatemala, this means that changes in the index of quality of capital, zq, are computed as a weighted average of investment of the four broad asset groups. These are (1) public and private construction, (2) imported capital goods and investment in machinery and equipment, (3) domestically produced capital goods, and (4) cultivated assets and major improvements to land. The formula used is:

$$(12) \qquad \Delta \log zq_t = \sum_{i=1}^{4} v_{i,t} \cdot (\Delta \log K_{i,t-1}) - (\Delta \log K_{t-1})$$

where K_i is the respective capital stock and the weights v_i are the relative capital rental rates. The index reflects changes in the composition of capital. If *all* components of the capital stock are growing at the same rate, quality remains unchanged. If *components* of the capital stock with higher capital rents are growing more rapidly, quality increases. Since data on the rental rates v_i is not readily available for Guatemala, estimates of these are, following Roldós (1997), based on the arbitrage relation:

$$(13) \qquad v_{i,t} = (1 + r_t) \cdot P_{i,t} - (1 - \delta_{z,i}) \cdot P_{i,t+1}$$

where P_i is a price index, $\delta_{z,i}$ the depreciation rate, and r_t is the economy-wide real interest rate. The price indices for the respective asset groups are taken from the Morán and Valle (2002) database. In order to take into account the volatility of the real exchange rate, which effects directly the relative price of the four types of capital, and to correct for measurement bias, the final series are smoothed by a 3-year moving average.

2. *Quality of Labor*

To quantify labor quality, an index hq is computed as a weighted average of labor within different levels of education. This formulation is consistent with the growth accounting literature that makes adjustments for education. It allows a more accurate indication of the contribution of labor to production. The index hq is defined as follows:

$$(14) \qquad hq_t = \sum_{j=1}^{3} w_j \cdot (L_{j,t} / L_t)$$

where L_j is the labor force with education level j (primary, secondary and tertiary) and w_j are the weights for the respective schooling level. The weights measure how the productivity effect of schooling varies with the level of education and are taken from the later regression analysis (Table 6). Interestingly, they correspond approximately with the private returns to schooling at each education level, as presented by Psacharopoulos and Patrinos (2002) for Guatemala.

Following OECD (2001a) another possibility to compute an implicit labor quality index would be to assume direct relations between skills and occupations, to rank occupations by their skill intensity and then use information on the occupational distribution of labor over time. In this case, skilled labor and less skilled labor have to be weighted by their respective relative labor productivity to account for differences in skills. For the case of Guatemala, similar to equation (14), this can be done by weighting labor inputs of different industries with the share that each type of labor occupies in total labor compensation.

Figure 4. Guatemala: Comparison of Labor Quality Indices, 1970-2002
(in percent, relative to base year 1970)

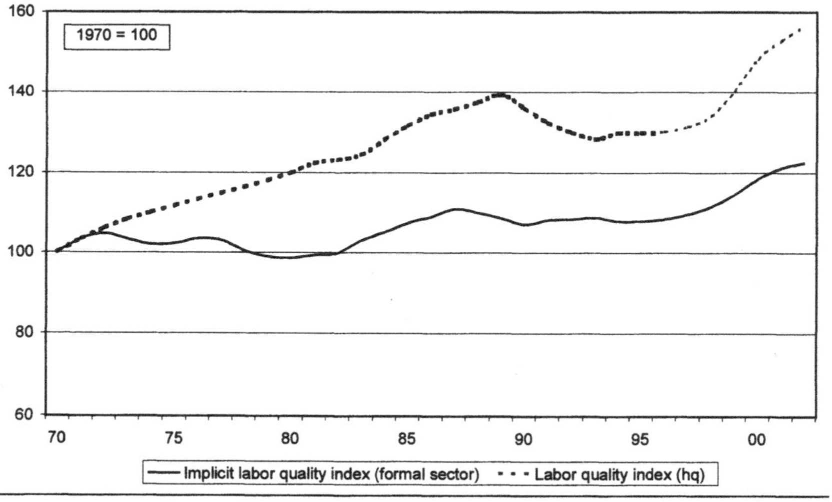

Source: Author's calculations based on *Banco de Guatemala* (2003) data (implicit labor quality index), and human capital stock estimate for labor quality index (hq).

However, it should be kept in mind that this kind of implicit differentiation of labor is a rather incomplete substitute for labor quality. It can only take into account some of the quality changes of labor input and does not allow the sources of the change to be identified. Moreover, the eight industry categories available from *Banco de Guatemala* (2003) statistics only apply to the *formal* sector. As such, they ignore approximately 75 percent of the population working in the informal and rural economy. Placing less emphasis on educational improvements in *primary* schooling — the working population of the IGSS is typically better educated than the population in the informal and rural sectors — the implicit labor quality index is biased downwards.[20] Nevertheless, for illustrative purposes, Figure 4 compares both indices. What is striking is the apparent similarity between both measures of labor quality despite completely different sources of data. This suggests that the time series properties of the human capital stock and its respective weights may be of reasonable quality.

3. Comparison of Both Indices

Finally, Figure 5 compares the estimated indices of the quality of labor, hq, and capital, zq. The descriptive analysis yields three important outcomes. First, the index of labor quality presents a clear upward trend, reflecting improvements in educational capital and a shift to more skilled jobs. However, as a consequence of the civil strife, labor quality slightly declined during the early 1990s but begins to increase again after 1998.

Figure 5. Guatemala: Indices of Capital and Labor Quality, 1970-2002
(in percent, relative to base year 1970) [a/]

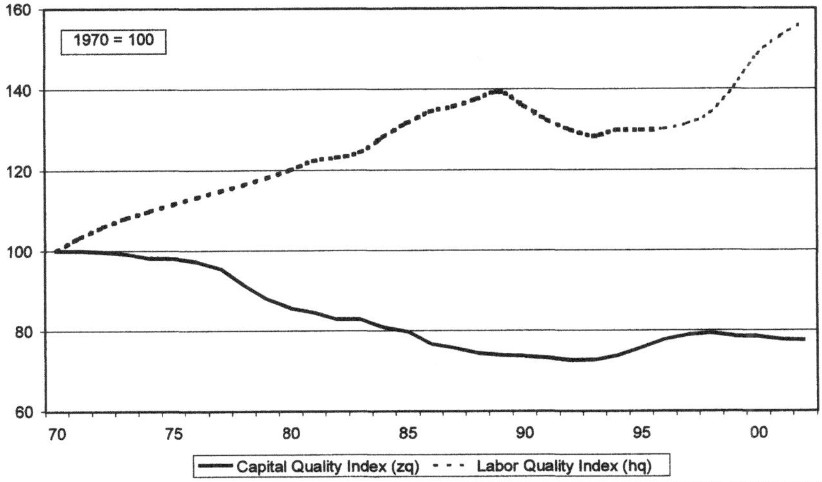

Source: Author's calculations. a/ Changes in capital quality reflect the fact that investment with comparatively higher rental rates (imported capital goods as well as machinery and equipment) decreased during the civil war but eventually climbed up again.

20 This is because primary school enrollment has increased substantially over time (see Table 3).

Second, the quality of capital has decreased over time. In particular after 1977, the data suggests that capital quality declined dramatically. In the mid 1990s, the advent of the Peace Accords led to an improvement, followed, however, by a stagnant pattern. In any case, for the period under observation, the quality of Guatemala's capital stock declined by about 20 percent. The exact reasons underlying the deterioration are unclear and require further research. Prominent explanations are the destructive impact of the internal military conflict, and a negative investment climate due to an unstable policy environment and lack of good governance.

Third, a comparison of both indices shows an apparent gap between the evolution of the quality of capital and the quality of labor. This could imply that the deterioration of quality of capital is associated with, among other factors, the decreased output growth during the last decades. In other words, there is a missing complementarity between the country's skills and its technology base. The next chapter will take a closer look at the empirical determinants of growth in Guatemala.

V. Empirical Evidence for Guatemala

This chapter presents the main empirical evidence regarding the relationship between education and growth in Guatemala. Section 1 introduces the empirical methodology. Section 2 reports the findings for average years of schooling and growth. Given the apparent shortcoming of aggregate measurements of human capital, section 3 examines separately the effects of primary, secondary and tertiary schooling on growth. Finally, section 4 compares the returns to education at the macro level with the microeconomic evidence.

A. Methodology

The empirical methodology for the following sections is based on the human capital augmented growth model of Mankiw et al. (1992). This model considers human capital as an independent factor of production. It can be represented in a Cobb-Douglas production function with constant returns to scale:

(15) $$Y_t = A_t \cdot K_t^{\alpha} \cdot H_t^{\beta} \cdot L_t^{(1-\alpha-\beta)}$$

where Y represents output and A is the level of technology or total factor productivity.[21] K, H and L are physical capital, human capital and labor. Multicollinearity between capital and labor is avoided by standardizing output and the capital stock by labor units, which also impose the restriction that the scale elasticity of the production factors is equal to unity. Converted into a logarithmic expression, the production function can be estimated in its structural form:

(16) $$\log y_t = \log A_t + \alpha \cdot \log k_t + \beta \cdot \log h_t + u_t$$

where the lower case variables y = Y/L and k = K/L are output and physical capital in intensive terms, and h = H/L stands for average human capital. At first glance, the formula already appears suitable for estimation. However, some problems arise since it is well known that most macroeconomic time series contain unit roots and that the regression of one non-stationary series on another is likely to yield spurious results. As reported in Appendix one, the data for the case of Guatemala is no

21 Further research may focus on a specification less restrictive than a standard Cobb-Douglas production function to allow a higher degree of precision for the determination of the technical coefficients. For example, factor shares are not necessarily constant, and the elasticity of substitution can be less than 1. A potentially interesting avenue is Jones (2003). He presents a production function that exhibits a short-run elasticity of substitution between capital and labor that is less than 1, and a long-run elasticity that equals to 1.

exception. The estimation bias can be removed by transforming the time series to stationarity. This can be done by first differencing. In any case, this will create its own problems, notably because of the risk of losing valuable information on the long-run relationships of the variables.

One approach to dealing with this dilemma is to employ an error-correction model which combines long-run information with a short-run adjustment mechanism. This methodology has been used successfully in alternative growth studies. Examples of this are Nehru and Dareshwar (1994), Morales (1998), and Bassanini and Scarpetta (2001). The error-correction model can be estimated in different ways. Banerjee et al. (1993) show that the generalized *one-step* error-correction model is a transformation of an autoregressive distributed lag model. As such, it can be used to estimate relationships among non-stationary processes. Based on Hendry's (1995) concept of general-to-specific modeling, the error-correction model of the human capital augmented production function for Guatemala can be specified as follows:

$$(17)\qquad \begin{aligned}\Delta \log y_t &= \gamma_1 \cdot \Delta \log k_t + \gamma_2 \cdot \Delta \log k_{t-1} \\ &\quad - \gamma_3 \cdot (\log y_{t-1} - \alpha \cdot \log k_{t-1} - \beta \cdot \log h_{t-1} - \log A_{t-1}) + u_t\end{aligned}$$

For Guatemala, in line with much empirical cross-country research, the short-run effects of schooling on growth have been found insignificant and are as such excluded from the regressions. This suggests that only the *level* of human capital has a long-run effect on economic *growth*. As it stands, the equation can be estimated by ordinary least squares (OLS) or instrumental variables (IV) techniques, but the coefficients cannot be formed without knowledge of α and β. However, one can estimate the re-parameterized form:

$$(18)\qquad \begin{aligned}\Delta \log y_t &= c + \gamma_1 \cdot \Delta \log k_t + \gamma_2 \cdot \Delta \log k_{t-1} \\ &\quad + \gamma_3 \cdot \log y_{t-1} + \gamma_4 \cdot \log k_{t-1} + \gamma_5 \cdot \log h_{t-1} + \textstyle\sum_j \delta_j \cdot dummy_{j,t} + u_t\end{aligned}$$

Estimates of the parameter γ_3 can now be used to calculate the required elasticities α and β. The loading coefficient γ_3 contains additional information because it can be interpreted as a measure of the speed of adjustment in which the system moves towards its equilibrium on the average. In addition, Banerjee et al. (1998) argue that in a single equation framework a significant coefficient serves as a test for cointegration. Notice that the technology parameter, A, is allowed to change overtime as a function of different variables, Z:

$$(19)\qquad \log A_t = f(Z_t)$$

where in its simplest formulation the technology level is proxied by a constant term, c, and a series of dummy variables. In a later chapter, proxy variables with respect to growth of trade openness, bad governance, time trends and other variables will be included in the equation. The majority of the following regressions include three dummies.[22] First, a 1963 impulse dummy captures a positive one-off effect stemming from expectations regarding the Central American Common Market (MCCA). Second, a 1982 impulse dummy takes into account a negative one-off effect stemming from the peak of internal war. Third, a 1977 step dummy which models a structural change in the long-run relationship of the variables. A Chow breakpoint test does not reject the null hypothesis of no structural change during that year (p = 0.000). In fact, the 1977 dummy is always negative, very significant, and most likely corrects for the deviations resulting from the civil strife. Interestingly, this finding is consistent with the quality index of the capital stock series showing a decreasing trend since 1977.

B. Average Years of Schooling and Growth

Table 5 shows the results for the average years of schooling specification. The adjusted R^2 of the error-correction model is rather high and indicates a good data fit. Test statistics do not indicate any serial correlation or misspecification at conventional levels. The residuals have been found to be normally distributed and to follow stationary patterns. If not mentioned otherwise, these properties apply equally to subsequent regressions.

The loading coefficient is highly significant and suggests a moderate speed of adjustment towards the long-run growth path, equal to about 25 percent of the deviations per year. After any specific shock to the economy it would, on the average, take approximately 10 years to reach the level of output consistent with long-run growth (with differences to be less than 10 percent). In the subsequent regressions, however, the magnitude of the coefficient — but not its significance — was found to be fragile with respect to the econometric specification. The asymptotic critical values of the t-ratio for the coefficient are taken from Banerjee et al. (1998). The significance level suggests a cointegrating relationship of the

22 Evidently, the Guatemalan time series are full of distortions, for example the 1976 earthquake and major political events. However, a sparse inclusion of dummy variables is the preferred econometric formulation. Other settings will be described in the following chapters. It is important to emphasize that the basic results are not sensitive to the dummy variables. That is, the omission of the impulse dummies (1963 and 1982) does have little impact on the qualitative results. However, it is important to model the structural break.

variables.[23] The results are satisfactory considering the distortions caused by the internal military conflict and the simplicity of the assumptions used to construct the time series in the context of data uncertainties. At first sight, this seems astonishing. However, the good performance of the model may be due to the small size of the economy, and that the overall data uncertainties are not as severe as is commonly believed.

The most striking result is that human capital, as measured by average years of schooling, has a highly significant, positive and strong impact on long-run growth. Column 1 reports the implicit long-run coefficients estimated by OLS.[24] Since education levels are likely to respond to growing employment opportunities and increased income, column 2 shows the regression results when IV techniques are applied. In this case, lags of the explanatory variables are used as instruments. Compared to the OLS estimate, the quality of the results does not vary much with the IV estimation. The estimating parameters are in both cases significantly different from zero and the regressions, as test statistics indicate, show a satisfactory performance. However, the absolute value of the human capital coefficient is slightly reduced. By contrast, the implicit elasticity of the capital coefficient is sharply reduced. The endogeneity problem, thus, does not distort the estimate but has an impact on the magnitude of the coefficients. In the IV specification, the estimated long-run effect of a 1 percent increase of average schooling on GDP per unit of labor is 0.33 percent. As such, it is roughly consistent with a priori expectations on the magnitude of the factor share of human capital. The results in terms of the human capital augmented Cobb-Douglas production function are approximately as follows:

$$(20) \qquad Y_t = A_t \cdot K_t^{1/3} \cdot H_t^{1/3} \cdot L_t^{1/3}$$

where the reported parameter values will serve as the base in a later growth accounting exercise. Notice that despite different methodologies the capital elasticity is broadly in line with empirical analyses which estimate a Cobb-Douglas production function for Guatemala (see Box 3). The capital elasticity, however, was found to be sensitive regarding the setting of the dummy variables. By

23 Notice equally that the human capital parameters are highly significant and compare favorably with the critical values provided by Pesaran et al. (2001). This is reassuring given the small sample size of 50 observations and the consequently low power of the ADF tests, where the stationarity properties of the repressors may not be known with certainty.

24 The long-run coefficients can be obtained by dividing the estimated parameter through the value of the loading coefficient, for example 0.084/0.241□0.351. Discrepancies are due to rounding.

contrast, the human capital coefficient was robust. These issues will be explored in more detail in the following analyses.

Table 5. Production Function for Guatemala: Average Years of Schooling Specification, 1951-2002

	Dependent variable: Percent change of GDP/worker	
	OLS	IV [a/]
Explanatory variables	(1)	(2)
Constant	-0.077**	-0.077**
	(-4.74)	(-3.76)
Percent change of capital/worker	0.871**	0.774**
	(30.2)	(5.74)
Percent change of capital/worker [-1]	0.120**	0.169*
	(3.28)	(2.58)
log GDP/worker [-1] [b/]	-0.241**	-0.269**
	(-5.87)	(-5.28)
log capital/worker [-1]	0.107**	0.099*
	(3.76)	(2.29)
log average years of schooling [-1]	0.084**	0.090**
	(5.00)	(4.54)
Step dummy 1977	-0.041**	-0.039**
	(-4.47)	(-3.38)
Impulse dummy 1963	0.057**	0.056**
	(4.69)	(4.15)
Impulse dummy 1982	-0.077**	-0.087**
	(-4.88)	(-4.09)
Long-run elasticity of capital	0.444	0.366
Long-run elasticity of schooling	0.351	0.334
Adjusted R^2	0.964	0.956
F-statistic	170.5	40.67
Durbin Watson [c/]	2.003	2.112
S.E. of regression	0.012	0.013
N	51	50

a/ Lags of the independent variables are used as instruments. b/ Asymptotic critical values of the t-ratio are from Banerjee et al. (1998). c/ A Breusch-Godfrey test finds no evidence for the presence of first, second and third order correlation in the residuals.

t-statistics in parenthesis. ** Significant at 1%, * significant at 5%.

Source: Author's calculations.

Box 3. Empirical Growth Studies for Guatemala: A Review

There are no studies for Guatemala that empirically assess the direct impact of education on economic growth over time. However, some standard growth accounting regressions exist that partially confirm the findings of the present study.

Prera (1999) and the World Bank (1996) came up with rough capital share estimates of about 0.4 and 0.6, respectively, while estimating a Cobb-Douglas production function. The World Bank provides neither a detailed methodology nor its data sources. The study from Prera faces several constraints regarding these issues. Particularly the fact that he ignores the existence of unit roots within the time series context and the low significance of the estimated parameters places doubt on the reliability of the results. Morán and Valle (2002) face the same problems. In addition, their parameter estimates must be considered carefully because of a short time period. The capital share is estimated about 0.3. Segovia and Lardé (2002) find a similar capital share using a first differences specification. Although the methodologies and data sources differ, the results partially suggest that the capital share for Guatemala is in agreement with empirical studies for other developing countries. According to Bosworth et al. (1996), capital shares are typically considered to be in the order of 0.3-0.4.

Some growth accounting studies for Guatemala also exist. Results differ and no firm conclusions can be drawn. The main discrepancies stem from the assumed or estimated factor shares, distinct time periods and, in particular, from data issues. Most studies rely on international data sets. They make no adjustments for the quality of inputs and are not concerned too much about data problems in the light of the civil strife. In general, studies tend to find that the role of total factor productivity growth was moderate and decreasing for recent periods. (with the exception of Bailén 2001, see for example Bosworth et al. 1996, Edwards 2000, Gregorio 1992, Loayza et al. 2002, Morán and Valle 2002, Nehru and Dhareshwar 1994, Segovia and Lardé 2002, Prera 1999, and World Bank 1996).

Particularly interesting is the work of Sakellariou (1995) who claims to use the Lucas (1988) model of endogenous growth. While analyzing microdata from the 1989 household survey, Sakellariou tests external effects of education on wage differentials. Unfortunately, the study suffers from a limited number of industry categories and human capital variables. Consequently, the regressions turn out to be statistically insignificant and strong conclusions cannot be drawn. However, Sakellariou goes as far as finding that the analysis does not reject the hypothesis that external effects of human capital investment could be present in Guatemala.

Finally, there are two additional findings of interest. First, even in the IV estimate, physical capital accumulation has a rather high impact on short-run growth. This suggests that measures to stimulate investment, for example by improving the investment climate, are likely to have an immediate impact on short-run growth. Second, the interception is significantly negative. Since the constant is expected to proxy for technology, a negative parameter in the sense of 'technological regress' is hard to understand. However, a loose interpretation for this finding would be that during the past 50 years, on average, the economy was not particularly efficient. One reason for that might be the conflicting political and social environment of Guatemala.

C. Schooling and Growth by Education Level

Using education data by levels may be preferable for a number of reasons. In particular, the growth impact of different forms of educational capital may vary. Columns 1-6 in Table 6 present the results of the production function augmented for human capital. The education level of the labor force enters separately into the estimation. The share of the labor force with primary, secondary and tertiary education is used here as the relevant unit.

It may be argued that *average years of schooling* by level of education should be used instead of labor force *participation*. In any case, with the given data, this would not change the results. Ideally, one would also include primary, secondary and tertiary education into the same equation in order to assess their joint impact on growth. However, due to strong collinearity, the estimation only supports the inclusion of one education level.[25] As can be appreciated from the test statistics the regressions perform quite well. Notice that the estimate for primary education includes a time trend starting in 1985, the year of Guatemala's transition to civilian rule. The inclusion of the trend variable was motivated to avoid serial correlation in the residuals, but does not have an impact on the magnitude of coefficients.

Table 6 presents both OLS and IV estimates. The endogeneity problem seems to be more pronounced for primary education, and in particular for physical capital. However, the qualitative results do not vary substantially. In all specifications the schooling variables are highly significant and positively correlated with growth. Interestingly, the significance levels increase with secondary and tertiary education. Regarding the long-run elasticities, the accumulation of primary schooling appears

25 In principle, the inclusion of a time trend for 1999 and an interaction term for secondary and tertiary schooling would allow incorporating all three levels of education at a time. Tentatively, such an exercise yields similar qualitative results on the impact of each level of education on growth — albeit primary schooling becomes insignificant. In addition, due to the multicollinearity problem, this specification was found to be rather sensitive and performs less well than the results displayed in Table 6.

to be most important for growth, followed by secondary and tertiary education. This finding should *not* be interpreted as implying that other levels are unimportant. This is particularly true given the tight connections between the various forms of educational capital and the retrospective character of the empirics.

Nevertheless, the evidence is in line with the limited cross-country studies on this topic. Recall that Gemmel (1996), Petrakis and Stamatakis (2002) and Papageorgiou (2003) plausibly suggest that the importance of post-primary education increases with the level of development. Similarly, de Ferranti et al. (2002) argue that in countries classified as adopters, such as Guatemala, policies should first focus on a critical threshold level of primary schooling, coupled with open trade policies. The intuition is here that different stages of technological transition require distinct policy priorities. A sufficient coverage *and* quality of primary education are regarded as the minimum prerequisite to adopt technologies. By contrast, in countries where basic skill requirements are fulfilled and firms are making significant adaptations or innovations, the creation of more specialized skills ought to be the priority. In addition, the results here partially confirm the earlier micro-level evidence for Guatemala.[26]

Finally, it is interesting to observe the changes of the physical capital coefficients by level of education. In the IV specification for primary and secondary schooling, capital only enters as weakly significant. By contrast, the coefficient for physical capital becomes very significant and alters its long-run elasticity if tertiary education is entered into the estimate.

To the extent that this effect does not merely reflect statistical arbitrariness, a possible interpretation would be that the productivity of physical capital is affected by tertiary schooling. These findings support the conjecture of Romer (1990b) that the level of scientific education should be correlated with the rate of growth and the share of output devoted to investment in physical capital. It should be kept in mind, however, that the reliability of tertiary education data is comparatively poor in Guatemala. Moreover, according to Anderson (2001), low quality and internal inefficiency plague university education. Hence, some care should be taken before drawing too strong conclusions from the observed changes.

---

26 For Guatemala, Psacharopoulos and others have extensively investigated the returns to schooling, sometimes by level of education. Such exercises are summarized in Psacharopoulos and Patrinos (2002), Haeussler (1993) and World Bank (1995c). The studies generally report high private returns to primary schooling, but are merely based on ENS (1989) or earlier data, and typically do not care about sample selection bias.

Table 6. Guatemala: Effect of Schooling on Growth by Level of Education, 1951-2002

	Dependent variable: Percent change of GDP/worker					
	j = primary		j = secondary		j = tertiary	
	OLS	IV	OLS	IV	OLS	IV
Explanatory variables	(1)	(2)	(3)	(4)	(5)	(6)
Constant	0.087**	0.082**	0.127**	0.140**	0.096**	0.141**
	(3.43)	(2.83)	(4.20)	(3.60)	(3.78)	(4.43)
Percent change of capital/worker	0.871**	0.766**	0.875**	0.757**	0.872**	0.785**
	(28.8)	(5.14)	(29.5)	(5.12)	(28.6)	(6.02)
Percent change of capital/worker [-1]	0.113**	0.157*	0.128**	0.181*	0.083*	0.143*
	(2.94)	(2.42)	(3.33)	(2.51)	(2.21)	(2.32)
log GDP/worker [-1] [a/]	-0.242**	-0.264**	-0.213**	-0.234**	-0.224**	-0.327**
	(-5.51)	(-4.88)	(-5.43)	(-4.64)	(-5.20)	(-6.00)
log capital/worker [-1]	0.107**	0.088	0.091**	0.074	0.120**	0.155**
	(3.47)	(1.65)	(3.22)	(1.61)	(3.72)	(3.63)
log participation of education level$_j$	0.103**	0.092**	0.049**	0.052**	0.023**	0.033**
in labor force [-1]	(3.89)	(2.79)	(4.59)	(3.92)	(4.27)	(5.20)
Trend 1985	0.002**	0.002**	...	...	...	...
	(3.38)	(3.15)				
Long-run elasticity of capital	0.445	0.333	0.426	0.319	0.538	0.474
Long-run elasticity of schooling in education level$_j$	0.426	0.349	0.230	0.220	0.104	0.101
Adjusted R^2	0.962	0.953	0.962	0.948	0.960	0.962
F-statistic	141.8	35.85	159.9	33.56	152.6	49.02
Durbin Watson [b/]	1.756	1.978	1.944	2.055	1.790	2.205
S.E. of regression	0.012	0.014	0.012	0.014	0.012	0.012
N	51	50	51	50	51	50

Note: The regressions include a 1977 step dummy and impulse dummies for 1963 and 1982, significant at 1%. a/ Asymptotic critical values of the t-ratio are from Banerjee et al. (1998). b/ A Breusch-Godfrey test finds no evidence for the presence of first, second and third order correlation in the residuals.

t-statistics in parenthesis. ** Significant at 1%, * significant at 5%.

Source: Author's calculations.

D. Mincerian Human Capital Specification

An important question is how the effect of schooling at the macro level compares with the microeconomic evidence. The macro returns could be higher because of externalities from education. For example, if post-primary schooling leads to technological progress that is not captured in the private returns to education, or if education produces externalities in the form of the reduction of crime, more informed political decisions, better health and so on. To reconcile the macro effect of schooling with the micro level, Cohen and Soto (2001) estimate the following production function:

(21) $$Y_t = A_t \cdot K_t^{\alpha} \cdot HM_t^{(1-\alpha)}$$

where Y is output, A total factor productivity, K physical capital, and HM human capital. As first suggested by Bils and Klenow (2000), the micro evidence derived from a log-linear Mincer (1974) formulation can be used to specify the aggregate human capital stock as follows:

(22) $$HM_t = e^{\psi \cdot h_t} \cdot L_t \Leftrightarrow hm_t = e^{\psi \cdot h_t}$$

where hm_t is the human capital per worker, h_t is average years of schooling and ψ corresponds to the returns to education. This Mincerian approach has become popular in the literature since the work of Bils and Klenow.[27] The specification is a straightforward way of incorporating human capital into the production function in a manner that is consistent with the standard semi-logarithmic formulation for estimating returns to schooling at the micro level.

Nevertheless, Temple (2001) argues that the parameter ψ may not be interpreted as the social returns to schooling because it does not incorporate the opportunity costs of the resources used in educational provision. Still, it remains of considerable interest since an empirical estimate provides a way of either confirming or rejecting the importance of education suggested by micro studies.

For the Guatemalan case, the econometric specification is similar to the previous equations. The production function is first converted into a logarithmic expression:

(23) $$\log y_t = \log A_t + \alpha \cdot \log k_t + (1-\alpha) \cdot \psi \cdot h_t$$

Then, the production function is transformed into an error-correction formulation, which allows the long-run schooling parameter to be identified:

27 The working paper version was circulated prior to 2000. A caveat here is the missing role of experience.

(24) $$\Delta \log y_t = \gamma_1 \cdot \Delta \log k_t + \gamma_2 \cdot \Delta \log k_{t-1} - \gamma_3 \cdot (\log y_{t-1} - \alpha \cdot \log k_{t-1} - (1-\alpha) \cdot \psi \cdot h_{t-1} - \log A_{t-1}) + u_t$$

Finally, the error-correction model is re-parameterized and includes a series of dummy variables:

(25) $$\Delta \log y_t = c + \gamma_1 \cdot \Delta \log k_t + \gamma_2 \cdot \Delta \log k_{t-1} + \gamma_3 \cdot \log y_{t-1} + \gamma_4 \cdot \log k_{t-1} + \gamma_5 \cdot h_{t-1} + \sum_j \delta_j \cdot dummy_{j,t} + u_t$$

Notice that the implicit return to schooling can be calculated with knowledge of α and γ_3. In principle, this approach would also allow the productivity effect of schooling to be differentiated by education level, as mentioned by Wößmann (2003). Unfortunately, the results here were found unstable for disaggregated education data. This is presumably due to the missing logarithmic transformation of the schooling variables.

Insofar, the specification provides an attractive way for comparing macro and micro evidence on the returns to schooling, but in a time series context tends to produce fragile parameter estimates. Nevertheless, when using aggregated data on human capital the regressions perform quite satisfactorily. Table 7 presents the results. Controlling for endogeneity does not distort the empirics. In the IV specification 1 additional year of schooling increases income per worker by approximately 18.4 percent.[28]

This number suggests that the macro return to schooling in Guatemala is rather high, but it compares favorably with earlier microeconomic evidence. For example, the World Bank (1995c) reports a private return to schooling of 14.9 percent for Guatemala.[29] There is evidence for much lower returns in the informal sectors and for decreasing patterns over time, but the magnitude of the coefficient is echoed in Funkhouser (1997). An estimate from Haeussler (1993) based on 1989 survey and Ministry of Education data suggests that, depending on the schooling level and underlying assumptions, the social return to schooling lies in a band between 13-19 percent. Finally, these results also confirm the cross-country evidence from Cohen and Soto (2001). They essentially find that in macro and micro regressions the effect of education on income is of similar magnitude.

---

28 According to the Table, the implicit return to schooling can be calculated as follows: $(0.034/0.240)/(1-0.240) \approx 0.184$. Discrepancies are due to rounding.

29 Based on ENCOVI (2000) survey data the World Bank (2003a) reports an overall rate of return of 6 percent.

Table 7. Production Function for Guatemala: Mincerian Human Capital Specification, 1951-2002

	Dependent variable: Percent change of GDP/worker	
	OLS	IV
Explanatory variables	(1)	(2)
Constant	-0.068**	-0.072**
	(-4.28)	(-3.78)
Percent change of capital/worker	0.865**	0.752**
	(28.7)	(6.05)
Percent change of capital/worker [-1]	0.104**	0.163*
	(2.77)	(2.56)
log GDP/worker [-1] [a/]	-0.200**	-0.240**
	(-5.35)	(-4.94)
log capital/worker [-1]	0.069*	0.058
	(2.56)	(1.45)
Average years of schooling [-1]	0.029**	0.034**
	(4.56)	(4.28)
Step dummy 1977	-0.035**	-0.035**
	(-3.97)	(-3.40)
Impulse dummy 1963	0.058**	0.058**
	(4.63)	(4.11)
Impulse dummy 1982	-0.070**	-0.080**
	(-4.24)	(-3.85)
Long-run elasticity of capital	0.343	0.240
Effect of 1 additional year of average schooling	0.219	0.184
Adjusted R^2	0.962	0.953
F-statistic	159.2	41.08
Durbin Watson [b/]	1.858	2.133
S.E. of regression	0.012	0.014
N	51	50

a/ Asymptotic critical values of the t-ratio are from Banerjee et al. (1998). b/ A Breusch-Godfrey test finds no evidence for the presence of first, second and third order correlation in the residuals.

t-statistics in parenthesis. ** Significant at 1%, * significant at 5%.

Source: Author's calculations.

VI. Additional Explanatory Variables and Robustness Check

This chapter seeks to answer some basic questions. How much confidence should be placed on the previous results? Evidently, given certain data restrictions and distortions caused by the civil war, a key issue is if the previous findings can be used to derive firm policy conclusions. In addition, another important aspect is considered: does the conditioning information set cause the schooling coefficients to change?

In order to answer these questions, the chapter is organized as follows. Section 1 tests the stability of the variables. By comparing the results with alternative sources, section 2 includes time trends, and analyzes the reliability of the human and physical capital stock data. Section 3, the bulk of the chapter, includes additional variables explaining growth. An overview of the alternative data is presented in Figure 7. Additional variables are the quality of capital, trade openness, terms of trade, and imported capital goods. This section also examines the effect of life expectancy as a companion indicator for human capital. In addition the role of military expenditures is analyzed, which, among others things, may serve as a proxy for bad governance in Guatemala. The chapter then closes with a brief summary of the findings.

A. Stability of Coefficients

Given the distortions of the economy by the civil strife and other events, it is imperative to evaluate the stability of the coefficients. For example, comparing data from different points of time could cause coefficients to show dramatic jumps. In this case, it would be almost impossible to interpret the magnitude and sign of the coefficients. In order to test for instability, this section evaluates parameter stability using recursive least squares. This allows a year-by-year comparison of the coefficients since ever larger subsets of the time series data are used in the regression.

With reference to the production function augmented for human capital, Figure 6 visualizes the recursive coefficients of the regression (Table 5) estimated by OLS. Also shown are the standard error bands around the coefficients. The coefficients do not display significant variations when more data is added to the equation. This is in particular true for the schooling parameter and indicates stability. In the light of permanent shocks to the Guatemalan economy, it is reassuring to note that the coefficient plots do not show significant jumps since the error-correction specification here is capable of digesting these disruptive events. Due to space limitations Figure 6 does not include the recursive coefficients for the 3 dummy variables, although they have been found to be equally stable. Parameter stability was found satisfactory as well using a Mincerian human capital specification (Table 7) or employing disaggregated data on educational attainment (Table 6).

Figure 6. Parameter Stability: Recursive Coefficients — Production Function with Average Years of Schooling Specification, 1988-2002

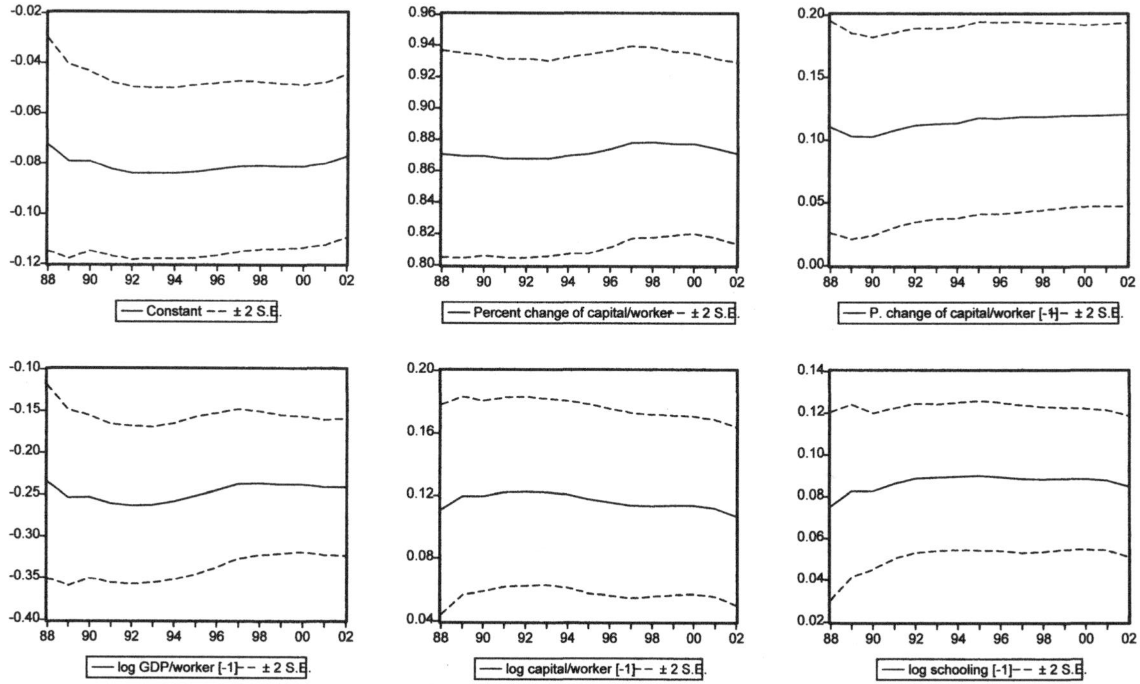

Note: Based on the OLS estimate presented in Table 5, column 1.

B. Alternative Data Sources

The estimates in this study ultimately rely on constructed time series. Consequently it is possible to ask: May the earlier results be related to arbitrary improvements during the stage of data construction? In order to pre-empt any suggestions of data mining, in particular with reference to the human and physical capital stock, this section discusses the use of alternative data sources. The benchmark for the subsequent variations in the data is the production function augmented for human capital (see Table 5).

The results of the sensitive tests are reported in Table 8. In general, the following regressions do not perform as well as the earlier estimates but still satisfactorily pass conventional tests. A Breusch-Godfrey serial correlation test suggests the possibility that the estimates (only in column 1 and 4) might present mild evidence ($p<0.15$) of first order serial correlation. Since the indication was weak and would make little impact, no correction for it was attempted. In addition, the nature of the following exercise does not necessitate absolute precision but rather enriches the earlier findings. The following results suggest in general that the findings are not sensitive to the conditioning data set but rather strengthen the final conclusions about the importance of human capital.

1. *Inclusion of Time Trends*

Column 1 of Table 8 presents the original estimate for average years of schooling (Table 5), and also includes two time trends in order to account for the possibility of missing explanatory variables. The inclusion of the trend variables was motivated by a look at the residual plot of the earlier estimates. They show moderate variations during these time periods, in particular since 1999. The inclusion of the trend variables does not have a substantial impact on the significance level of the long-run elasticities, albeit the magnitude of the coefficients is moderately affected. While the schooling coefficient decreases minimally, the physical capital coefficient is augmented. The time trend for 1985 is significantly positive but there is a negative trend since 1999. Interestingly, both time periods are related to political events. 1985 is the transition year to civilian rule. 1999 is the election year of the Alfonso Portillo government, where compromised representatives of the former military nomenclature are suspected of wielding political power.

The results of the sensitive tests are reported in Table 8. In general, the following regressions do not perform as well as the earlier estimates but still satisfactorily pass conventional tests. A Breusch-Godfrey serial correlation test suggests the possibility that the estimates (only in column 1 and 4) might present mild evidence ($p<0.15$) of first order serial correlation. Since the indication was weak and would make little impact, no correction for it was attempted. In addition,

Figure 7. Guatemala: Additional Explanatory Variables of Growth, 1950-2002

(a) GDP and Capital Stock (5 percent depreciation), Billions of 1958 Quetzals

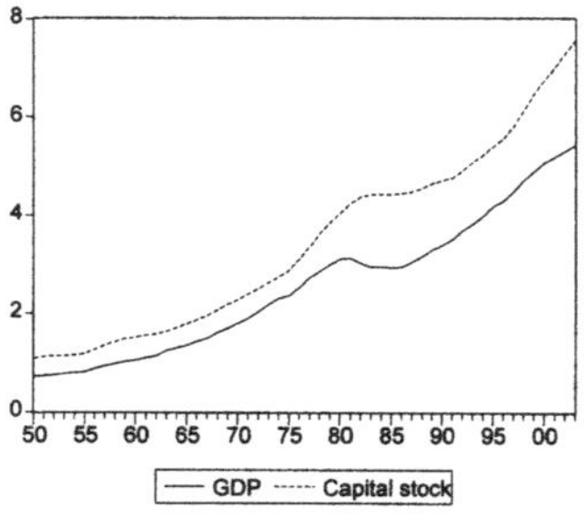

(b) Annual Growth of GDP and Capital Stock (in percent)

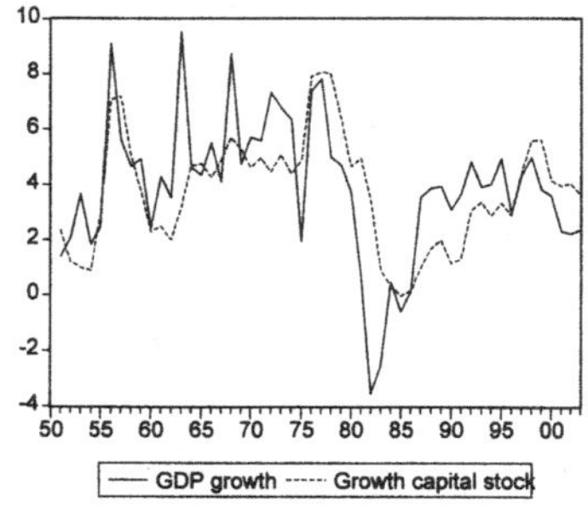

(c) Participation of Primary, Secondary and Tertiary Education in Labor Force (share)

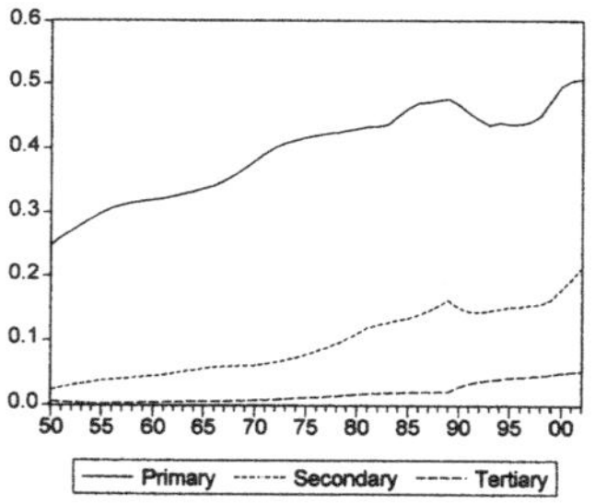

(d) Life Expectancy at Birth (years)

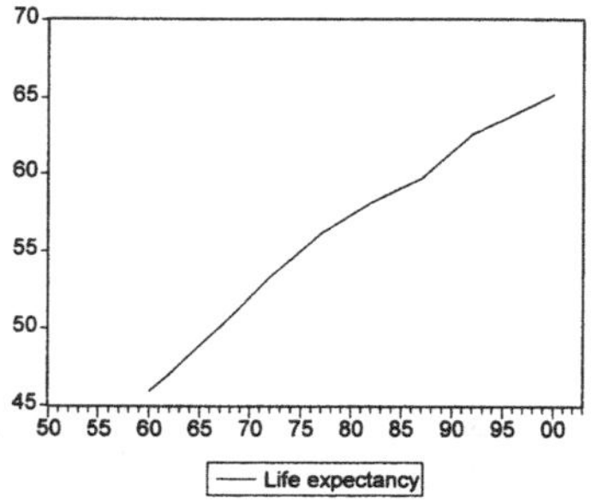

(e) Imported Capital Goods/Investment and Military Expenditure/GDP (shares)

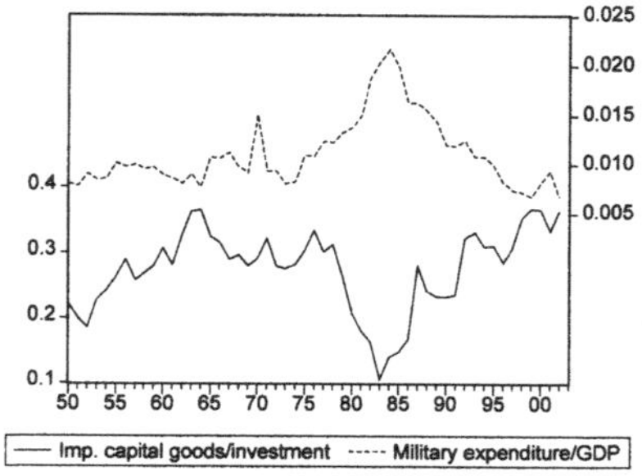

(f) Annual Growth of Terms of Trade and Trade Openness (in percent)

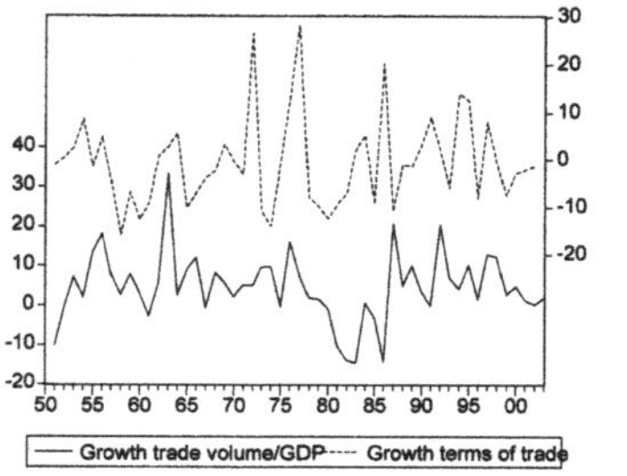

Data sources: See Appendix One.

the nature of the following exercise does not necessitate absolute precision but rather enriches the earlier findings. The following results suggest in general that the findings are not sensitive to the conditioning data set but rather strengthen the final conclusions about the importance of human capital.

2. *Inclusion of Time Trends*

Column 1 of Table 8 presents the original estimate for average years of schooling (Table 5), and also includes two time trends in order to account for the possibility of missing explanatory variables. The inclusion of the trend variables was motivated by a look at the residual plot of the earlier estimates. They show moderate variations during these time periods, in particular since 1999. The inclusion of the trend variables does not have a substantial impact on the significance level of the long-run elasticities, albeit the magnitude of the coefficients is moderately affected. While the schooling coefficient decreases minimally, the physical capital coefficient is augmented. The time trend for 1985 is significantly positive but there is a negative trend since 1999. Interestingly, both time periods are related to political events. 1985 is the transition year to civilian rule. 1999 is the election year of the Alfonso Portillo government, where compromised representatives of the former military nomenclature are suspected of wielding political power.

To the extent that this association is correct, a loose interpretation would suggest that in Guatemala the strengthening (weakening) of civilian rule has a significant positive (negative) impact on long-run growth. While at first sight this interpretation appears plausible, however, it is obvious that other factors are important as well. Moreover, the growth-enhancing channel of democratic rights might be operating indirectly on some independent variables, such as educational attainment. This complicates the analysis. Hence, further research is needed to strengthen this hypothesis.

3. *Alternative Capital Stock Data*

Column 2 of Table 8 includes capital stock data with a 4 percent depreciation rate rather than the 5 percent thumb value assumed throughout this study. The data with 4 percent depreciation is essentially identical to the Nehru and Dareshwar (1993) capital stock series, despite some minor discrepancies — when compared with data from *Banco de Guatemala* — on investment. Assuming 4 percent depreciation of the capital stock has little impact on the results, although in the IV specification the significance of the capital coefficient is weakened. This suggests that a 4 percent depreciation is rather on the low side.

Column 3 includes the capital stock estimate built with disaggregated investment data originally constructed to compute the quality index for capital. This series is robustly correlated with growth. The long-run elasticities for physical and human capital are slightly higher than with the standard estimate of the capital

Table 8. Guatemala: Robustness of Results — Alternative Data Sources

	Dependent variable: Percent change of GDP/worker					
	Includes time trends starting in 1985 and 1999	4 percent depreciation of capital stock	Disaggregated capital stock estimate [b]	Barro and Lee (2001) education data [c]	Cohen and Soto (2001) education data [c]	Population 15-64 instead of labor force data
	IV	IV	OLS	IV	IV	OLS
	1951-02	1951-02	1971-02	1951-00	1961-02	1951-02
Explanatory variables	(1)	(2)	(3)	(4)	(5)	(6)
Constant	-0.071**	-0.075**	-0.042*	-0.073**	-0.061**	-0.013
	(-4.05)	(-3.46)	(-2.57)	(-4.31)	(-4.43)	(0.66)
Percent change of capital/worker	0.865**	0.780**	0.827**	0.730**	0.847**	0.507*
	(8.44)	(5.59)	(33.0)	(10.3)	(9.18)	(2.44)
Percent change of capital/worker [-1]	0.119*	0.168*	0.167**	0.160**	0.138**	...
	(2.41)	(2.54)	(4.37)	(3.28)	(3.16)	
log GDP/worker [-1] [a]	-0.259**	-0.243**	-0.333**	-0.279**	-0.272**	0.040
	(-6.14)	(-4.88)	(-7.06)	(-5.45)	(-5.40)	(0.72)
log capital/worker [-1]	0.113**	0.078	0.180**	0.080*	0.108*	-0.127*
	(3.19)	(1.63)	(5.47)	(2.40)	(2.10)	(-2.02)
log average years of schooling [-1]	0.074**	0.083**	0.130**	0.133**	0.072**	0.026
	(4.54)	(4.58)	(6.65)	(4.86)	(5.53)	(1.53)
Trend 1985	0.002**	...	...	...	...	...
	(2.83)					
Trend 1999	-0.008*	...	-0.008**	...	...	...
	(-2.50)		(-3.63)			
Long-run elasticity of capital	0.436	0.322	0.541	0.288	0.399	N.A.
Long-run elasticity of schooling	0.287	0.344	0.392	0.476	0.266	N.A.
Adjusted R^2	0.972	0.958	0.982	0.955	0.975	0.648
F-statistic	57.55	43.28	180.4	59.61	67.88	14.92
Durbin Watson	2.440	2.162	2.174	2.441	2.151	1.879
S.E. of regression	0.011	0.013	0.009	0.013	0.010	0.014
N	50	50	31	49	40	51

Note: The regressions include a step dummy for 1977 and impulse dummies for 1963 and 1982 significant at 1%. a/ Asymptotic critical values of the t-ratio are from Banerjee et al. (1998). b/ Includes 1976 and 1982 impulse dummies significant at 1%. c/ Data is interpolated. t-statistics in parenthesis. ** Significant at 1%, * significant at 5%. Source: Author's calculations.

stock. Due to the limited number of observations the regression could only be run by OLS. Thus, the coefficients are likely to be upwardly biased. Altogether, varying the assumptions about the depreciation rate moderately changes capital elasticities but does not change very much the role of human capital on growth.

4. *Alternative Schooling Data*

The most interesting sensitive test concerns the validity of the conclusions on the importance of human capital to growth. Column 4 uses interpolated education data from Barro and Lee (2001). Column 5 includes the interpolated time series from Cohen and Soto (2001) into the regressions. In both estimates human capital, as measured by average years of schooling, is robustly correlated with growth. In addition, the parameter estimate yields a long-run elasticity in the range of 0.29-0.39. This magnitude is similar to the benchmark results obtained in the earlier estimate. Given the interpolated nature of these sources, a too strong interpretation of the associated changes makes little sense. Insofar, the sign and significance of the variables are more important than their magnitude. All in all, employing alternative data on human capital confirms the earlier conclusions about the importance of education on growth.

5. *Population Instead of Labor Force Estimate*

The regression in column 6 employs population data (15-64 years) instead of the labor force. Alternatively ILO labor force estimates could be used. The time series properties, however, are almost identical, and population statistics refer to a longer time period. In any case, the results are rather disappointing. That is, the significance of the coefficients and the overall fit of the model are poor. In order to ameliorate the estimate, the lag structure of the short-run capital coefficients was modified.Human capital still enters positively but is only weakly significant. A puzzling finding is that long-run capital accumulation has now a negative impact on growth, which is a counterintuitive and implausible result. Overall, given the absence of fluctuations and considering the civil war, Guatemalan population data seems to be a poor proxy for labor as well.

C. Additional Explanatory Variables

When the conditioning set of data in the regressions is modified, it is interesting to observe changes in the explanatory variables, such as schooling. For example, the production elasticities of human or physical capital could be larger than their factor shares because of presumed externalities. The benchmarks of the following analyzes are the results in chapter five. When possible, the following paragraphs differentiate for the effect of primary, secondary and tertiary schooling.

Table 9. Guatemala: Effect of Schooling on Growth by Level of Education Considering Quality of Capital and Trade Openness, 1971-2002

	Dependent variable: Percent change of GDP/worker					
	j = primary		j = secondary		j = tertiary	
	OLS [c/]	OLS [c/ d/]	OLS [c/]	OLS [c/ d/]	OLS [c/]	OLS [c/ e/]
Explanatory variables	(1)	(2)	(3)	(4)	(5)	(6)
Constant	-0.048[+]	-0.065**	0.042**	0.031**	0.125**	0.112**
	(-1.93)	(-3.19)	(4.07)	(3.33)	(3.19)	(4.08)
Percent change of quality-adjusted capital/worker	0.833**	0.862**	0.791**	0.838**	0.832**	0.868**
	(26.5)	(31.9)	(25.9)	(29.2)	(25.8)	(36.4)
Percent change of quality-adjusted capital/worker [-1]	0.158**	0.182**	0.153**	0.162**	0.106*	0.050
	(3.20)	(4.50)	(3.11)	(3.97)	(2.63)	(1.64)
log GDP/worker [-1] [a/]	-0.342**	-0.266**	-0.322**	-0.332**	-0.694*	-0.571**
	(-5.32)	(-7.48)	(-5.37)	(-6.56)	(-4.89)	(-5.64)
log quality-adjusted capital/worker [-1]	0.181**	0.106**	0.119**	0.141**	0.352**	0.283**
	(3.19)	(3.81)	(2.95)	(3.91)	(4.08)	(4.58)
log participation of education level$_j$ in labor force [-1]	0.094[+]	0.163**	0.075**	0.063**	0.071**	0.056**
	(1.72)	(4.28)	(3.90)	(3.84)	(3.03)	(3.39)
Step dummy 1977	...	...	-0.034**	-0.024*	-0.049**	-0.051**
			(-2.88)	(-2.38)	(-3.92)	(-5.62)
Step dummy 1984	...	...	...	...	0.032**	0.030**
					(4.11)	(5.44)
Step dummy 1986	0.026*	...	...	...	...	...
	(2.37)					
Percent change of trade volume/GDP	...	0.141**	...	0.117**	...	0.017
		(4.20)		(3.20)		(0.68)
Long-run elasticity of capital	0.529	0.401	0.370	0.424	0.507	0.496
Long-run elasticity of schooling in education level$_j$	0.274	0.614	0.233	0.188	0.103	0.098
Adjusted R^2	0.972	0.982	0.970	0.980	0.976	0.988
F-statistic	132.7	180.0	124.3	148.1	150.9	232.1
Durbin Watson [b/]	2.023	2.007	2.028	1.787	1.961	1.979
S.E. of regression	0.011	0.009	0.011	0.009	0.010	0.007
N	31	31	31	31	31	31

a/ Asymptotic critical values of the t-ratio are from Banerjee et al. (1998). b/ A Breusch-Godfrey test finds no evidence for the presence of first, second and third order correlation in the residuals. c/ Includes impulse dummies for 1976 and 1982 significant at 5%.

d/ Includes 1986 impulse dummy significant at 1%. e/ Includes impulse dummies for 1975 and 1996 significant at 5%.

t-statistics in parenthesis. ** Significant at 1%, * significant at 5%, [+]significant at 10%. Source: Author's calculations.

1. *Quality-Adjustment Capital*

Column 2 of Table 10 shows an OLS estimate for the period 1971-2002 when the capital stock is adjusted for quality. For comparative purposes, column 1 presents the same regression but without such an adjustment. Following de Ferranti et al. (2002) the intuition behind this exercise is that embodied technological change could have a positive impact on the returns to education, in particular for post-primary schooling. However, in the case of Guatemala, the overall effect seems to be the opposite. An increase in the long-run elasticity for physical capital and a decrease of the importance of education on growth is found.

To interpret this puzzling finding recall that the index of capital quality actually measures a decay by about 20 percent. In contrast, human capital and hence labor quality, have increased substantially over time. This may point in the direction of a missing capital-skill complementarity in Guatemala, which would tend to reduce the returns to education. Interestingly, this effect impacts mainly on primary education. If one compares the respective elasticities of Table 6 (columns 1, 3 and 5) and Table 9 (columns 1, 3 and 5) the econometric results suggest that introducing quality adjustments for capital have little effect on secondary and tertiary education. Nevertheless, given the limited sample size of only 31 observations a word of caution is required here. These findings should be strengthened by additional research.

2. *Trade Openness*

Growth is often thought to be enhanced by trade openness. Apart from comparative–advantage arguments, it is argued that openness expands potential markets, facilitates the diffusion of technological innovations, improves managerial practices and promotes domestic competition, all of which increase efficiency. Considering the small size of the Guatemalan economy trade openness is of particular interest. For case of Latin America, Loayza et al. (2002) present evidence suggesting a significant relationship between trade openness and growth.

Column 3 of Table 10 suggests that the growth rate of trade openness is positively and significantly related to Guatemalan GDP growth. By contrast, the elasticities for physical and average human capital do not show significant variations. This finding changes, however, if disaggregated data on educational attainment is entered into the estimate. Table 9 reveals that the inclusion of the growth rate of trade openness alters the coefficient for primary education, while secondary and tertiary schooling remain more or less unchanged (columns 2, 4 and 6). The parameters for post-primary schooling are of a similar magnitude as those in the earlier estimate which did not consider trade openness (Table 6, columns 1, 3 and 5). Interestingly, in both cases, the coefficients for post-primary schooling are of almost identical magnitude, which is also an indication of robustness. The fact that trade affects only primary education may suggest that, over the past decades, general education and basic technical skills have been the key determinants for the diffusion of technological innovations. Or, more generally, the people with primary education seem to benefit particularly from the effects of trade openness.

Somewhat surprisingly, the econometric evidence reveals that trade openness, as measured by the trade volume over GDP, exhibits a short-run effect on growth. The long-run coefficient was found insignificant and as such excluded from the model. A possible interpretation of this finding points in the direction of Rodríguez and Rodrik (2000). They cast doubt on the robustness with respect to measurement concepts and specifications of the bulk of the empirical evidence on this topic. Instead, they suggest exploring alternative causal interpretations. For example, an additional indirect channel might be that more-open economies adopt better policies and institutions that explain part of the effects of openness on growth. Following this interpretation, hitherto, trade openness in Guatemala has not been associated with political change (see also Box 1).

Column 3 indicates that improvement in the terms of trade, that is, a higher growth of the ratio of export prices to import prices, seem to enhance short-run economic growth. In line with the effect of trade openness, the long-run coefficient was found insignificant. However, the positive impact of terms of trade growth must be regarded with some caution. This is essentially because its significance was found fragile considering the conditioning set of variables that enter into the regression.

3. *Foreign Capital Goods*

International trade may have an additional impact on growth through the imports of foreign capital goods. Lee (1995) emphasizes that developing countries can increase the efficiency of capital accumulation and thereby the rate of growth by importing relatively cheap foreign capital goods from higher income countries. Taking into account this potential avenue of trade on growth, the ratio of capital imports to total investment is used as a proxy variable for the efficiency of capital accumulation. The regression of column 4 in Table 10 indicates that the composition of investment is indeed an important determinant for long-run growth in Guatemala. The implied elasticity suggests that a 1 percent increase in the ratio of capital imports to total investment increases output by about 0.10 percent. This supports the idea of Lee that more use of imported capital goods increases the efficiency of capital accumulation. Therefore, any trade distortion that restricts the importation of capital goods damages the economy in the long run. Such distortions also include disincentives for trade, such as a climate that discourages investment. Thus, continuing political instability and a climate of violence dampens the prospective for growth not only for the present, but also for future.

Table 10. Guatemala: Additional Explanatory Variables to Growth

	Dependent variable: Percent change of GDP/worker					
	Without quality adjustment for capital [b]	With quality adjustment for capital [b]	Terms of trade and trade openness [b]	Capital imports/ investment [c]	Life expectancy instead of schooling [d]	Military spending/ GDP
	OLS 1971-02	OLS 1971-02	OLS 1951-02	IV 1951-02	IV 1961-00	IV 1951-02
Explanatory variables	(1)	(2)	(3)	(4)	(5)	(6)
Constant	-0.080**	-0.120**	-0.073**	-0.070**	-1.266**	-0.215**
	(-4.62)	(-3.66)	(-5.49)	(-3.69)	(-5.16)	(-3.85)
Percent change of capital/worker	0.818**	0.793**	0.891**	0.929**	0.784**	0.846**
	(28.1)	(27.6)	(35.7)	(8.84)	(9.96)	(8.31)
Percent change of capital/worker [-1]	0.170**	0.171**	0.115**	0.118*	0.134**	0.140**
	(3.92)	(3.61)	(3.56)	(2.20)	(2.95)	(2.81)
log GDP/worker [-1] [a]	-0.230**	-0.408**	-0.227**	-0.316**	-0.307**	-0.316**
	(-5.40)	(-5.83)	(-6.76)	(-5.96)	(-5.34)	(-6.38)
log capital/worker [-1]	0.070*	0.167**	0.095**	0.206**	0.135**	0.159**
	(2.13)	(3.77)	(4.10)	(4.24)	(2.81)	(4.35)
log average years of schooling [-1]	0.105**	0.149**	0.086**	0.092**	...	0.102**
	(4.94)	(4.46)	(6.00)	(5.19)		(6.20)
log life expectancy [-1]	...	...	...	...	0.316**	...
					(5.09)	
log military expenditure/GDP [-1]	...	...	...	...	...	-0.024*
						(-2.42)
Imported capital goods/investment [-1]	...	...	...	0.032**	...	...
				(2.73)		
Percent change of trade volume/GDP	...	...	0.089**	...	...	...
			(3.57)			
Percent change of terms of trade	...	...	0.037*	...	...	...
			(2.39)			
Long-run elasticity of capital	0.306	0.409	0.420	0.653	0.439	0.501
Long-run elasticity of schooling	0.458	0.365	0.378	0.289	N.A.	0.323
Adjusted R^2	0.976	0.974	0.977	0.965	0.969	0.972
F-statistic	158.2	140.3	191.7	45.82	61.45	57.49
Durbin Watson [e]	1.785	2.013	2.303	2.308	2.208	2.365
S.E. of regression	0.010	0.011	0.009	0.012	0.011	0.010
N	31	31	51	50	39	50

Note: The regressions include a step dummy for 1977 and impulse dummies for 1963 and 1982 significant at 1%. a/ Asymptotic critical values of the t-ratio are from Banerjee et al. (1998). b/ Includes a 1976 impulse dummy significant at 1%. c/ Includes a time trend starting in 1999 significant at 5%. d/ Data is interpolated. e/ A Breusch-Godfrey test finds no evidence for the presence of serial correlation in the residuals.

t-statistics in parenthesis. ** Significant at 1%, * significant at 5%. Source: Author's calculations.

Notice that the inclusion of the variable alters the coefficients for capital accumulation but has little impact on the elasticity of average years of schooling. Unfortunately, measuring the impact of foreign capital goods on schooling by level of education was hampered by implausibly high, albeit positive, parameter estimates for schooling. Tentatively, such an exercise reveals an altering of the coefficients for primary education but has little impact on secondary and tertiary schooling. This clearly supports the earlier finding of the effect of trade openness on growth by level of education

4. Life Expectancy

Given the incomplete nature of education to proxy for human capital, a look at the effect of the health status yields important insights. Column 5 includes life expectancy at birth into the regression. The schooling variable is removed due to collinearity. The health variable is highly significant and has a very strong impact on long-run growth. The estimate suggests that a 1 percent increase in life expectancy would increase output by about 1.04 percent. Barro (2001) suggests that the variable has such a strong impact on growth because it may proxy for features other than health, such as social capital, better work habits and a higher level of skill. The elasticities could be biased due to the reliance on interpolated data sources. Nevertheless, the results support the view that human capital policies in Guatemala should place a strong emphasis on the health status of the population. This finding is equally echoed by the World Bank (2003a) that places Guatemala among the worst performers in terms of health outcome in Latin America, and particular poor in child nutrition.

5. Military Expenditures

Given the strong influence of military rule in Guatemala's recent history, it is finally imperative to discuss the role of military expenditure on growth.[30] This issue is particularly important since in the light of Guatemala's low tax burden military expenditures will necessarily be met at the expense of other government services, such as education and health. Military spending shows the priority given to other fiscal functions by the government and serves as an indicator of the military's power as a lobby. As such, *Guatemalan* military expenditures may also indicate political corruption and other aspects of bad government.

---

30 As a share of GDP, military expenditure in Guatemala is not excessively high, ranging from 0.7 up to 2 percent. However, its share of government expenditures is quite significant. According to Scheetz (2000) it has varied from approximately 14 up to 31 percent (in the 1980s) in terms of total resources controlled by the Treasury.

However, a number of channels by which military spending can influence growth have been identified. According to Deger and Sen (1995), the defense sector can take skilled labor away from civilian production, but it can also train workers. It could crowd out resources for investment and impact negatively on the efficiency of resource allocation, but also provide positive externalities for the civilian sector, such as infrastructure development. It can stipulate civil strife, but also generate an increase in national security and strengthen property rights. Thus, the role of military expenditure is ambiguous and the direction of the overall effect remains an empirical question.

Given the historical and political context of Guatemala, however, it is hard to believe that military expenditure plays a positive role on economic growth. According to the Commission for Historical Clarification (1999) an overwhelming number of violent actions during the civil war was attributed to members of the army. In addition, forced displacement and mandatory civil defense patrols (*Patrullas de Autodefensa Civil* — PACs) diverted a significant share of the economically active population from productive activities. Guatemalan defense spending reached its height during the peak of the civil war and declined in the advent of the peace process. They eventually began to rise again in 2000.

Even without econometric analysis, a look at Figure 7e reveals that output growth is essentially opposite to the ratio of military expenditure to GDP. Moreover, the negative correlation of the share of foreign capital goods to investment suggests that a higher ratio of military expenditure to GDP is associated with a decrease in the efficiency of capital accumulation. When military expenditures are included into the regression, column 6 of Table 10 reveals a significant negative impact on long-run growth. The implicit elasticity suggests that a 1 percent increase in the defense burden decreases output by approximately 0.08 percent. Considering the negative correlation with imported capital goods (r=-0.69) and the effects of the internal war, however, the true magnitude of military expenditures on long-run growth may be underestimated.

D. Summing-Up

For the case of Guatemala, sensitive tests reveal that the relationship of human capital and growth proves stable. Parameter stability of the coefficients is acceptable and employing alternative data in fact strengthens the findings. An important aspect is that the health status of the country exhibits a strong impact on long-run growth. In the light of Guatemala's recent history, it does not come as a big surprise that military expenditure has hampered growth. One important point here is that it crowds out investment. By contrast, imported foreign capital goods exhibit a significant impact on long-run growth via an increase in the efficiency of capital accumulation. In agreement with the previous chapter, primary schooling has the strongest impact on productivity growth, and is particularly affected by adjustments for the quality of capital and the growth of trade openness.

VII. Sources of Growth

The following paragraphs apply a modified growth-accounting framework to explore some basic facts of economic growth in Guatemala. Growth accounting can be very informative by providing a consistent decomposition of economic growth among its proximate sources. As such, growth accounting is a useful framework to explain a country's growth experience and may provide a basis for medium-term recommendations.

The chapter is divided into three sections. Section 1 briefly describes the methodological framework. To facilitate comparisons section 2 presents alternative measures of the sources of growth for Guatemala. After giving the results of a traditional Solow (1957) decomposition, indices for the quality of inputs are considered. Section 3 extends the basic growth accounting framework to disaggregate by level of education.

A. Growth Accounting Framework

Growth accounting is a technique that seeks to identify the sources of economic growth. The standard aggregate production function that generates the growth accounting equation is:

$$(26) \qquad Y_t = A_t \cdot K_t^{\alpha} \cdot L_t^{(1-\alpha)}$$

where Y, K and L represent output, physical capital stock and labor input, respectively. The term A is total factor productivity (TFP) and reflects the relative efficiency of the inputs to produce a given amount of output. The production function is assumed to have constant returns to scale and the markets are assumed to be competitive. In this framework, the growth rate of output can be represented as:

$$(27) \qquad \frac{\Delta Y_t}{Y_{t-1}} = \frac{\Delta A_t}{A_{t-1}} + \alpha \cdot \frac{\Delta K_t}{K_{t-1}} + (1-\alpha) \cdot \frac{\Delta L_t}{L_{t-1}}$$

where output growth is divided into components attributable to changes in the factors of production. TFP growth is a residual that represents the component of growth that is not explained by increases in the factors of production, but rather by productivity gains. The production function elasticities can give estimates of factor shares that are used to weigh the relative contribution of the inputs growth rates and to obtain straightforward estimates of the residual. Based on the results of the earlier regressions, the capital share, α, is taken to be equal to $^1/_3$. According to Bosworth et al. (1996) the econometric results are quite consistent with the evidence for other developing countries. Reliable estimates typically yield capital shares in the range of 0.3-0.4.

Estimates of Solow residuals are sensitive to the precision of the estimated factor shares, measurement errors, and adjustments for utilization and quality. For the case of Guatemala, as will be apparent in the next section, it is crucial to explicitly account for the quality of inputs.[31] Within the basic framework, changes in the quality of labor and physical capital are picked up in TFP. As such, TFP growth is overstated and the contribution of inputs is understated. In order to explicitly account for changes in the quality of inputs, the standard sources of growth equation is extended:

$$\frac{\Delta Y_t}{Y_{t-1}} = \frac{\Delta A_t}{A_{t-1}} + \alpha \cdot \left(\frac{\Delta K_t}{K_{t-1}} + \frac{\Delta zq_t}{zq_{t-1}} \right) + (1-\alpha) \cdot \left(\frac{\Delta L_t}{L_{t-1}} + \frac{\Delta hq_t}{hq_{t-1}} \right) \tag{28}$$

where zq_t and hq_t are quality indices of capital and labor, respectively.

Another important consideration, not captured by the basic framework, is to account for the contribution by level of education. Barro (1998) describes extensions of the basic growth accounting framework to allow for disaggregation across different factor types. Incorporating primary, secondary and tertiary education into the production function augmented for human capital gives:

$$\frac{\Delta Y_t}{Y_{t-1}} = \frac{\Delta A_t}{A_{t-1}} + \alpha \cdot \left(\frac{\Delta K_t}{K_{t-1}} \right) + \sum_{i=1}^{3} \beta_i \cdot \left(\frac{\Delta H_{i,t}}{H_{i,t-1}} \right) + (1 - \alpha - \sum_{i=1}^{3} \beta_i) \cdot \left(\frac{\Delta L_t}{L_{t-1}} \right) \tag{29}$$

where H_i indexes for primary, secondary and tertiary schooling. The capital share for physical capital is $^1/_3$. Likewise, the shares for human capital, β_i, are taken from the earlier regression estimates disaggregated by level of education. To ensure comparability with the aggregate case, however, the coefficients are scaled so as to preserve the aggregate human capital share of approximately $^1/_3$. Consequently, the implicit shares for the aggregate case are 0.17 for primary, 0.11 for secondary and 0.05 for tertiary schooling.

Finally, before taking a look at the results, it is important to emphasize some methodological caveats of growth accounting. TFP reflects a whole range of factors since it captures everything that is not accounted for. It is hard to distinguish the effect of technological change from that of improved resource allocation, or from bias resulting from model deficiencies and poor data quality. Thus, TFP estimates may be affected by scale economies and can be sensitive to data perpetuation.

---

31 Accounting for the degree of utilization of factor inputs is equally important. A common proxy is to use the unemployment rate. However, in the case of Guatemala with its extremely poor data on unemployment, such an adjustment is more likely to introduce measurement error than to correct for it.

In addition, findings in the area of growth accounting require careful interpretation because the technique does not provide information about the interdependencies of the variables. For instance, an increase of output growth could be due to a percentage change in educational attainment. This would not imply that, in the absence of educational improvements, the growth rate would have been precisely the same percentage point lower. Quite the contrary, education could impact on output growth due to fertility, attitudes and labor force participation, investment and productivity. Therefore, growth accounting should be treated with caution and only be regarded as a useful technique for examining growth.

B. Sources of Growth in Traditional Framework

Table 11 presents a basic decomposition of GDP growth for Guatemala for 1951-2002. TFP is measured as the residual representing the component of growth not explained by labor or capital accumulation. There are no adjustments for the quality of inputs. The results suggest that growth in Guatemala is largely due to the accumulation of inputs. Labor plays the dominant role in explaining about 50 percent of Guatemala's growth rate of GDP, followed by the accumulation of capital with approximately 32 percent. Growth of TFP — unadjusted for the quality of inputs — was about 18 percent.

Introducing quality change in factor inputs brings the relative roles of capital and labor into a sharper focus. Table 12 presents a decomposition of GDP growth for 1971-2002. Average annual growth was about 3.5 percent, while it was 3.9 percent during the whole five decades. Compared to the basic growth accounting framework, the results change dramatically. In particular, quality-adjusted labor now explains about 78 percent of the growth rate of GDP, compared to 50 percent explained by the unadjusted labor variable. This finding unambiguously suggests that the effect of the increase of education, now captured by the labor quality index, was the main driving force behind TFP growth during the past decades. By contrast, quality-adjusted capital only explains about 28 percent of growth, compared to 32 percent explained by the unadjusted variable. Consistent with earlier findings, the decrease of capital accumulation in explaining GDP growth reflects the deterioration of the quality of the country's physical capital base. This is most likely associated with the disastrous effect of the civil war and a negative investment climate, among other factors.

The finding of a negative rate of TFP growth of about 6 percent for the period 1971-2002 is a somewhat odd result. Rather than 'technological regress' it should be interpreted as an indication of the declining efficiency of the economy, due to the conflicting political and social environment of the country. Notice that TFP growth is consistent with the earlier regression results. In most specifications the constant term was found to be significantly negative.

Table 11. Guatemala: Decomposition of GDP Growth in Basic Framework, 1951-2002 (in percent) [a/]

Time Period	GDP Growth Rates	Contribution of		
		Capital	Labor	TFP
1951-55	2.3	0.6	-2.3	4.0
1956-60	5.4	1.7	4.0	-0.3
1961-65	5.3	1.1	3.8	0.3
1966-70	5.8	1.7	3.6	0.5
1971-75	5.6	1.6	2.2	1.9
1976-80	5.7	2.3	5.4	-2.0
1981-85	-1.1	0.6	-2.0	0.2
1986-90	2.9	0.4	3.1	-0.5
1991-95	4.3	0.9	1.2	2.2
1996-00	4.0	1.5	0.8	1.6
2001-02	2.3	1.3	1.6	-0.7
Average	3.9	1.2	2.0	0.7
		32%	50%	18%

Source: Author's calculations. a/ Discrepancies are due to rounding.

Table 12. Guatemala: Decomposition of GDP Growth Adjusted for Quality of Inputs, 1971-2002 (in percent) [a/]

Time Period	GDP Growth Rates	Contribution of		
		Capital	Labor	TFP
1971-75	5.6	1.5	3.6	0.5
1976-80	5.7	1.5	6.4	-2.1
1981-85	-1.1	0.2	-0.7	-0.5
1986-90	2.9	-0.1	3.5	-0.4
1991-95	4.3	1.1	0.6	2.6
1996-00	4.0	1.8	2.6	-0.4
2001-02	2.3	1.1	3.4	-2.3
Average	3.5	1.0	2.7	-0.2
		28%	78%	-6%

Source: Author's calculations. a/ Discrepancies are due to rounding.

How stable are these findings? The TFP estimate was found sufficiently robust. A sensitivity analysis based on alternative assumptions on the factor shares yielded TFP growth estimates ranging from –4 percent (capital share 0.4 and labor share 0.6) to –1 percent (capital share 0.5 and labor share 0.5). The associated changes of the contribution of labor and capital was negligible. Applying alternative data sources to calculate the residual was not found to be helpful. The robustness tests of the regression analyses clearly indicate that both the labor (based on IGSS data) and capital variable (5 percent depreciation) provide a higher explanatory power than other sources.

C. Disaggregation by Education Level

Table 13 shows the results of the extended growth accounting exercise for the period 1951-2002. The human capital variables now enter directly into the production function by level of education. They capture improvements in the country's skill base, which were formerly measured by quality-adjusted labor. At first sight, the overall results are somewhat similar to the decomposition of GDP growth in the traditional framework. With about 32 percent explaining growth, the role of physical capital accumulation is moderate.

Table 13. Guatemala: Decomposition of GDP Growth with Education Level Disaggregation, 1951-2002 (in percent) [a/]

Time Period	GDP Growth Rates	Contribution of					
		Capital	Labor	Education			TFP
				Primary	*Secondary*	*Tertiary*	
1951-55	2.3	0.6	-1.1	*0.0*	*0.7*	*-1.1*	3.2
1956-60	5.4	1.7	2.0	*1.3*	*1.1*	*1.1*	-1.7
1961-65	5.3	1.1	1.9	*1.2*	*1.2*	*0.7*	-0.8
1966-70	5.8	1.7	1.8	*1.4*	*0.8*	*0.7*	-0.5
1971-75	5.6	1.6	1.1	*0.9*	*0.9*	*0.7*	0.5
1976-80	5.7	2.3	2.7	*1.5*	*1.7*	*0.8*	-3.4
1981-85	-1.1	0.6	-1.0	*-0.3*	*0.1*	*0.0*	-0.6
1986-90	2.9	0.4	1.5	*0.8*	*0.8*	*0.6*	-1.3
1991-95	4.3	0.9	0.6	*0.1*	*0.2*	*0.5*	2.0
1996-00	4.0	1.5	0.4	*0.7*	*0.5*	*0.2*	0.6
2001-02	2.3	1.3	0.8	*0.6*	*1.3*	*0.3*	-2.1
Average	3.9	1.2	1.0	*0.8*	*0.8*	*0.4*	-0.3
		32%	25%	*19%*	*21%*	*10%*	-7%

Source: Author's calculations. a/ Discrepancies are due to rounding.

At second sight, the contrast to the traditional framework is apparent. Table 13 suggests that human resources are the main engine of growth. In fact, the human capital variables alone explain approximately 50 percent of output growth. Of these, the main contribution comes from secondary education with about 21 percent. This is closely followed by primary education, which explains about 19 percent of growth. The contribution of tertiary education was only 10 percent.

Insofar, *both* primary and secondary schooling constitute major determinants of GDP growth. The fact that secondary education constitutes the dominant role reflects its rapid increase in the share of the economically active population. Approximately 20 of the labor force has had secondary schooling in 2000, compared to only about 2 percent in 1950. The increase of primary schooling in the labor over time was much slower. As evidenced on Table 3, during the past five decades it has essentially doubled.

Table 14. Guatemala: Decomposition of GDP Growth with Education Level Disaggregation and Adjusted for Quality of Capital, 1971-2002 (in percent) [a/]

Time Period	GDP Growth Rates	Contribution of					
		Capital	Labor	Education			TFP
				Primary	*Secondary*	*Tertiary*	
1971-75	5.6	1.5	1.1	*0.9*	*0.9*	*0.7*	0.6
1976-80	5.7	1.5	2.7	*1.5*	*1.7*	*0.8*	-2.5
1981-85	-1.1	0.2	-1.0	*-0.3*	*0.1*	*0.0*	-0.2
1986-90	2.9	-0.1	1.5	*0.8*	*0.8*	*0.6*	-0.7
1991-95	4.3	1.1	0.6	*0.1*	*0.2*	*0.5*	1.8
1996-00	4.0	1.8	0.4	*0.7*	*0.5*	*0.2*	0.4
2001-02	2.3	1.1	0.8	*0.6*	*1.3*	*0.3*	-1.8
Average	3.5	1.0	0.9	*0.6*	*0.7*	*0.5*	-0.2
		28%	25%	*18%*	*21%*	*14%*	-6%

Source: Author's calculations. a/ Discrepancies are due to rounding.

Finally, Table 14 presents a decomposition of GDP growth by level of education. Capital is here adjusted for quality. Notice that the quantitative results for the period 1971-2002 are almost identical to Table 12. Capital explains 28 percent of growth, compared to 78 percent explained by labor and education. Of these, secondary education plays the dominant role, followed by primary and tertiary education. Thus, the results of the different accounting exercise were found consistent over time.

Figure 8 plots the annual TFP growth rates for the period 1951-2002. It contains two measures of TFP. The dotted line indicates TFP growth adjusted for the quality of labor. The thin solid line presents TFP growth adjusted for the quality of capital and labor. Both lines show similar patterns. Productivity growth is volatile according to Figure 8. Also, it is apparently not free of measurement errors. For instance, the strong increase in 1981 is probably best interpreted by data deficiencies. Therefore, to facilitate the interpretation of the results, the bold trend line was included using the Hodrick-Prescott filter. Productivity growth has been positive, although slightly decreasing until the late 1950s. This was followed by a substantial deterioration from the early 1960 until the end of the 1980s. In the 1990s, TFP growth became positive again, but from 1999 on has eventually decreased.[32] All in all, Figure 8 obviously suggests that TFP growth in Guatemala was closely associated with political events.

Figure 8. Guatemala: Evolution of Total Factor Productivity, 1951-2002 (annual growth rates, in percent)

Source: Author's calculations.

D. Comparison of Results with International Evidence

How do these estimates compare to other Latin American countries? Appendix One summarizes the results of a study that applies a comparable methodology. Loayza et al. (2002) focus on the growth performance of 20 Latin American and Caribbean countries. Similar to the approach used here, they adjust for changes in the quality of labor associated with increased educational attainment.[33] Consistent

32 This finding is in agreement with other recent growth accounting studies for Guatemala, which are presented in Box 3.

33 Roldós (1997) examines the growth experience for Chile, and adjusts for changes in the quality of labor *and* capital. These results are in Appendix One.

with international evidence, Loayza et al. find that during the 1990s the recovery in output growth for the 'best' performers in the Latin American region was driven by increases in their rates of TFP growth, and less so by factor accumulation.

However, in most Central American countries TFP growth was only moderate. In some cases it was even negative. While TFP growth in Guatemala appears to be on the high side compared to its Central American neighbors, it is worth recalling that the estimate presented in Appendix One does not take into account quality changes of the physical capital stock. Given the decay of Guatemala's quality-adjusted capital stock, TFP growth is likely to be overstated. In addition, a one-to-one comparison is hampered by the nature of the different data sources.[34] Overall, Guatemala's growth experience shows some similarities with its neighbors, in particular with Costa Rica and El Salvador. During the 1990s these countries have experienced much faster growth than during the 1980s. In particular, quality-adjusted labor — associated with increased educational attainment — was the main source of growth.

34 For example, Loayza et al. (2002) rely on the Barro and Lee (2001) data set on educational attainment.

VIII. Conclusion

Human capital has a highly significant and positive impact on long-run growth in Guatemala. The importance of human capital is substantial. An increase by 1 percentage point of average years of schooling would raise output by about 0.33 percent. The effect is of similar magnitude to that in micro studies. A disaggregated analysis by level of education reveals that primary schooling is most important for productivity growth, followed by secondary schooling. Over the past decades, it appears that general education and basic technical skills have been the main determinants for the diffusion of technological innovations, and people with primary education have particularly benefited from policies that promote competitiveness, such as trade openness. The stability of the error-correction model with respect to data issues and endogeneity concerns are the main reasons for confidence in the overall results. The robustness is even more remarkable in the context of heavy distortions within the Guatemalan economy.

Accounting for the sources of growth supports the importance of human capital in Guatemala. Such an exercise reveals that the increased skill level has been the main driving force behind productivity growth, and that education explains more than 50 percent of output growth during the past five decades. A differentiation by level of education suggests that the growth of secondary schooling was the predominant factor, closely followed by primary education. Tertiary education ranks last. Due to an environment of social and political conflict, however, total factor productivity has been slightly negative over the past decades. The evolution of productivity growth is linked to political events — such as the civil strife and military rule — and suggests a declining efficiency of the economy over time.

The study contains additional findings of interest, which ultimately point towards the importance of an institutional and political environment conducive to growth. They can be summarized as follows:

First, Guatemala's growth process was accompanied by the exclusion of large parts of society from wealth and by underlying social conflict. The growth rates of the sectors that employ the poor and rural people lagged behind other sectors of the economy. Extreme social imbalances and weak institutions for conflict management gave rise to an internal military conflict that imposed high costs for long-run growth. Regarding Guatemala's future growth prospects, a key factor for reducing the vulnerability of the economy to external shocks is to reduce inequality and to strengthen democratic institutions.

Second, mean education of the labor force has increased over time, although it suffered from the civil strife. The attention to education since the Peace Accords has only compensated the loss of human capital caused by the civil war, but does not represent a major improvement regarding the long-run growth of human capital. This means that considerable more effort is needed to strengthen the country's human capital base. The strong impact of life expectancy on growth suggests that human capital policies should not only focus on the expansion of the quantity as well as the quality of primary and secondary education, but in particular also place a great deal of emphasis on the health status of the population.

Finally, there is evidence of a missing complementarity between Guatemala's skills and its technology base. That is, for the period 1970-2002 the quality of Guatemala's physical capital stock decreased by about 20 percent. Prominent explanations for this decline are the destructive impact of the civil war, and a negative investment climate due to an unstable policy environment and a lack of good governance. The apparent gap between the evolution of quality of labor and physical capital could be a key factor for decreased output growth during the past decades. Decreased efficiency in capital accumulation also tends to reduce the returns to education, in particular for primary schooling. Hence, measures to stimulate investment and imports of foreign capital goods — for example by reducing trade distortions and improving the investment climate — are important complementary factors to human capital policies.

Part Two

What Drives Habitat Loss in Guatemala? An Inquiry into the Causes of Deforestation with an Emphasis on the Role of Education

Guatemala is a country with low levels of human capital and a modest per capita growth performance over the past decades — and it is relatively abundant in forest resources, which have been consecutively converted into agricultural land during the course of its history. To what extent have these factors a common ground? From a theoretical perspective, the processes in Guatemala have similarities with those described by Birdsall et al. (2001). Exploring the nexus between human capital accumulation, economic growth and natural resource abundance, she argues that skill accumulates at a slower rate in resource-abundant countries than in resource-deficient ones. This is because resource abundant countries tend to concentrate incomes and assets, while reducing employment and investment opportunities outside the agricultural sector. If there is little dynamism outside agriculture, high inequality, poor quality of schools and little demand for education prevails. When the boom in the resource sector ends, low human capital endowment, as well as low-quality schools, leave the country without the skilled workers and entrepreneurs needed for developing efficient, non-resource based firms. Having fewer chances to diversify the economy, these effects tend to prevail in small countries.

In fact, much can be learned from the Guatemalan case. The development of the country's agricultural sector — and here in particular regarding coffee and livestock — makes nearly a textbook example for rent seeking and income concentration among elitist groups. Resource rents from agricultural and livestock expansion were accumulated in the hands of the government, the military nomenclature and by a small number of businessmen. Guatemala's resource abundance in terms of forest and agricultural land has tempted governments and entrepreneurs to disregard policies that promote social development and human capital accumulation. In addition, there is ample evidence documented by UNDP (2000) and Luján (2000) that the overwhelming part of the indigenous and campesino population was actively discriminated against in labor and educational policies in order to create a low-wage rural labor force. These policies led, according the World Bank (2003a), to one of the greatest levels of inequality in terms of the distribution of income and land in the Latin American hemisphere. The situation finally exploded into a bloody conflict lasting three-decades. As stressed in the previous part, this civil strife had additional negative consequences on the country's human capital base and growth performance.

Past agricultural policies dominated by rent seeking entrepreneurs have not only provoked inequality, caused low schooling and hampered Guatemala's long-term growth perspectives. They also had important repercussions on rural livelihoods, the current structure of land use and deforestation. These issues are focussed on next. More specifically, Part Two explores the factors and underlying causes that led to the comparatively high levels of deforestation and habitat destruction in the countryside. A particular focus is laid on the role of human capital, an issue widely neglected in the deforestation literature. With this in mind, Part Two also offers an empirical analysis.

It is important to emphasize here that the following analysis should be considered as an independent, original contribution, and to outline the scope and limitations. First, analyzing the causes of habitat loss requires the reader to make a perspective change. Analytically, following Kaimowitz and Angelsen (2002), it seems to be most promising to address the underlying causes of habitat loss and the specific role of human capital from a household or regional-level perspective.

Second, this study investigates selected economic *decision* parameters of deforestation. It also analyzes the socio-economic context in which deforestation is taking place. However, it is *not* the aim here to document the complex interactions between income growth, poverty reduction programs and deforestation. On the one side, somewhat simplistically, the overall tone of the study may lead the reader to believe a view that income growth and poverty reduction would be conducive for a policy aimed at reducing habitat loss in Guatemala. On the other side, however, there are clearly tradeoffs that would have to be considered in *future research* and would need *distinct methodologies*, such as Computable General Equilibrium (CGE) approaches. For example, higher incomes may result in an increased demand for forest resources, energy consumption and could boost environmental pollution. Regarding poverty, in fact, the results of the following part suggest that there even could be unpleasant conflicts between poverty alleviation programs and habitat conservation practices.

Finally, in what follows, there is no answer offered to the question of why arresting deforestation and conserving biodiversity in a poor country like Guatemala should deserve a prominent place. For many people, habitat conservation and deforestation issues are not even considered to be the biggest problems facing the country. Given that not much is known about the genuine value that can be attached to biodiverse forest resources, potentially powerful arguments usually stress the importance of a safety belt for impoverished people, the need to tackle global climate change, and the importance of having an option value for future generations. For the case of Guatemala, it is also interesting to note that forest resources in terms of watersheds are significant since, reportedly, the country produces about $^1/_3$ of its electrical energy from hydro-electric power plants. Nevertheless, the arguments that justify natural resource conservation in poor countries like Guatemala are beyond the scope of this study.

"Maderas preciosas por lo preciosas. Palos medicinales en montón. Como la guerrilla con los hombres en la guerra, así acaba el maicero con los palos. Humo, brasa, cenizal. Y si fuera por comer. Por negocio. Y si fuera por cuenta propia, pero a medias en la ganancia con el patrón y a veces ni siquiera a medias. El maíz empobrece la tierra y no enriquece a ninguno. Ni al patrón ni al mediero. Sembrado para comer es sagrado sustento del hombre que fue hecho de maíz. Sembrado por negocio es hambre para el hombre que fue hecho de maíz..."

Miguel Angel Asturias, Hombres de Maíz, 1949

I. Introduction

Over the past decades, decline and extinction of species have emerged as major environmental issues.[35] Given the importance attached to habitat modifications as a threat to biodiverse natural resources, and in order to keep a broad range of options for future generations, analyzing the processes that determine land use decisions within a country is essential. Like many other countries, Guatemala has experienced a dramatic loss of forest cover during the past decades. In fact, according to the FAO (2001) deforestation in Central America is higher than elsewhere in the world, and the annual percent loss of forest cover in Guatemala is higher than in countries predominantly in the public eye, such as Brazil or Indonesia. Within this context, the aim of this part is twofold.

First, it investigates the socio-economic factors that determine the deforestation process in Guatemala. Clarifying the role of the economic parameters of deforestation makes it possible to propose policy interventions that will mitigate the loss of biodiversity. Needless to say, little rigorous analytical work for Guatemala exists. Most evidence comes from scattered literature, which is usually focused on

---

35 I have greatly benefited from interviews and discussions with David Kaimowitz (Center for International Forestry Research), Norman Schwartz (University of Delaware), Douglas Southgate (Ohio State University), Julia Johannsen, Michael Markussen and Regina Birner (University of Goettingen), Juventino Gálvez (*Universidad Rafael Landívar*), Gisela Gellert and Silvel Elías (*Facultad Latinoamericana de Sciencias Sociales*), Juan Carlos Godoy (*Ministerio de Ambiente y Recursos Naturales*), Maynor Estrada (FAO), Edgar Pineda (UNDP), Odgen Rodas and Adelso Revolorio (*Plan de Acción Forestal* — PAFG), Karla Donis de Girón (*Instituto Nacional de Bosques* — INAB), Jorge Minera (*Banco de Guatemala*), Augusto Rosales (*Fundación Rigoberta Menchú Tum*), Celia Marcos (*Asociación de Investigaciones y Estudios Sociales* — ASIES), Margret Dix (*Universidad del Valle*), Reginaldo Reyes (*Oficina Técnica de Biodiversidad del Consejo Nacional de Areas Protegidas* — OTECBIO) and Ivo Bockor (GTZ).

a particular issue, location, or time period, and the analysis tends to be highly speculative. It is worth noting that the deforestation process in Guatemala, which according to Southgate and Basterrechea (1993) has much in common with its Latin American counterparts, also provides an interesting and unique case study. Generally, due to the difficulties in terms of data availability, the empirical analysis of deforestation in the developing world has been concentrated on medium and large countries, which are politically stable, and of comparatively higher levels of economic wealth. However, this kind of selection bias may impact the results of empirical studies, and influence the conclusions and policy decisions drawn from them. Thus, a closer look at a small, poor, and unstable country such as Guatemala is inherently valuable.

Second, this study documents the correlation between schooling and forest clearing and indicates an interesting policy lever, namely, if more schooling could reduce forest clearance, it could also, in theory, provide an interesting 'win-win' scenario, reducing poverty and stimulating income growth at the same time. Godoy and Contreras (2001) have also pointed out that the extra costs of bringing schools to remote areas might be less than financing new and expensive programs to conserve more tropical forest. In general, there are currently very few deforestation studies that shed any light on the role of human capital. This is surprising, but may reflect disciplinary parochialism, since researchers of education seem to be *not* concerned about environmental issues, and investigators working on deforestation seem to know *little* about the effects of human capital.

To examine the causal structure of deforestation, and the specific role of human capital, this study is divided into three parts: a conceptual analysis of the factors associated with deforestation, a qualitative assessment of deforestation patterns in Guatemala, and an empirical analysis.

In Chapter II the relationship between deforestation and biodiversity loss is clarified, and the reader is given an overview of relevant theoretical and empirical underpinnings. The conceptual framework provides *working hypotheses* for the empirical analysis on Guatemala to come later. It covers a variety of socio-economic parameters, including the potential role of education. One of the main findings is that the effects of economic parameters on deforestation are rather ambiguous. Consequently, in order to arrive at policy-relevant conclusions, closer *empirical* analysis is essential. In this regard, a number of studies suggest that market links are strengthening even in remote forest areas. Part Two therefore establishes the hypothesis that, in principle, education can play a significant role in reducing the pressure on forests and contribute to the conservation of biodiversity.

Chapter III provides an extensive qualitative assessment of deforestation patterns in Guatemala, and identifies coherent trends and causes over time. Due to the complexity of the various driving forces behind deforestation, the literature is quite scattered, and a series of qualitative interviews were conducted to complement it. One of the key findings is that deforestation in Guatemala is correlated with the discriminatory labor and educational policies. Agricultural policies of the past have caused poverty and rural underdevelopment and, in turn, have had important repercussions on the current structure of deforestation. After an episode of agricultural expansion and, as documented by Schwartz (1995a), government sponsored colonization, it appears that the encroachment of smallholders can now be regarded as the main direct source of deforestation. Unfortunately, the conflict-ridden situation is aggravated by the return of the civil war refugees, and the massive expansion of protected areas by non-participatory management policies of several environmental movements.[36]

Chapter IV validates the hypothesis derived from the previous analysis about the socio-economic parameters of deforestation. The chapter consists of an unique analysis of three different data sets designed to eliminate potential aggregation and data quality bias. Overall, the results are found to be consistent, not to show significant bias, and to provide interesting insights into the underlying socio-economic parameters of deforestation. In particular, the use of survey data for Guatemala's main agricultural frontier region, the Petén, strengthens the validity of the empirical results. In fact, the number of observations of this survey exceeds some of the existing empirical evidence from household-level analysis. Insofar, the findings may have implications beyond this pure case study.

Finally, chapter V summarizes the results, provides policy recommendations, and indicates directions for future research. The two clearest and most important findings are first, that indeed schooling does show a significant effect on the reduction of deforestation. For the Petén, Guatemala's main agricultural frontier, the effect is more pronounced for basic education up to 3 years. The fact that schooling reduces forest clearing is probably closely associated with improved access to rural non-agricultural activities. However, since it is also evident that many other factors are important determinants of deforestation, providing better access to educational services is obviously only one ingredient towards reducing pressure from the forest. Second, contrary to common belief, agricultural intensification techniques seem to increase the demand for additional land in Guatemala. Insofar, these results call into question some of the current agricultural

---

36 In practice, not on paper, Guatemala's 1999 National Biodiversity Conservation Strategy focuses nearly exclusively on protected area issues. It was made without proper consultation of the indigenous groups, who represent the overwhelming share of the rural population. Personal communication with Anne Dix, *Universidad del Valle*, July 4, 2001.

development projects promoted by non-governmental organizations and bilateral donors.

II. Explaining Deforestation and Biodiversity Loss

This chapter provides a conceptual framework to explore the causes of deforestation and biodiversity loss and is organized as follows. Section A explains the relationship between biodiversity loss and forest cover change. Section B compares subsistence and market-based models of deforestation to provide a range of hypotheses on the potential effects that changes in economic parameters have on deforestation. Section C incorporates formal education into this framework. Section D provides a review on the deforestation literature, and focuses particularly on case studies for Mexico, Belize, Honduras and Bolivia. The main conclusion drawn from this chapter is that the effects of economic parameters on forest cover loss are ambiguous. However, the empirical evidence tends to suggest that the relative profitability of agriculture does play a role in deforestation. In addition, despite conflicting mechanism and scarce empirical evidence, it is argued that, in principle, schooling has the potential to reduce pressure on the forests.

A. Deforestation as Proxy for Biodiversity Loss

The absence of baseline data and methodologies makes it difficult to gather reliable information on biodiversity loss.[37] According to the United Nations Environment Programme (UNEP 2002), much of the available information is qualitative and anecdotal, and studies typically rely on habitat degradation. This includes the conversion of forests, classified by UNEP as the single most important factor causing loss of species in tropical and sub-tropical countries. Uncertainties in the assessment of biodiversity loss are, however, a function of uncertainty in the rate of deforestation itself. It is worth noting that there are a number of additional factors related to biodiversity loss. Among these are pollution, the unsustainable harvesting of natural resources, climate change, and the invasion of exotic species. The relative importance of these factors differs between regions and ecosystems. In terms of data availability and given the underlying causal structure of habitat loss in Guatemala, this study focuses on deforestation.

The rational to see deforestation as a major cause of biodiversity loss is provided by the theory of island biography. McArthur and Wilson (1967) visualized the number of species on an island as a balance between species gains by

---

37 Biodiversity refers to the variability among all living organisms from all environments, including terrestrial, marine and other ecosystems, and the ecological complexes of which they are part. Following the UN Convention on Biological Diversity (1992), this includes diversity between species, within species and of ecosystems, as well as human cultural diversity. For details and a critique on the convention, see Brühl (2002) as well as Boisvert and Caron (2002).

immigration and losses through extinction.[38] Using this concept, they developed a quantitative model to explain the number of species on islands. The model implies that habitats will contain more species if the area available to species increases or the immigration rate increases. The model is commonly — and quite loosely — extended to forest reserves, which are considered as islands in a sea of altered habitat. The species-area relationship, upon which island biography is based, is often used to make *pragmatic* estimates of the extinction of species resulting from deforestation. It is usually expressed in the form of a simple power law:

$$(30) \qquad S_t = c \cdot A_t^{\,z}$$

where S is the number of species, A the area, and c is a parameter that depends on the taxon group, the population density, and the biogeographical region. In particular, the predicted magnitude of the extinction of species in relation to the loss of forest area is a function of the z-factor. The latter can be interpreted as the elasticity of species diversity with respect to the area. Empirically, the z-factor is estimated to lie somewhere between 0.15 and 0.35. Thus, the empirical evidence points to diminishing returns in species diversity with increasing area. Because little is known about c, studies using the species-area relationship tend to eliminate it through the following reworking of the equation:

$$(31) \qquad \frac{S_t}{S_0} = \frac{A_t^z}{A_0^z}$$

where t stands for the current time period and zero for a reference time period. In an empirical examination of this relationship, Plotkin et al. (2000) demonstrate that it is a very good approximation at broad scales. It is less accurate, however, as a rule of thumb at finer resolutions.[39] Thus, the application of these equations can be problematic, and its simplicity is subject to a series of critiques.

(1) Broad confidence bands. A variation in z creates broad confidence bands. Since the model is very sensitive to the z values, it allows for a wide envelope of extinction given a similar magnitude of deforestation (see Table 15). Unfortunately, an understanding of the factors that affect the value of z is still incomplete. Islands

38 The species-area curve was postulated by Arrhenius (1921) but did not enjoy popularity until the work of McArthur and Wilson (1967). Details of the theoretical and empirical underpinnings can be found in Connor and McCoy (1979). A caveat is that the relationship captures only the species component of biological diversity.

39 For an empirical case study on Guatemala, confirming the effect of deforestation on species loss, see Renner (2003).

tend to have somewhat higher factors compared to continental areas. In other words, the factor increases, as the area under consideration becomes smaller. When the z values are low, the relationship predicts that much of the land area can be deforested before the slope of the extinction curve increases rapidly. With a value of z being 0.25, a 95 percent reduction of the size of an island, say forest, should roughly produce a halving of the number of species. Conversely, at high z values, the model would suggest that the extinction rate is almost proportional to the deforestation rate. However, Lugo et al. (1993) mention that the relationship cannot predict rates of species extinction that are faster than deforestation rates because the z-factor must then be higher than the available empirical data suggest is possible.

Table 15. Relationship Between Deforestation and Species Loss

Deforestation (percent lost of primary forest cover)	Species loss to extinction (percentage lost of initial)		
	z = 0.35	z = 0.25	z = 0.15
10	3.6	2.6	1.6
25	9.6	6.9	4.2
50	21.5	15.9	9.9
75	38.4	29.3	18.8
90	55.3	43.8	29.2
95	65.0	52.7	36.2

Source: Author's calculations based on equation (31).

(2) Overestimation of extinction rates. When deforestation is taking place, the partial depletion of a specific area must not necessarily destroy the species completely. In addition, it can be argued that there are not only two states of the land, that is, deforested and forested land, but more. Since not all the logged forest need be considered unforested land, part will become secondary forest through human intervention or will be open to natural regeneration. For example, after fleeing, species can return and invade sites through successful natural mechanisms. Therefore, Lugo et al. (1993) suggest that the use of the species-area relationship overestimates extinction rates as it fails to take into account these additional parameters.

(3) Omission of habitat diversity. Finally, the species-area relationship has limitations since the curves are based on single taxa. Habitat diversity is not accounted for in the model, except for the implicit assumption that larger areas have more habitats. Therefore, it is likely that assemblages of species will exhibit different relationships from area to area as compared to individual taxa because the

curves are not necessarily additive. For the cases of low or high species diversity at a specific site, the direction of the measurement bias is not immediately apparent.

With consideration of the restrictions just mentioned above, however, there usually appears to be a strong correlation between the size of an area and the number of species to be found in that area. Hence, tropical deforestation is likely to cause a considerable degree of extinction. Therefore, the species-area relationship provides powerful arguments for being concerned about deforestation in terms of biodiversity loss. Before proposing interventions to mitigate this important cause of biodiversity loss, it is necessary to analyze more closely the process of land conversion.

B. Is Deforestation Subsistence or Market Driven?

Deforestation and land use changes do not lend themselves readily to a simplistic causal analysis. The following paragraphs present a conceptual framework for land use changes and deforestation. Models of agricultural expansion in countries that are affected by deforestation can differ with respect to their behavioral and market assumptions. The implicit reasoning in these models is that *agricultural* expansion takes place into forested areas. In reality, of course, this must not always be the case. Although this section does not consider other important sources of deforestation, they should be kept in mind, for example, the expansion of livestock or logging via large-scale and state sponsored activities. Nevertheless, when agricultural expansion is the main direct source of deforestation the following approaches provide useful insights.

Two important and partly contradicting sets of models are outlined next. Section 1 briefly presents the subsistence approach. Section 2 presents the basic market approach. As somewhat extreme categories, they are considered useful to explore the range of hypotheses on deforestation resulting from changes in economic parameters. Section 3 extends the market approach. Finally, section 4 compares both model classes.

1. Subsistence Approach

As its point of departure, this approach assumes that people satisfy their subsistence requirements mainly from agricultural production. The objective of the household is assumed to be to minimize labor efforts given a predefined subsistence target. In essence, the key assumption is that households seek to meet a pre-established consumption target and loose all interest in working once having reached these goals. Among others, Kaimowitz and Angelsen (2002) claim that this assumption seems to be rather unrealistic, even in remote frontier agricultural contexts.[40] Nevertheless, this assumption underlies many popular studies and policy recommendations. Therefore, it is important to briefly outline the main implications.

In the simplest version, it is supposed that no markets exist and that the subsistence requirement is fixed. Uncultivated land or forest is thought to be under open access. With family labor as the only input besides land, the household produces for its own consumption. Given the simplifying assumption of fixed labor inputs, varying according to the life cycle of the household, there is little choice left to the household because there is only one decision variable left: agricultural land. In this case, the area of cultivation has to be expanded until the subsistence target is met. While many policy recommendations and arguments in the popular debate are grounded on this subsistence thinking, there are rather few analytical models. Stryker (1976) and Dvorak (1992), as well as Angelsen (1995; 1999) present models of the subsistence approach. The main implications of these are summarized below. In general, productivity, population growth, distance costs, and subsistence requirements determine the magnitude of land use changes.

First, an increase in the value of production will reduce deforestation since the subsistence income can be obtained from a smaller area. Higher agricultural productivity or higher output prices will therefore reduce deforestation. Second, given a subsistence requirement per capita, total area of cultivation is proportional to population. Population growth will boost deforestation as it increases the overall consumption requirement. The effect of population growth can, however, be modified by technological progress and will not lead to more deforestation if the rate of population growth is lower than the rate of productivity growth. Third, improved accessibility leads to an increased area of cultivation and is thus likely to promote deforestation. This is because there are costs related to the clearing of new land, as well as costs entailed in having a larger area to cultivate, for example in both walking distances and transportation requirements.

Finally, an increase in the subsistence requirement will expand the agricultural frontier. Whereas a basic subsistence requirement could be defined in nutritional terms, it may also have cultural and social elements. Angelsen (1999) hypothesizes that the integration of the subsistence sector into a larger market economy expands the subsistence requirement and, hence, increases deforestation.

---

40 This critique has led to the development of Chayanov-type models, in which household are assumed to maximize their utility in terms of preferences for income *and* leisure time. Chayanov-type models with the assumption of existing non-farm employment have been developed by Nakajima (1986), Singh et al. (1986) and more recently Angelsen (1999) and Walker et al. (2002). For a discussion see the later section 'Policy Implications of the Models.'

2. Market Approach

Compared to the subsistence model, the market (or open economy approach) is based on a different kind of reasoning that was pioneered by von Thünen (1826). He suggests that deforestation occurs because people find it profitable. Modeling rural land use in concentric cycles around a city in which all goods and services are marketed, von Thünen argues that the land is put into use according to how it will yield the highest returns. The increasing transportation costs from locations with greater distance from the market place will lead to decreasing land value and decreasing intensity of cultivation, until the land value decreases to zero and an 'uncultivated wilderness' begins. Applying this principle, von Thünen was able to deduce that different commodities would be produced in distinct zones, and he identified the principle by which commodities were assigned to particular zones.

Based on the von Thünen approach, von Arnsberg (1994), Angelsen (1995; 1999) and Angelsen et al. (2001) present a static framework for areas that are affected by deforestation. Following Singh et al. (1986) the key assumption is that production decisions can be separated from consumption decisions. This allows production decisions, including land use, to be analyzed as profit maximization problems. Profits that come from production (or land rent) are defined as the gross value of production minus all costs of production:

$$r = p \cdot X - w \cdot L - q \cdot D - c \cdot K \qquad (32)$$

where

r	=	land rent
p	=	price per unit of output
X	=	output related to technological level or soil fertility
w	=	opportunity cost of labor
L	=	labor input
q	=	costs related to the location of the field
D	=	distance from the village to the field
c	=	price of capital
K	=	capital requirements

The relationship between land rent and distance is illustrated by the left curve, the so-called bid-rent curve, in Figure 9. An interesting feature is that it can be given both a local and a regional level interpretation. At the local level in a village surrounded by forest, the main distance costs would be to walk to the field. Some locations may have too high distance costs to make cultivation profitable. At the regional level, a more abstract interpretation would be to let the abscissa in the

Figure 9 represent all forestland within a larger area, ranked according to accessibility.

The bid-rent curve refers to the maximum rent someone would be willing to pay (or to bid) for land at a given distance in a competitive market. Keeping other factors constant, land rent declines as distance increases and eventually reaches zero. The basic premise here is that all forest land with a positive rent will be cleared and transformed into agricultural production, given that people are free to move. Thus, point d^* delineates the distance at which land rent is zero and thus defines the agricultural frontier.

Figure 9. The Agricultural Frontier

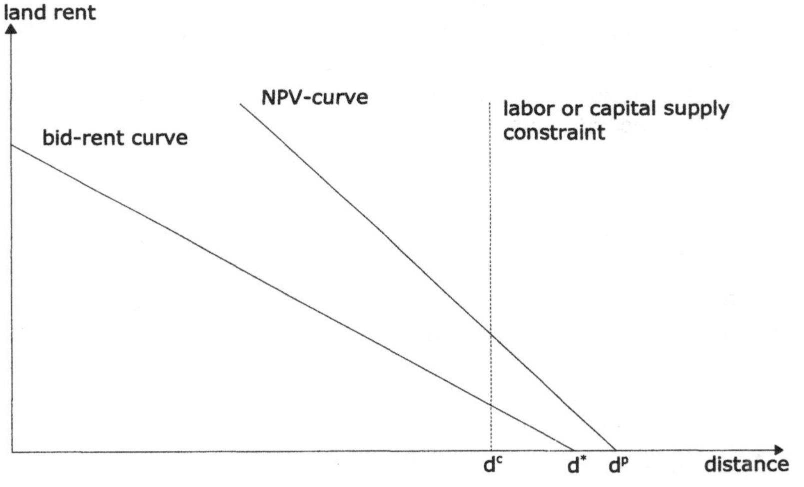

Source: Adapted from Angelsen (1995) and Angelsen et al. (2001). The Net Present Value (NPV)-curve is explained in the later section 'Extensions of the Market Approach.'

Any change in the variables, which increase the profitability of agriculture, moves the curve to the right and will therefore increase deforestation. Higher output prices, a lower price of capital and lower transport costs, particularly influenced by the availability of road infrastructure, will boost deforestation. A forest area in a remote frontier region will remain forested as long as transportation and access costs are so high that agricultural activities on the land will not generate a profit. In addition, better soil quality and higher output prices should increase deforestation. Finally, technological progress may augment deforestation, since it could either be labor saving or increase the production of agricultural output.

The open economy approach assumes that all prices are exogenous. That is, deforestation agents behave as if their actions have no impact on prices. While this assumption may be analytically convenient, it carries powerful implications, including the assumption of a perfect labor market where individuals can find employment at an exogenously determined wage rate. Labor is considered to migrate freely between the farm and the non-farm sectors to ensure labor supply and demand at the predetermined wage rate.

Compared to the subsistence approach, one of the key changes here is the introduction of a labor market into the underlying assumptions. The wage rate in alternative employment gives the opportunity to consider the cost of labor used in agriculture. According to the market approach, a lower wage rate in alternative employment will increase agricultural land use. Angelsen (1995) argues that the opportunity costs of labor should be thought of in a broad sense and can include types other than self-employment in agriculture. For instance, alternative employment could comprise not only wage labor from the non-farm sector but also, in the case of temporary migrants, the income from labor-intensive farming or from other occupations at the place of residence.

3. Extensions of the Market Approach

The reasoning inherent in the basic premises of the market approach can be modified and extended in order to achieve a more realistic view of the processes involved in deforestation. Three extensions are considered in the following paragraphs. Property rights often play a prominent role in the debate on resource degradation, and should therefore be incorporated into the model. In addition, regarding the possible imperfections in rural labor and capital markets, it will be interesting to see what happens in the case of labor or capital constraints. Finally, a qualification is made regarding the effects of increased agricultural productivity on land use changes.

(1) Property rights. In theory, an important economic instrument for overcoming excessive deforestation is the establishment of property rights because to do so would eliminate the problem of open access. In practice, however, the establishment and enforcement of property rights can be expensive, possibly even more costly than the value to be protected. As a consequence, in areas that are affected by deforestation, de facto property rights are often established by so-called 'improvements' of the land. In most cases, this involves forest clearing. Under such circumstances, farmers are not only looking at immediate benefits. They are also expecting a future surplus from agricultural production.

Following Angelsen (1995), the *future* production surplus can be summarized in the net present value (NPV), and is illustrated by the right curve in Figure 9. The reason why the NPV-curve intersects the abscissa to the right of the bid-rent curve is straightforward. Since it is expected that the land rent increases over time, the net present value at distance d* must be positive, and the NPV-curve lies above the bid-rent curve. Competition among farmers for new land will ensure that all forest with a positive net present value is going to be cleared. Thus, the agricultural frontier will be found at point d^p, where the net present value is zero. Forest is cleared even if it has a negative rent during the first years. The potential loss is outweighed by the positive land rent of the future. In this sense, from an individual point of view, early clearing is necessary to establish property rights. If no clearing occurs, others would take the land. Consequently, a system where clearing gives property rights will move the agricultural frontier beyond a pure open access regime, and can therefore stimulate deforestation.[41]

(2) Market imperfections. As has been stressed by Angelsen et al. (2001), the absence or imperfection of markets can have important consequences. With regard to the labor market, family labor often finds few alternatives outside the farm and many households cannot afford to hire labor. Therefore, at the different stages of its family cycle, the amount of labor the household has available limits the amount of land use. The vertical line illustrates this case. Instead of d^* the actual forest frontier will be at d^c.

Contrary to the basic model, this would imply that the availability of certain types of non-farm employment might not have an unambiguous effect on deforestation: in the unconstrained world, non-farm opportunities increase the opportunity cost of labor. This, in turn, makes land expansion more expensive and causes the agricultural frontier to contract. In the constrained world, however, farmers can use increased wage earnings to hire labor or purchase cattle, all of which would increase deforestation. In a similar manner the availability of capital can constrain the expansion of the agricultural frontier. Programs targeting poor farmers who initially behaved as if they were credit-constrained could therefore boost deforestation.

(3) Technological progress. When the supply of labor or capital constrains the expansion of agricultural area, the type of technological process involved becomes important. Technological change that allows farmers to use less of their scare factor will boost deforestation. By contrast, innovations that are labor-intensive will reduce deforestation. For example, when households have a limited amount of

41 Guatemala has a quasi-open access situation. Agricultural and forest land is mostly in private or state property. However, property rights are often not enforced, and 'illegal' encroachment plays a great role.

labor at their disposal, labor-intensive technological change should reduce the cultivated area and hence decrease deforestation.

However, this kind of reasoning needs to be relativised. Van Soest et al. (2002) explore in detail the relation between technology that affects the agricultural sector and deforestation. Looking at various land-use decisions models of rural households, they conclude that it is questionable to talk in general terms about the effects of agricultural technology and deforestation. Whether and how technological change affects forest clearing depends not only on the form of the change, but also on the presence of market imperfections, the institutional setting, and the specification of the underlying theoretical model.

In line with the reasoning of the previous section, technological progress is more likely to encourage deforestation when farmers behave as profit maximizers rather than subsistence oriented producers, the new technology is labor saving and can be applied in agricultural frontier contexts, or both labor supply and the demand for agricultural products are elastic. Insofar, the net effects of technological change in agriculture on deforestation can be either positive or negative. Quite often, however, they are rather ambiguous and can vary substantially within the local situation. As will be shown in a later section, attempts to assess this issue empirically have yielded equally mixed results — or been unable to even establish any significant relationship.

The issue is further complicated by the fact that technological progress is unlikely to affect only one household. If a large number of households adopt new technologies, this could have important repercussions beyond the micro-effects envisaged so far. The regional-level effects can either diminish or enlarge the impact of new technologies on households decision variables. Angelsen et al. (2001) identify two major types of these effects. (i) The first one operates via changes in prices. (ii) The second one operates through migration to or from the agricultural frontier.

(i) The overall price effects are likely to depress the micro-level effects. Depending on whether the increase in agricultural productivity outweighs the decline in price induced by the raise in aggregate supply, farmers revenues may go up or down. On the one hand, technological innovations affecting crops not very sensitive to changes in supply, as is probably the case for most export crops, may cause agricultural activities to expand at the expense of forests. On the other hand, in the case of crops produced mainly for the domestic market, the price decrease may outweigh the productivity increase. In other words, the more farmers produce, the less they earn per unit and, hence, the less incentive they have to clear additional forest.

(ii) Another important mechanism that might impact on deforestation is migration. The key reasoning is here that technological progress can be region-specific. For example, if agricultural productivity rises outside the forest region and farmers both inside and outside the forest region produce the same crop, and sell it to the same market, deforestation may decrease. This is because there is an incentive to move away from the agricultural frontier as frontier farmers expect to receive lower revenues.

As illustrated in Figure 10, the effects of technological change (which is assumed to raise the household's income) on deforestation depend on the number of households at the forest margin. Figure 10 suggests that households compare the level of income that they can expect in different regions in order to choose where to live best. Furthermore, there are two regions, that is the upland and the lowland. The expected per capita income in each region declines as the number of people in one region rises. The span of Figure 10 is total population.

The basic premise is that people will migrate from one region to another until each region has the same level of income. This is illustrated by point L_1. An increase in agricultural technology can influence the location of the curves. Better agricultural technology that applies to the forested lowland area but not elsewhere will shift the lowland income curve upward.

Figure 10. Migration and Income Differences

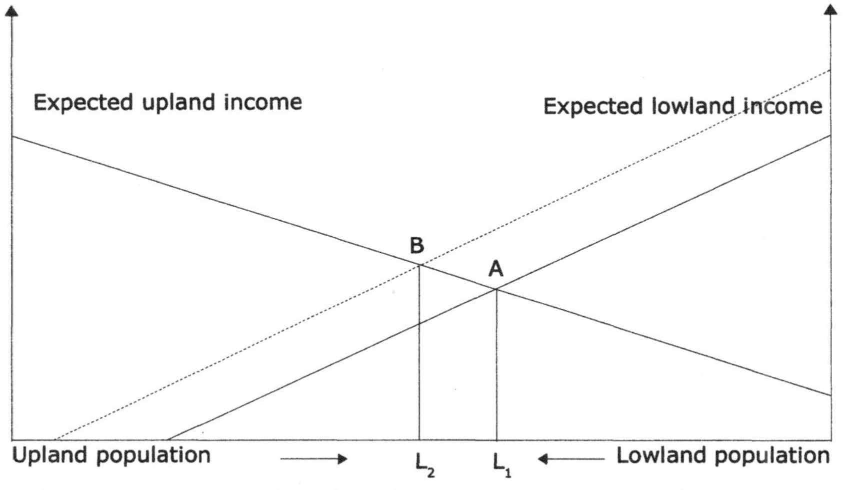

Source: Adapted from Angelsen et al. (2001). The span is total population.

An example for this would be the promotion of sustainable agriculture practices via the establishment of Integrated Conservation and Development Projects (ICDPs), or better access to markets via road construction. The dotted line in Figure 10, where L_2 is the new equilibrium, reflects this. A consequence of technological change — making agriculture more attractive in only one region — would be increased migration flow (from L_1 to L_2) and deforestation. Thus, taking into account the potential of technological change to attract households to the agricultural frontier, the risk of deforestation increases. By contrast, creating socio-economic incomes outside the forest margin could be a tool to impede forest degradation. A shortcoming with this kind of reasoning is the focus on only one decision parameter affecting migration. Obviously, numerous non-economic factors may also impact on rural migration. This kind of reasoning will be picked up in Section C of this chapter by discussing the role education and other variables can have on the decision to migrate.

4. Policy Implications of the Models

Given the previous analysis of the subsistence and market approach, one can conclude that the effects from policies influencing economic parameters of deforestation are far from being straightforward. Some policies reduce pressure on forests and can simultaneously be accused of increasing deforestation. The hypotheses about the effects from changes in economic variables on deforestation are summarized in Table 16. To simplify a bit, the subsistence approach yields a population and a productivity-based explanation, while the open economy approach emphasizes the relative *profitability* of frontier agriculture, and the importance of alternative employment opportunities.

In the subsistence approach, population growth will unambiguously result in higher deforestation. In the market approach, population does not enter explicitly. However, Angelsen et al. (1999) argue that a higher population level may have effects by lowering wages and raising food prices. In addition, population can be influenced by the availability of infrastructure, soil quality and socio-economic factors. In an empirical model, effects of population may therefore be captured indirectly by these variables. Within the open economy approach, the population parameter should, in general, be considered to be partly endogenous.

The hypotheses for the effect of output prices and, in particular, the technological level is the opposite in both approaches. On the one hand, technological progress — due to agricultural intensification or other factors — can be justifiably considered as reducing pressure on forests since food requirements can be met with ever-smaller cultivation plots. On the other hand, this agricultural intensification may increase profitability, lead to agricultural expansion, and, hence, increase deforestation. Nevertheless, as discussed in the previous section, extensions of the market approach reveal the rather complex relationship between improved technology and land use change. Also, the role in land use changes that alternative employment and availability of capital do have becomes less obvious or clear in the presence of capital and labor constraints.

Table 16. Hypotheses on Deforestation Derived from Subsistence and Market Approach

Increase of	Effect on deforestation	
	Subsistence approach	Market approach [a/]
Population	+	(+)
Subsistence requirement	+	N.A.
Output prices	N.A.	+
Productivity	–	+
Distance costs	–	–
Price of capital	N.A.	–
Opportunity costs of labor	N.A.	–
Expectations about land rent	N.A.	+

Source: Adapted from Angelsen (1999). a/ Basic model, see text for qualifications. Brackets indicate uncertain effects due to endogeneity. N.A. = not applicable.

Since policy recommendations depend critically on the approach chosen, the question arises whether the subsistence or market approach is more realistic in an agricultural frontier context. As pointed out by Angelsen (1999), the distinction is extremely important. Many of the popular policy descriptions that emphasize population growth and poverty as the main driving forces of deforestation seem to rely on subsistence thinking. Perhaps this is because, if agricultural intensification can take pressure off forests, it can also offer an easy policy entrance for promoting the 'win-win' scenario within that critical triangle of environmental sustainability, productivity growth, and poverty alleviation. In practice, however, subsistence reasoning often predominates with its simple and clear logic and its unambiguous policy implications. An explicit discussion of these quite different basic approaches, however, is difficult to address empirically and has been limited.

Stryker (1976) argues that the subsistence approach may be the most appropriate for a traditional economy, whereas the market approach may give a better explanation for a modern or a commercial economy. Based on a case study from Indonesia, however, Angelsen (1995) concludes that this point of view may be misleading. While the subsistence model can accurately describe the individual farm household's response in certain circumstances, particularly in the short-run, to apply it on the aggregate level is questionable for two reasons in particular. First, even traditional agrarian societies seem to be increasingly integrated into a larger market economy (see also Box 4 for the Guatemalan case). Consequently, commercialization and the modernization of village life might create increased cash income needs even in remote rural areas. Second, in the case of rural migration, the market approach might give a more realistic description of frontier agricultural systems, particularly of long-term effects.

Box 4. Penny Capitalism: Sol Tax's Ethnographic Research on Guatemala

An early advocate of seeing rural habitants as integrated into a market economy was the anthropologist Sol Tax (1953). His ethnographic research from the 1930's and 1940's is about the indigenous Guatemalan Panajachel economy, located next to the famous Lake Atitlán. Tax argues that the socio-economic life of indigenous communities is deeply imbedded in a competitive market. Moreover, he claims that the Panajachel economy is not dominated by irrational beliefs, cultural or religious influences. In his introduction to Penny Capitalism he notices: *"The title is intended to be catchy, but it should also convey in two words what the book describes: a society which is 'capitalist' on a microscopic scale... In most 'primitive' societies about which anthropologists write, people behave in our terms irrationally, since they try by devices strange to us to maximize different, hence curious, satisfactions. This happens not to be the case in the part of Guatemala about which I write..."* Tax's work about the Guatemalan indigenous economy has been used by Theodore Schultz as major evidence in support of his efficient-but-poor hypothesis. For a critique and a more complete discussion, see Schweigert (1994).

In the context of developing countries, the two approaches are often criticized for their assumptions regarding household behavior and the functioning of markets. In response to this problem, part of the literature prefers to rely on Chayanov-type models in order to overcome the somewhat rigid basic assumptions of the other models. The theoretical foundations for this approach were laid down by the Russian Economist Chayanov (1925) who studied peasant farming practices in Russia after the October Revolution of 1917. Chayanov's study, which in a broader sense was meant to apply to non-industrial, non-market rural societies without land constraints and without well-developed labor markets, lay dormant for decades until it was translated into English in 1966. Subsequent advances in the theory have since been made in the agricultural household literature by Singh et al. (1986) and

Nakajima (1986). Recently, Angelsen (1999) and Walker et al. (2002) have developed analytical approaches based on a Chayanov-type model.

However, using this model for the deforestation problem also tends to give ambiguous results. At the risk of oversimplification, in particular the model of Angelsen (1999) can be understood as a combination of a pure subsistence model in compliance with elements of the market approach. Depending on the functional form and underlying assumptions, either subsistence (income) or market (farm firm) effects dominate. If the income effect dominates, the model moves toward the subsistence approach. If the market effect dominates, the model comes analytically close to the open economy approach. When an imperfect labor market, however, is introduced, the subsistence effect inclines to get weaker and the response in the Chayanov-type model becomes quite similar to the open economy approach. Consequently, despite its stylized and partly unrealistic assumptions, the market approach should not be simply discounted. To one degree or another, it could also apply to a more realistic and complex setting.

C. Potential Effects of Education

Researchers have long been studying the causes and consequences of land use changes. Surprisingly, there are very few studies that shed light on the role education might play in the clearing of forests. [42] So far, only a set of studies from Ricardo Godoy *explicitly* try to assess how education might impact on deforestation. Interesting as they are, these attempts are primarily an empirical contribution, and do not explicitly explain why schooling might be associated with forest clearing. Godoy and Contreras (2001) argue that this may reflect disciplinary parochialism. Investigators working on deforestation typically know little about the broad spectrum of the effects of human capital, and researchers of education are generally not concerned about environmental issues.

A first step in filling this gap is provided in the following paragraphs. The discussion will be based on the framework of the subsistence and market approach. A substantial number of variables are directly or indirectly affected by schooling, and they are sometimes linked together. Therefore, in order to keep the discussion tractable, a focus will be placed on selected parameters. These include the opportunity costs of labor (section 1), population growth (section 2), productivity (section 3), and subsistence requirements (section 4). Output prices are assumed to

---

42 Godoy and Contreras (2001: 650) emphasize: *"So far attempts to explain the path linking formal education and conservation have relied on narrative rather than theory or on quantitative evidence... We know of no study focused on why and how schooling could affect conservation."*

be exogenous and are therefore not taken into account. At the aggregate level an increase in education may not be associated with changes on economic variables, such as distance costs and the expectations of land rent. Consequently, these parameters are not considered.

1. Opportunity Costs of Labor

The availability of alternative employment with comparatively higher returns than self-employed agriculture raises the opportunity cost of labor. Simulations from Angelsen (1999) and Bluffstone (1995) based on land use models suggest that rural non-farm employment is the single most important factor among a household's decision parameters. Given the robust and uncontroversial evidence that individual earnings are positively and significantly associated with schooling, it is possible that — within the framework of the market approach — schooling could operate on household's deforestation behavior mainly via its effect on rural wages. This is embedded within the framework of Mincer's (1974) human capital earnings function.

As reviewed in Psacharopoulos and Patrinos (2002), a broad array of studies in many different countries has confirmed that better educated individuals earn higher wages than their less educated counterparts. The reported rates of return for another year of schooling typically lie somewhere between 5 and 15 percent, and tend to fall with the level of socio-economic development, and level of education. Despite the overwhelming evidence of a positive correlation between education and earnings, there are some difficulties within the context of the present study. They refer to the magnitude of the returns to schooling, the causality of schooling and individual earnings, and the interpretation of the empirical evidence.

(1) Magnitude of the returns to schooling. There is an ongoing debate on the level of the returns to education in developing countries. It is not immediately apparent why a relatively high rate of returns to primary education in many low-income countries is frequently associated with a stationary economic environment. If technology and knowledge advances, then the demand for skilled labor should grow relative to the demand for less skilled labor, and consequently the potential for high returns to education should exist.[43] In a stagnant environment, however,

43 This *may* be equally true for Guatemala. The World Bank's (1996) basic education study, written under the authority of George Psacharopoulos, finds an overall rate of return to schooling of about 14.9 percent. By contrast, the World Bank's (2003a) poverty assessment, placing much emphasis on the rural economy and based on the ENCOVI (2000) survey, finds an overall rate of return to schooling of only 6 percent.

one would expect the returns of education to be low. Huffman (2001) presents evidence that education in selected rural labor markets of low-income countries does, in fact, have little effect on the wage rate.

One explanation for the empirical evidence in Psacharopoulos and Patrinos (2002) could be due to systematic biases in favor of the urban or formal sectors, particularly for countries with large rural economies. As noted by Foster and Rosenzweig (1996), the studies from Psacharopoulos are regularly based on cross-sectional wage data from very unrepresentative samples. In addition, these studies frequently rely on the most basic earnings equations where only a few variables are included and the sample selection is not corrected for bias.

(2) Causality of schooling and individual earnings. A much-debated controversy lies in giving the association of schooling and earnings a causal interpretation. Higher earnings observed for better-educated individuals could be caused by their education or could be due to the fact that those individuals with greater ability have chosen to acquire more schooling. If more able individuals have relatively higher returns regardless of extra education, and choose to spend more time in school, then the effect of education will be overstated. This argument would provide a plausible reason for a correlation between ability and years of schooling, even if schooling has no effect on earnings.

Although few doubt that signalling may play some role in explaining educational wage differences, its overall importance remains controversial. Card (2001) notes that definitive answers are not yet available. However, estimates of the returns to education based on analysis of twins' earnings as well as estimates using instrumental variables techniques suggest that the ability biases seem to be very modest in magnitude. Moreover, in the context of a developing country like Guatemala, it should be noted that the ability-debate sounds somewhat exaggerated — given the systematic exclusion of the rural and poor from public education services.

(3) Interpretation of the empirical evidence. According to Card (1999), not much is presently known about the exact mechanisms by which education might contribute to higher earnings. The simplest interpretation of the evidence from earnings functions is that more educated individuals are more productive. In a static agricultural environment, however, more education does not necessarily make a better farmer, and accumulated experience may be a better investment than schooling. Limited evidence from developing countries supports this argument. For example, in comparative case studies on several Latin American countries, Lopez and Valdés (2000) find that the impact of education on rural earnings is quantitatively small, and in some cases even insignificant. This implies that

additional schooling does not contribute to higher income where smallholder's activities only require limited skills.[44]

However, as Foster and Rosenzweig (1996) show, the returns to schooling can increase as a country goes from a traditional agriculture toward modernization, and thus creates a technological and economic environment requiring information acquisition, technology evaluation, and continual adjustments to change. Furthermore, poor returns to education in the rural sector do not mean that people that migrate to urban areas will also obtain low education returns.

As will be discussed in the next paragraphs, one important aspect of rural education is to facilitate migration to urban areas. In addition, the evidence from Lopez and Valdés (2000) as well as Huffman (2001) indicates that relatively higher returns to schooling are obtained in employment outside agriculture. More schooling, in turn, raises the probability of working in certain types of non-farm activities.[45] Given the contribution of schooling to non-farm income, frequently an important source of rural income, the net impact of education can still be substantial. Since in rural economies women tend to allocate more of their time than men to non-farm activities, female education is of particular interest.

In sum, given the positive contribution of schooling on wages and non-farm employment (requiring skills obtained by formal education), one should, tentatively, expect a decreasing effect on deforestation. However, it should be remembered that in the case of severe labor market constraints non-farm employment might also have an ambiguous outcome (e.g. farmers could use increased wage earnings for hiring labor or purchasing more cattle).

2. Population

An increase in education should lower population pressure. In the subsistence approach, and to some extent also in the market approach — through its impact on wages and food prices — this could imply a decrease in deforestation. There are

---

44 In line with this argumentation, Johannsen (2003) claims that formal schooling has a positive albeit qualitatively small impact on rural livelihoods in Guatemala. Consequently, she stresses the importance of informal learning and experience, in particular for low-productivity activities. Nevertheless, the finding of a limited role for education stands in contrast with other studies, such as Vakis (2002).

45 The effect of schooling on the probability of working should be larger in the non-farm sectors than those that require skills. In line with most of the literature, Lopez and Valdés (2000) do not distinguish between different types of non-farm employment in terms of productivity levels.

two other separate effects, which, nevertheless, pull in the same direction. These are population growth and rural to urban migration.

(1) Population growth. In the long run, increased educational endowment is expected to lower population growth. Dasgupta (1995) and Schultz (2001) show that in a broad spectrum of developing countries there is uncontroversial evidence for a strong negative correlation between literacy and fertility. Reductions in fertility occur with improvements in a wide range of socio-economic conditions, such as access to family planning services, the provision of health care, reduction in child mortality, but above all with the education of woman, and the promotion of female literacy. There are a number of reasons why better female education in particular should lower fertility. Schooling can improve the work opportunities for woman, which in turn makes it more costly in time to have children. In addition, education and employment may also delay marriage, and the time available to rear children. Finally, education makes woman more receptive to information about contraception and may improve their status or bargaining power and capacity to make their own choices.

(2) Rural to urban migration. Pressure on forests should be reduced with a shrinking size of the rural population and, hence, the labor force available for agriculture. This is because education encourages migration into urban areas. Starting from the assumption that migration is primarily an economic phenomenon, Harris and Todaro (1970) postulate that migration proceeds in response to urban-rural differences in the expected income. The fundamental premise is that migrants consider the various labor market opportunities available to them in the rural and urban sectors, and choose the one that maximizes the expected gains from migration. In this regard, human capital characteristics play a key role since they influence both wages and the likelihood of obtaining an urban job.

Mazumdar (1988) and Agesa (2000) review the vast empirical literature on this topic. Although data limitations often hamper empirical research on migration, the results generally support Todaro-expected income-migration theories. That is, in most cases, differentials in average wages or incomes between regions are significant for explaining rural to urban migration flows. Rural to urban migration depends on many factors such as distance, wage and unemployment rates, individual educational characteristics but in particular, the average levels of human capital in source and destination areas. In general, rural workers with relatively more human capital skills are more likely to migrate. Furthermore, educated migrants are better able to compete in urban labor markets.

However, as pointed out by Agesa (2000), the link between schooling and migration may often be weak. In the institutional and socio-economic context of developing countries, migrants cannot expect to secure a better-paying urban job immediately. On entering the urban labor market, comparatively less educated rural migrants might either become totally unemployed, or might seek casual and part-time employment. Consequently, in deciding to migrate, the individual must balance the probabilities and risks of being unemployed or underemployed for a considerable period of time against the positive urban-rural income differential. Even though there is a worthwhile income differential, the individual potential migrant may not choose to seek a job in the urban area if there is a low probability of successfully obtaining a job there.

Moreover, the perspective that migration decisions are taken by isolated actors, but not by larger units of related people, seems to be unrealistic. That is, migration represents a loss of human resources for the household as labor is withdrawn from farm production. Numerous non-economic factors may also influence the migration decision. For example, considering the Guatemalan case, high levels of urban violence and ethnic discrimination would relativise the incentive for urban migration.

An issue that is widely neglected — and due to the lack of data not well documented — is the extent of *rural to rural* migration. Lucas (1997) points out that this is rather surprising, given the fact that the rate of rural to rural migration in many developing countries proves far higher than urban to rural migration. As pointed out in Figure 10 (in the previous section), intra-rural migration may have many properties in common with urban-rural migration, since it can enhance income opportunities as well. Bilsborrow (1992) compares the magnitude of different types of internal migration in developing countries, including Guatemala. In almost all cases, rural to rural migration exceeds rural to urban migration flows. Therefore, migration into new rural environments can be a key mechanism of environmental degradation and deforestation.

3. Productivity

Education of farm labor has a potential for enhancing agricultural production, especially in an environment that is friendly to technological change. According to Schultz (1988), education may affect agricultural productivity in a number of different ways. A useful distinction is between cognitive skills — which affect technological and allocative efficiency — and non-cognitive skills.

(1) Technological efficiency. Within cognitive skills, a distinction can be made between the formation of general skills, such as literacy and numeracy, and the transmission of specific knowledge. For example, literacy qualifies for following

written instructions for chemical inputs or other aspects of modern farm technology. Numeracy permits calculations of correct dosages and may assist in making other planning decisions. These cognitive effects of education may increase the output produced by a given combination of inputs.

In addition, a distinction can be made between the increase of productivity due to the education of the workers and that due to the education of the decision-makers about the farm. In practice, however, the distinction between farm workers and farm managers is likely to be obsolete in smallholder agriculture because decisions may be made collectively by all household members who work at the farm. All of these factors are arguments for technological efficiency. Huffman (2001) argues one should be cautious in not overstating the effects of education in this regard. For enhancing technological efficiency, experience seems likely to be a more important form of human capital than schooling.

(2) Allocative efficiency. More important, functional literacy may also change allocative efficiency by altering the selected combinations of outputs and inputs. This may be particularly important in disequilibria, when prices or technology are changing. Educated farmers may have a greater propensity to adopt agricultural innovations, for example, modern inputs or new crops. If education alters input and output mixes, this may be because education alters farmer's ability to use particular mixes or to change their preferences. In addition, there may be effects in the ability to finance and plan the household. If schooling gives better access to rural credit markets and more remunerative activities like non-farm employment, it may increase the funds available to the household to purchase market inputs and seeds.

(3) Non-cognitive effects of education. Regarding the non-cognitive effects, education can also change people's attitudes and practices such as discipline, acceptance of hierarchy, punctuality, teamwork and working at a timetable — although this might be more important in the context of industry than in agriculture. However, particularly in developing countries, education may increase people's achievement-orientation, giving them greater awareness of the possibility to improve living standards. There may also be a greater openness to new ideas and modern practices. However, it can also be argued that education leads to disdain for agriculture, as students aspire to formal sector employment.

(4) Empirical evidence on education and agricultural productivity. Although there are several mechanisms through which education may affect agricultural productivity in developing countries, whether or not the effects are large and significant is an *empirical* matter. Hayami and Ruttan (1985) as well as Jamison and Lau (1982) summarize some of the *early* evidence, which makes one cautious

about claiming a positive effect of schooling on agricultural productivity. Overall, the results are rather mixed. Not all studies found a statistically significant effect from farmers' schooling on farm output. Nonetheless, the estimated effects are often positive, and sometimes fairly large. The insignificant effects might be due to several reasons. On the one hand, researchers were focussing on technological efficiency rather than allocative efficiency effects. On the other hand, schooling levels, or the variance in schooling levels, may have been too small.

Later studies had more success. For example, using longitudinal Indian rural household data, and area-specific information on crop yields and schooling, Foster and Rosenzweig (1996) show that primary school rates were positively and significantly related to the growth of crop yields. More importantly, their results also indicate that the returns to primary schooling increase during a period of rapid exogenous technological progress. Such increases induce private investment in schooling, net changes in wealth and wages, and in the availability of schools. Their results point out that policies resulting in greater technological change *and* increased education should be viewed be as *complementary*. In such an environment, educated individuals are better able to take advantage of technological change. These results can also explain the findings from Lopez and Valdés (2000). That is, the relatively small impact of education on agricultural productivity in these Latin American countries could be due to the rather stagnant agricultural context. Under such circumstances, more education does not pay off.

In general, as summarized in Huffman (2001), most of the recent empirical studies found that farmers' schooling is positively and significantly associated with farm productivity, but tends to have higher values through the effects of allocative efficiency rather than technological efficiency. The positive allocative efficiency effects are closely associated with a farming environment where technologies are changing. However, education can help farmers to get more from their inputs, to cope better with political and legal problems, to manage their farms better, and to get higher prices for their goods and pay lower input prices even without new agricultural technologies. Another common finding is that schooling has a greater impact on productivity where production is multi-input and multi-output. Finally, an important topic is the applicability of educational programs in the agricultural context. In developing countries, more weight is often placed on the formation of general skills, and there are few attempts to reform the curriculum so as to teach specific agricultural knowledge.

All in all, one can say that there is a potential for a positive effect of schooling on agricultural productivity, but that this relationship between the two is quite complex. In a stagnant agricultural environment with low innovation more schooling probably has negligible effects on agricultural productivity. In addition, as has been pointed out in the previous section, the effects of agricultural innovation on deforestation itself are far from being clear. In this respect, the impact of schooling on deforestation via increased agricultural productivity remains ambiguous.

4. Subsistence Requirements

Schooling probably raises the farm household's consumption and subsistence requirements. As summarized in Godoy (2001), there is strong ethnographic evidence to support this hypothesis. In a comparative analysis of several indigenous villages in Latin America, he finds that an improved education in the formerly isolated indigenous households is almost always associated which an integration into the larger market economy. Increased market integration, in turn, often causes commercialization of village life and a subsequent increase in peasant's consumption requirements. This finding is in line with the case study of Angelsen (1995) for Indonesia. The results from Godoy's study also indicate that the effect of education on deforestation is often a non-linear one. Increased market integration seems to initially increase and then decrease deforestation. Overall, the final effect of education on deforestation is unclear.

In the long run, when rural migration is taken into account, more schooling may result in an increase in local consumption and deforestation. As Godoy et al. (1998a) argue, migration may raise rural income through the net remittances of cash and goods from the city. These remittances may increase the consumption of forest goods (such as timber to build more durable and prestigious houses) but may also make innovations and technological progress in farming possible. Insofar, the deforestation effect is intermediate.

Lucas (1997) argues that, overall, the effect of remittances seems too small to have much effect on enhancing rural productivity. On the other hand, urban remittances may in fact lower the demand for forest goods since cheaper industrial substitutes for these goods are now available with this added resource. In fact, urban remittances could also prove to be an important factor for establishing 'high-productivity' rural non-farm activities. Overall, the effects of remittances are complex and have been little explored. Using a unique data set from China, the empirical results from Rozelle et al. (1999) suggest that migrant remittances partially offset the loss of labor to migration.

5. Summing-Up

This section has discussed some of the main avenues by which education can affect land use changes. The main conclusion is that schooling is likely to affect deforestation. However, understanding the magnitude and the direction of the effect remains preliminary. The qualitative results are summarized in Table 17.

Depending on the underlying model, the effect of schooling can work differently and is subject to uncertainty. It follows that whether and how schooling — and other parameters — may impact on deforestation is largely an *empirical* matter. This will be the subject of the following section. Nevertheless, two tentative conclusions emerge from this discussion.

Table 17. Potential Effects of Education on Deforestation in Subsistence and Market Approach

Changes on economic parameters due to an increase in education		Effect on deforestation [a/]	
		Subsistence approach	Market approach
Population	↓	–	(–)
Subsistence requirement	↑	+	N.A.
Productivity	↑	–	+
Opportunity costs of labor	↑	N.A.	–

Source: Author. a/ See text for qualifications. Brackets indicate uncertain effects due to endogeneity. N.A. = not applicable.

First, in a stagnant agricultural environment of smallholders — like in Guatemala — the productivity effects of schooling are probably of minor importance. If the dominant effect in the long run is to make a transition to non-farm work that indeed requires skills, education could reduce deforestation. In addition, particularly by encouraging migration to urban areas, schooling can lower population pressure. Therefore, a close look at the summarized evidence leads to the hypothesis that, according to the market approach, education has the *potential* to lower deforestation.

A second feature is that the interaction of potentially conflicting effects could imply education has non-linear effects on deforestation. Once a certain threshold is reached, schooling might stimulate certain types of non-farm activities and rural to urban migration. If these effects were relatively dominant, increased educational levels of rural households would lower deforestation. However, in an empirical model, it may be difficult to isolate and separate the diverse effects of schooling on deforestation. That is, there is a potential for an endogenous bias, which may constrain the econometric testing. Additionally, it is likely that the quantitative outcome could vary according to the local context or the country. In this regard, empirical case studies are of particular interest.

D. Controversial Empirical Evidence

Empirical work on deforestation simplifies complex and multidimensional processes. This is because it highlights only a few of the many variables and causal relationships involved in land use changes. Given the number of deforestation studies, the variability of their methodologies and their data sources, to synthesize the results is a complex task.[46] The methodologies used in each instance are often tailored to the specific data available and to the research question asked. One of the main findings in the literature is that the factors, interactions and magnitude of economic parameters affecting deforestation can vary significantly from one location to another. Quantitative models also are limited when addressing issues related to market failures and institutional factors.

Nevertheless, the following paragraphs explore some effects of socio-economic determinants on deforestation. The analysis is guided by the work of Kaimowitz and Angelsen (1999; 2002). Supplementary studies include Contreras-Hermosilla (2000), Barbier (2001), and Barbier and Burgess (2002). Most of the literature has been produced since the 1990s and focuses on cross-section analyses.

Section 1 gives a brief overview of strengths and weaknesses for different types of deforestation models. The term deforestation usually refers to a long-term complete removal of tree cover. Section 2 reviews the results from selected empirical studies — with a focus on Latin America. While some variables have an unambiguous effect on forest clearance, many of them often do not. Section 3 emphasizes two related studies for Mexico from Deininger and Minten (1999; 2002) in order to overcome the overall somewhat inconclusive results from empirical deforestation studies. Due to methodological and empirical strengths as well as to Mexico's geographic and socio-economic similarities, they are of utmost relevance for Guatemalan context. Section 4 reviews the few studies assessing the impact of schooling on deforestation. The most comprehensive empirical evidence comes from Godoy et al. (1997; 1998), Godoy and Contreras (2001), and Godoy (2001). Dealing explicitly with indigenous communities living in biodiversity-rich forest margins, the Godoy studies are of particular interest for the present study. His findings suggest that education does have the potential to reduce primary forest clearing.

1. Types of Deforestation Models

As a starting point, Kaimowitz and Angelsen (1999; 2002) suggest distinguishing between the potential explanatory variables at three different analytical levels:

---

46 This section places emphasis on regression models. As such, it does not consider a variety of other approaches, for example Computable General Equilibrium (CGE) models or linear programming. For a discussion, see Kaimowitz and Angelsen (2002).

(i) The direct sources of deforestation. Possible variables to be included here are the expansion of agricultural area, firewood collection and timber production. The measurement of the relative share of the various direct sources need not, in principle, be subjected to econometric analysis. If data is available, simple accounting can be sufficient. For the case of Guatemala, estimates will be presented in the following qualitative assessment of deforestation.

(ii) The immediate causes of deforestation. These variables influence the decisions by deforestation agents either on a regional or local level. Possible variables include wages, education, access costs and property rights, among many others.

(iii) The underlying causes of deforestation. Macro-level variables determine deforestation behavior through their influence on the decision parameters, but do not enter into the decision making/problem solving choices directly. Examples here include GDP per capita, economic and population growth.

In this hierarchy, the main cause-effect relationship would go from level (iii) to (ii) and from (ii) to (i). Problems can arise when variables at different levels are mixed, and due to the complex nature of deforestation issues this is sometimes the case in empirical studies. Some of the explanatory variables will then be functions of others and the interpretation of the cause-effect may be flawed. From a statistical point of view, it could result in high levels of multicollinearity.

According to this scheme for simplification, models of deforestation may be classified into four broad categories according to their aggregation level. The first three are cross-country, regional, and local level analysis. The fourth category contains those specific features provided by geographic information system (GIS) analysis, where the unit of investigation is typically a pixel of a certain size, rather than a decision-making unit. Each level or type of analysis has some advantages and drawbacks that will be discussed below.

(1) Cross-country analysis. The overwhelming empirical evidence of the effects from economic parameters on deforestation comes from cross-country regressions. This may reflect the ease of access to data, the analytical and computational simplicity and the desire to produce conclusions that are universally valid. Many of the empirical cross-country regression models are ad hoc approaches that lump together the available data. In addition, there is a tendency for cross-country regressions to not distinguish the different causal structures of deforestation. In principle, this kind of analysis allows the researcher to investigate

the relationship between the rate of deforestation, and the associated macroeconomic and institutional factors, such as economic growth, population growth, openness, trade policies, the political regime, indebtedness, devaluation rates, poverty and so on. Some of these factors vary only at the national level and thus may only be analyzed in a cross-country context. However, the main problems associated with cross-country analysis are the heterogeneity between countries and the poor quality of data.

The biggest methodological problem with cross-country deforestation regressions is heterogeneity. For example, while firewood collection appears to be an important source of deforestation in many African countries, it has less significance in Latin America where the main direct source of deforestation appears to be the demand for agricultural land. In Asia, logging seems to be relatively more important. In addition, it is doubtful that macroeconomic factors affect deforestation in the same way across all countries. If the assumption that the underlying forces driving deforestation are the same does not hold, cross-country analysis leads to doubtful policy conclusions.

For example, there is no consensus on the effect of economic growth and higher national incomes on deforestation. Higher incomes could be associated with less firewood consumption, more capital intensive agriculture, and more opportunities outside agriculture. Countries with higher incomes may also have a greater demand for forest conservation. On the opposite side, higher incomes could be associated with greater consumption of agricultural and forest products. Some authors hypothesize that there may be an Environmental Kuznets Curve. At low levels increased income leads to higher deforestation, but beyond a certain income threshold the opposite occurs. The empirical evidence for such a relationship is extremely weak. There are two studies explicitly investigating whether an Environmental Kuznets Curve exists for *species diversity*. Using panel regressions, Schubert and Dietz (2001) as well as Dietz and Adger (2003) find that the existence of such a Biodiversity Kuznets Curve cannot be empirically proven.

Most analyses are based on estimates from the Food and Agricultural Organisation (FAO) on forest cover change. While the latest FAO (2001) information from the Global Forest Assessment relies on aerial photography or satellite imagery, earlier information is considered to be unreliable. That is, the FAO based its Global Forest Assessments before 2001 on *population* projections in order to overcome inadequate forest data for many countries. This means that FAO country forest cover data is simply inappropriate to be correlated with demographic factors, as is done in many cross-country analyses. Moreover, in a cross-section context low deforestation levels can be interpreted differently. For instance, maintaining the level could reflect either that forests are intact, that the countries have little forest left to clear, or that the government officials simply had no new basis for the estimates, and therefore continued to report the same figures to the FAO even when the data was from a time period before that asked for.

It should not come as a big surprise that it has been difficult to get any robust policy conclusions out of cross-country deforestation regressions. The lack of significance for most variables is pervasive in this kind of literature. Given the overall disappointing results for cross-country deforestation analysis, the next paragraphs will see if country level studies have the potential to provide better insights. Figure 11 gives a graphical illustration of the following discussion.

Figure 11. Types of Deforestation Models

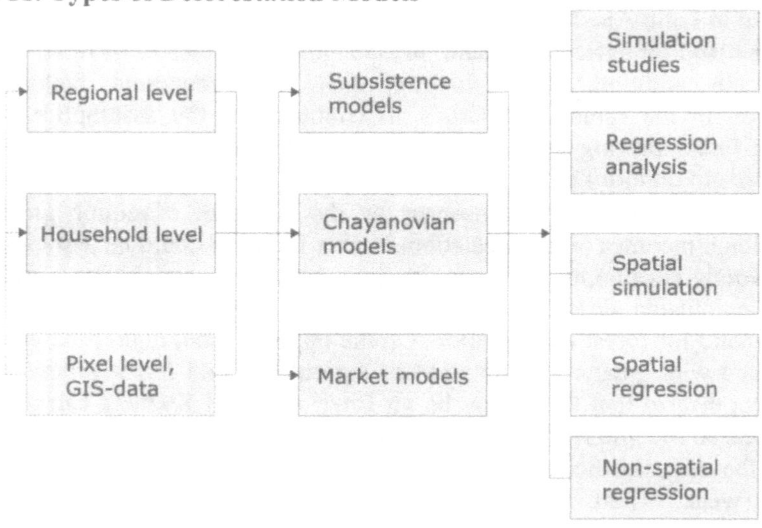

Source: Author's elaboration.

(2) Regional level analysis. Analyses at the regional level have several advantages. First, it is easier to obtain detailed data, at least in principle, which in turn permits better-specified statistical models. Compared to cross-country regressions, there is also a much closer geographical match between deforestation rates and the variables of interest. Second, historical factors that are country-specific can be taken into account. Finally, the results generally appear to have more obvious policy implications.

The disadvantage of such an analysis is that it is presumably impossible to investigate the effects of variables identical across a country or region. However, government policies can influence the manner in which national policies are implemented. For example, credit and infrastructure can be distributed differently across regions. If data of reasonable quality is available, however, differences in population characteristics, internal migration and population densities can best be analyzed at this level. Common scales used in regional analysis are either the municipal or district levels. Some regression models also include a spatial component using geographic information systems (GIS) data. However, non-spatial models are more common.

So far, the number of available studies is limited to a *handful* of developing countries. Studies at the national level are often plagued by poor data quality. Most of these countries are medium or large, politically stable, and with comparatively higher levels of economic wealth. For the case of Latin America, the focus has been on Brazil and to a lesser extent also on Mexico, Ecuador and Costa Rica. The models tend to support some of the initial hypotheses of the open economy approach. Overall, the examination by Kaimowitz and Angelsen (2002) reveals that one should be cautious about making too strong conclusions. Most studies in the regional category tend to have methodological problems, and suffer from data constraints. A notable exception is the Deininger and Minten (1999) study to be reviewed later.

(3) Local level analysis. Farm-level analyses are particularly useful because households are the actual decision-makers with respect to land. These models often may have the potential to provide detailed answers to the questions about the underlying causes of deforestation. They also can be important for complementing and validating larger scale models. Compared to the regional level analysis, the data is typically of higher quality.

Household empirical models do, in fact, provide evidence confirming some of the basic conclusions from the analytical approaches. In particular, lower transportation costs, better access to markets, and a shortage of non-farm employment are associated with higher deforestation. The studies from Ricardo Godoy that represent the scarce evidence for the influence of schooling on deforestation, are examples of such an approach, in particular Godoy and Contreras (2001). If data from agricultural frontier regions is applied, the drawbacks are the limited capacity to generalize across regions, the time consuming data collecting, and the costs of conducting household surveys in agricultural frontier regions. Probably for this reason there are currently relatively few of these models.

(4) Geographic information system (GIS) analysis. Not only the causes of deforestation and its magnitude, but also its location is important. The GIS has made it possible to analyze the location of deforestation, and its causes, at the pixel level. Sample points at this level are typically at 1-kilometer intervals or even smaller. Variables in GIS models include different types of land use, which are

regressed on distance to road, distance to markets, population density, soil quality, rainfall, topography and other physical-geographic characteristics. The GIS data can also be incorporated into local and regional level analysis. However, it tends to be less meaningful at higher aggregation levels. There are two main drawbacks of such an approach.

(i) With observations numbering in tens of thousands, GIS models are extremely data demanding. Since the dependent variable is typically a discrete category of land use (forest or non-forest), most models use Logit or Probit regression analysis. A common statistical problem here is spatial autocorrelation, because nearby locations are more similar than distant ones.

(ii) Economic variables do not always easily lend themselves to geo-referencing, and are sometimes simply ignored. In particular, GIS-models are not well suited to incorporate important less location-specific decision parameters, such as wage rates. Since these variables tend to be highly important in other settings, this is a serious limitation. Recent approaches, however, have made advances in this respect. If data is available, it is possible to combine geographic and socio-economic information at reasonable aggregation levels.

Spatial models do not only provide information on how much forest is likely to be cleared, and its causal structure. Once constructed and calibrated, a GIS model can predict the effects of infrastructure and settlement policies, protected areas, property rights, technology, and the environmental endowment. If geo-referenced household data is available, it may also assess the impact of socio-economic determinants commonly used in other models.

Chomitz and Gray (1996) did a seminal contribution for the southern part of Belize, which due to geographic and socio-economic similarities is also of interest for the present study. In multinomial Logit regressions based on the market approach, they predict the probability of three alternative land uses: natural vegetation, semi-subsistence agriculture and commercial agriculture. The results show that the probability of commercial agriculture drops with distance to market, while subsistence farmers are less sensitive to distance. However, even semi-subsistence farmers are moderately sensitive to market access. Chomitz and Gray also find a surprisingly strong influence of soil quality on subsistence farming. This contradicts the belief that subsistence farmers are insensitive to soil conditions or that they will colonize along any available road. A similar approach, to be presented later, has also been adopted by Deininger and Minten (2002).

Recapitulating, this section briefly reviewed strengths and weaknesses of different empirical approaches assessing deforestation. The higher the aggregation levels, the more numerous but also the more doubtful were the available studies. The GIS analysis is an elegant way to incorporate the spatial dimension of deforestation along with economic variables. However, these studies often deal with statistical problems and may miss important aspects of deforestation, such as less location-specific parameters. Local studies based on household data can give very important insights. Given the small number of these studies so far, however, it is difficult to generalize these findings to other areas.

2. *Effects of Economic Parameters on Deforestation*

Having presented some of the main avenues by which the process of deforestation can be investigated, this section looks at the impact of selected decision parameters on deforestation. To a certain degree, the empirical evidence tends to confirm some of the basic hypotheses from the analytical models. In particular, the importance of distance costs, market access, agricultural prices and the opportunity costs of labor stresses the relevance of the open economy approach. Moreover, some recent studies tend to have swept away the earlier conventional wisdom of the small-scale farmer driven to deforest for subsistence as a stylized special case. Instead, Vosti et al. (2002) argue that these studies reveal that market links are strengthening even in remote forest margins.

The tentative stylized outcomes of the following variables are guided by Pearce and Brown (1994), Contreras-Hermosilla (2000), Barbier (2001) and Kaimowitz and Angelsen (1999; 2002). At the risk of oversimplifying, the available evidence from most studies agrees on the effects of accessibility and the physical-geographic environment. To a lesser degree, there is also a growing consensus on the effects of the opportunity cost of labor, population growth, and agricultural prices.

(1) Road construction. The greatest single regularity in the literature is that road construction is correlated with higher deforestation (see for example Andersen 1997; Chomitz and Gray 1996; Chomitz and Thomas 2001; Deininger and Minten 1999, 2002; Nelson and Hellerstein 1997; Pfaff 1997; Pichón 1997). In most studies, better access to markets is also associated with higher deforestation (see for example Vosti et al. 2002). However, the high correlation between roads and deforestation may overstate the causal relationship. For example, lower distance costs and hence better market access could be there because an area has already been cleared and settled, rather than vice versa.

(2) Physical-geographic factors. Numerous GIS models also provide evidence that geographical factors strongly influence the deforestation outcome. In general, forests which are more suitable for agriculture because of their soil quality, better drainage or other advantageous factors are more likely to be cleared (see for

example Chomitz and Gray 1996; Chomitz and Thomas 2001; Deininger and Minten 1999, 2002; Müller and Zeller 2002; Pichón 1997; Pfaff 1997).

(3) Non-farm employment. Limited empirical evidence supports the hypothesis that greater non-farm employment opportunities reduce deforestation (see for example Godoy et al. 1997, 1998; Godoy and Contreras 2001; Godoy 2001; Pichón 1997; Vosti et al. 2002). It should be noted that the evidence seems to be somewhat restricted to the household level analysis and has yet not been fully validated in a regional context. Non-farm employment usually refers to the income obtained *outside* agriculture. In addition, there is usually no distinction between different types of non-farm employment. The effects of temporary *farm wages* obtained in the agricultural sector while working outside the own farm, typically another important source of income for rural households, are rarely addressed empirically.

(4) Population growth. In most empirical models population growth is negatively correlated with deforestation (see for example Andersen 1997; Barbier and Burgess 1996; Godoy et al. 1997, 1998; Godoy and Contreras 2001; Godoy 2001; Pfaff 1997; Pichón 1997). However, this effect sometimes disappears or become less significant when additional variables or instrumental variable techniques are taken into account (see for example Deininger and Minten 2002). Therefore, it is argued that population growth should be treated as an endogenous variable. For example, migration and hence population growth may be determined by infrastructure, distance to markets and soil quality. To some degree or another, government interventions, such as colonization policies, agricultural subsidies and tax incentives also affect migration. Consequently, population and migration affect deforestation, but in a more complex manner than is expressed by simply saying that population growth promotes deforestation.

(5) Agricultural output prices. The few studies that were able to include price measures find that higher agricultural output prices tend to stimulate forest clearing (for the Mexican example see Barbier and Burgess 1996; Deininger and Minten 1999, 2002). The reasoning that higher agricultural prices might not stimulate deforestation when farmers exhibit a preference for subsistence farming finds little empirical support.

Regarding other important economic parameters, such as agricultural productivity, availability of credit, input prices, the household's income and property rights, the results vary greatly. In many cases, the available evidence is mixed or insignificant, and does not allow firm conclusions to be drawn where analytical models provide inconclusive results. The relevance of each parameter seems to be location specific, and especially sensitive to data issues. In particular, the deforestation effect of agricultural intensification remains ambiguous (Angelsen et al. 2001).

A variable that does not enter explicitly in analytical models but that is of considerable interest is poverty. The importance of poverty is discussed extensively in the literature, albeit mostly at the qualitative level (see for example Vosti and Reardon 1997). Shifting cultivation by poor agriculturists is often considered to be the most serious threat to the forests. The assumption that shifted cultivators appear to be responsible for the main part of deforestation leads to the argument that broader socio-economic problems, which often lie outside the forest areas themselves, need to be addressed in order to tackle the deforestation process. However, the existing literature makes rather conflicting predictions regarding the poverty-deforestation nexus.

Poverty may not be a direct cause of deforestation but instead may operate as a constraining factor on the poorer rural households' ability to avoid resource degradation or to invest in mitigating strategies. Consequently, a rational strategy for poor rural households with limited access to alternative economic opportunities may be to extract short-term rents through resource conversion, as long as there are sufficient additional resources available in the frontier areas that can be relatively cheaply exploited and the costs of access remain low. Unfortunately, there is little *empirical* evidence on this topic. The studies reviewed in the next section argue that poverty and deforestation may be linked via the availability of non-farm employment in rural areas.

3. The Deininger and Minten Studies for Mexico

Probably one of the most comprehensive recent empirical analysis in the context of the determinants of deforestation in developing countries are two related studies from Deininger and Minten (1999; 2002) for Mexico. This is true for at least two reasons.

(i) Much of the empirical analysis on deforestation in developing countries is systematically limited due to the lack of sufficiently disaggregated data and absence of dynamic information on deforestation over time. Therefore, in many cases empirical models do not allow policy-relevant answers where theoretical models provide inconclusive results. The Mexican case, however, is a notable exception and provides a unique opportunity to study issues that have been at the heart of many empirical debates on deforestation in developing countries.

(ii) While many studies focus either on physical-geographic or on socio-economic data, the Deininger and Minten studies are able to incorporate both types of information. This, in turn, allows the authors to test to what degree their empirical results are affected by the omission of specific variables and makes it possible for them to assess empirically the impact of aggregation biases. Finally, while most of the empirical analyses in the literature are rather ad hoc, both studies are explicitly guided by the land-rent model (or market approach) explained in the previous section.

Deininger and Minten (1999) is a regional level deforestation study for the period 1980-1990. Applying Tobit regression analysis, it uses approximately 2,400 municipalities as the basic unit of analysis. Their later study, Deininger and Minten (2002), is for the southern states of Oaxaca and Chiapas. In a plot-level analysis for the same time period, the authors apply Probit-regression for more than 117,000 plots of 1 km^2 each, and are able to test for aggregation biases and the validity of their earlier results.

The empirical findings from both studies are similar and can be broadly divided into the effects of economic or policy variables, effects related to the security of property rights, and 'natural protection' factors. Table 18 provides a schematic overview of the qualitative effects. Given the physical-geographic, socio-economic and cultural similarities, in particular for southern departments of Mexico, it is argued here that the results could also serve as a rough guidance for factors affecting deforestation in the Guatemalan context.

(1) Economic variables. The effects of the economic variables are roughly consistent with expectations from the open economy approach. Lower distance costs, higher agricultural prices and better credit availability (though insignificant at the national level) increase deforestation. In particular, higher levels of poverty are significantly associated with increased deforestation. In terms of its magnitude, it is among the most important variables. The poverty variable is empirically proxied by the unskilled wage rate — reported to be almost synonymous with the level of poverty – and is instrumented by education, the availability of social services and environmental endowments. For the national level, Deininger and Minten also report that the availability of technical assistance has a deforestation-reducing effect. However, in the plot-level analysis for Oaxaca and Chiapas, the variable turns out to be insignificant.

(2) Security of property rights. Since communities rather than individuals hold a large share of Mexico's forest, an important question to be asked is whether these common tenure forms do provide less secure land tenure. Low levels of tenure security rights might be associated with higher levels of deforestation if individuals deforest to establish property rights. In this view, communal land tenure institutions (*ejidos*) are associated with an open-access problem and with high levels of

deforestation since security of tenure is seen to be equivalent to individual and formal titling. However, the empirical analysis shows that contrary to the 'tragedy of the commons' arguments, indigenous and community tenure forms reduce deforestation. This implies that strengthening communal models of resource management and their integration into the formal land tenure structure could actually provide an alternative to traditional land titling approaches of private property.

Table 18. Parameters Affecting Deforestation in Mexico

	Effect on deforestation [a/]	
	National level: Deininger and Minten (1999)	Plot level South Mexico: Deininger and Minten (2002)
Policy variables		
Higher distance costs	N.A.	–
Higher population density	N.A.	+
Higher levels of poverty (or lower unskilled wage rate)	+	+
Better availability of technical assistance	–	(–)
Higher agricultural prices	+	+
Better credit availability	(+)	+
Protected areas	–	–
Property rights		
More land under community tenure	–	–
Higher levels of indigenous population	–	–
Natural factors		
Unfavorable physical-geographic conditions	–	–

Source: Author based on Deininger and Minten (1999; 2002). a/ Brackets indicate that coefficients are not statistically significant at the 10% level. N.A. = not applicable

(3) Natural protection factors. Unfavorable physical-geographic factors, such as elevation, slope, rainfall and soil quality limitations constitute important natural protection factors for forest resources. Quantitatively, they are among the most important determinants of deforestation. In fact, the omission of all relevant policy variables would not significantly reduce the predictive power of the empirical model. In line with a priori expectations, protected areas reduce the probability of

deforestation. However, the coefficient turns out to be quantitatively small. Even though protection reduces the threat of deforestation, it fails to eliminate deforestation altogether. This suggests that the deforestation-reducing effect of protected areas could easily be overwhelmed by other factors.

Deininger and Minten also empirically assess the impact of aggregation biases and the omission of physical-geographic variables. This allows them to mimic regressions for studies with limited data availability and to obtain information on potential biases. Since neither the signs nor the significance of their results change in an important way, the authors conclude that in practice higher levels of aggregation due to data limitations might be tolerable.[47] This is an important finding for the later empirical analysis of the determinants of deforestation in Guatemala.

4. Educational Endowment and Deforestation

The direct impact of formal education on deforestation has rarely been assessed in empirical studies. An exception is a set of related studies from Godoy et al. (1997; 1998), Godoy and Contreras (2001), and Godoy (2001). Between 1992 and 1998, together with over 20 assistants, he collected household survey data in 65 indigenous villages in the lowland tropical rainforests of Bolivia, Honduras, and also to a lesser extent Nicaragua. In the context of the present study his findings are of particular interest because he deals explicitly with indigenous communities that live in biodiversity-rich forest margins.

Godoy et al. (1997; 1998) is an empirical analysis of approximately 100 indigenous households with relatively low levels of formal education in the Honduran rain forest. Applying various regression techniques and controlling for other variables, Godoy et al. find that schooling reduces primary forest clearing. In Godoy et al. (1998) the effect of schooling is found to be non-linear. With up to 2 years of schooling forest clearance declines, between approximately 2 and 4 years of education clearance increases, and beyond 4 years schooling deforestation again seems to be curbed. However, the results are not statistically significant.

In a similar analysis, this time for several hundred indigenous households of different ethnic groups in the Bolivian rainforest, Godoy and Contreras (2001) obtain significant results. After controlling for other variables, schooling is found to be a factor associated negatively with deforestation. This time, a linear relationship

47 However, the omission of relevant physical-geographic information may be associated with biases for the poverty variables. This could be due to the fact that the poor live predominantly in marginal areas with adverse environmental conditions.

has been assumed. Interestingly, none of the other human capital variables like literacy, competency in arithmetic or knowledge of Spanish were statistically significant. In an empirical estimation using the data set from Godoy — Pendleton and Howe (2002) are able to confirm these results.

Finally, Godoy (2001: Chapter 5) is a comparative cross-section analysis of 65 indigenous communities. Except for the Honduran communities, Godoy presents strong evidence of a negative and statistically significant relationship between schooling and deforestation. In most cases, the schooling variable, measured as average years of schooling obtained by the household head, is the single most important factor determining the clearing of primary forests.

While the findings provide some empirical support for the hypothesis that schooling should impact on deforestation, there are several problems with the approach from Godoy. First, besides the empirical evidence, the author fails to provide a convincing explanation for the deforestation reducing effect of schooling. This is particularly relevant given the strong quantitative effects of human capital on forest clearing. Second, the regressions suffer from endogenous biases. And finally, random sampling was not used to select households. All this implies that the results should be viewed as suggestive.

Besides the Godoy studies, there is little evidence to warrant generalization. In a plot-level analysis for the highlands of Vietnam, Müller and Zeller (2002) also find that better *access* to education exhibits a deforestation-reducing effect. By contrast, Pichón (1997) demonstrates for Ecuador that better-educated households might engage in more forest clearing. Along with a qualitative analysis, it will be up to the next chapter to see whether and how in Guatemala education is associated with deforestation.

III. Qualitative Assessment of Deforestation in Guatemala

While deforestation in Guatemala is a contemporary problem, land use changes in Guatemala and the processes involved cannot be understood without first looking at the historical and socio-economic context. In the next paragraphs it will be argued that agricultural expansion is correlated with the country's exclusionary labor and educational politics, since the elite believe their wealth to depend upon a low-wage and uneducated labor force. From the 19th century until about the early 1970s, the expansion of agricultural land was mainly due to the production of export crops. However, deforestation patterns have changed dramatically during the last decades. Since then, most of the forest cover loss can be attributed to managed and, more recently, to spontaneous colonization. These patterns, in turn, have their roots in the exclusionary labor and educational policies of the past which have caused rural poverty and underdevelopment.[48]

It is imperative to mention that any discussion of the deforestation process in Guatemala must acknowledge the information limitations. Much of the available evidence can only be found in some scattered literature, unpublished reports or booklets, and disperse individual files. Many of these sources have never been used to generate a consistent picture. Available information is often contradictory and varies greatly in accuracy. Moreover, there is no forest data collected in a systematic way and some earlier inventories are lost. In-depth studies of deforestation exist only for some parts of the Petén. Nevertheless, the following sections will piece together the available evidence. It will be argued that to some degree or another, coherent trends can be identified. Section A presents the historical context. Section B refers to the magnitude and spatial deforestation patterns. Section C addresses the question of the agents of deforestation for the decade of the 1990s. Finally, section D explores some elements of the underlying causal structure of land use decisions, as identified by the literature.

A. From Past to Present

From a historical perspective, Guatemala's deforestation process is tightly linked to the country's developmental path and its dualistic economic structure. The expansion of agricultural land and pasture was the major direct source of deforestation. The next paragraphs distinguish four different phases of deforestation. These can be related to the Mayan civilization and the Spanish colonial period (section 1), the production of export crops after independence from

48 The later outbreak of the civil war also had a great impact on deforestation patterns in Guatemala. For an in-depth political analysis of the war's origins, see Molketin (2002).

Spain (section 2), the massive spontaneous colonization processes since the 1960s (section 3), and the declaration of protected areas in the light of increased colonization up until today (section 4).

1. Mayan Civilization and Spanish Colonial Period

The historical deforestation pattern in Guatemala shows some similarities to current processes. Indeed, deforestation already occurred during the time of the Mayan civilization, and was concentrated, ironically, in the Petén region and in the lowlands of northern Guatemala (the same place where the overwhelming part of forest cover loss occurs today). The empire reached its peak in the period from 250 A.D. until 900, and then suffered a rapid decline in both population and cultural sophistication. The civilization was partially rebuilt in 1200, but this latter Mayan civilization again went into decline. Due to the soil characteristics in that region, which are not suitable for long-term agriculture, Cabrera (1995) claims that the Mayas were forced to practice shifting cultivation.

There are various hypotheses regarding the civilization's collapse, including political reasons. Culbert (1988) and O'Hara et al. (1993) argue that environmental decline played a key role. Much of the evidence is from carbon-dated core samples showing deforestation, drying, soil erosion, and reduced crop yields in major agricultural areas. By the early ninth century, agricultural output could no longer support the dense population in the region. This lead to migration out of the Petén, a decline in population, and the final collapse of the civilization.

The main unresolved question concerns the extent to which drying and soil erosion were the endogenous result of human activity, or if they arose from exogenous climate change. The evidence suggests that both factors were important. Most likely the agricultural shortfall was partly determined directly by the Maya as a result of deforestation and soil erosion. At the same time, the high population density they had achieved through their intensive agriculture left no margin of safety when climate conditions changed, even if just marginally. Shriar (2001) presents evidence suggesting that the population density in the Petén at the height of the Maya civilization was higher than that prevailing today.

At the time of the Spanish conquest in 1524, the Petén region had already been abandoned, and much of the population was concentrated in the highlands. Because of the relatively fertile grounds, the indigenous population likely depended on less extensive forms of agriculture. Due to the lack of precious metals, the Spanish rapidly directed their attention to agricultural production. Both the Spanish and the Mayan culture had a strong focus on agriculture, but the motivation for agricultural production was not the same. While the Mayan practiced agriculture to cover the living needs of the community and relied on a communal structure of property, the

Spanish exploited the land to export a small number of export crops, such as cacao and indigo. They based their land use on a structure of private property.

Box 5. Guatemala — Land of Trees

Some authors speculate that the origin of the word Guatemala comes from *Quauhtemalan*, which in Nathuatl means land of trees. *Quauhtemalan* is a translation of the word *K'ichee'* (*ki* = much, *chee'* = trees) by the indigenous Nathual accompanying the Spanish conquistadors (see Cabrera 1995 and Maya' 1995). *K'ichee'* is also one of the 21 indigenous languages spoken in Guatemala today. The etymological narrative suggests that forests covered the overwhelming part of the country when the Spanish arrived.

Initially, the process of colonization meant changes in the structure of property rights. According to Luján (2000), these changes consisted of the Spanish appropriation of agricultural areas and the consequent expulsion of the Maya people to less fertile areas, particularly to the highlands. However, the Spanish allowed the indigenous to rely on communal forms of land tenure. Cabrera (1995) argues that moderate deforestation during this period was principally due to two reasons. First, Spanish immigration from Europe and the need to create a surplus from production for the crown resulted in a moderate increase in farm land. Second, the expropriation of indigenous agricultural land may already have encouraged shifting cultivation, because the indigenous were expulsed to areas hardly appropriate for agriculture.

2. Production of Export Crops

The massive expansion of agricultural land began after independence from Spain in 1821. Forests were considered useless and opened to distribution. 'Using' the land was the mechanism to assure property rights. Consequently, privileged landowners allowed the indigenous and campesinos to clear forest and plant their own crops for a limited period of time. After a while, the landowners introduced commercial crops. The peasants moved on and repeated the process. Until the 1970s, the massive expansion of agricultural land was due to the production of relatively few export crops, such as coffee, and later also sugar cane, banana, cotton and cattle. Deforestation during this period was concentrated in southern Guatemala, and in the parts of the highlands suitable for coffee production. Historical data showing the rapid increase of major export crops can be found in Luján (2000) as well as SEGEPLAN and MAGA (1984).

Cabrera (1995) discusses several factors that favored the loss of forest cover during that period. First, governments provided cheap credit for agricultural expansion and gave incentives for European immigration. This credit advantage was the origin of the German coffee producers, particularly in the highlands of the Department Alta Verapaz. Second, deforestation was initially associated with the expansion of the coffee sector. However, the diversification of export crops beginning in the 1940s additionally spurred the expansion of agricultural land.

Most qualitative research agrees that increased agricultural production due to the conversion of forest areas contributed to Guatemala's agricultural growth rates until the mid 1970s (Elías et al. 1997; Schweigert 1993; Valenzuela de Pisano 1996; World Bank 1996). However, according to the World Bank (2003a), exclusionary patterns of development can be attributed to past agricultural policies. Insofar, these policies not only had important historical consequences for the distribution of incomes, but they are still relevant today. Key elements, as summarized below, refer to mass land expropriations as well as the discrimination of the indigenous and campesinos regarding labor and education. Luján (2000) remarks that the historical practice of expropriating land from the indigenous gained momentum with the *Reforma Liberal* in 1871. Legal instruments encouraged the conversion of communally held indigenous lands into individually titled holdings. A central aim was the formation of large plantations, in particular for coffee. Since the ideal terrain for coffee occurs between 800 and 1,500 meters of altitude, the indigenous peoples who had been cultivating this land were once again compelled to locate to less fertile grounds. Diversification of export crops brought additional expropriations for the peasants.[49]

In 1950, according to the World Bank (2003a), communal lands accounted for 12 percent of agricultural land. This share dropped to 4.8 percent in 1964 and only about 1 percent in 1979. However, the number of farm families between 1950 and 1979 possessing parcels of land too small to provide subsistence incomes increased by 37 percent, and the number of landless peasants increased to about $^1/_4$ of the rural workforce. Estimates from 1979, the last published agricultural census, indicate that less than 2 percent of the population owned at least 65 percent of the land. With an estimated Gini coefficient of 0.85 for the distribution of land in 1979,[50] the World Bank (1996) places Guatemala highest on the list for land

49 Today, Southgate and Basterrechea (1993) argue that large-scale land redistribution, an issue of faith for many observers, cannot be regarded as panacea for Guatemala. That is, there is simply not enough land available to give all rural households a farm large enough to support an entire family.

50 According to the World Bank (2003a), this compares with 0.82 for El Salvador, 0.81 for Panama, 0.80 for Costa Rica and Nicaragua, 0.77 for Honduras and Bolivia, and 0.61 for Mexico. The figures in Appendix Two illustrate that there have not been significant distributional changes during the past 50 years. As a consequence, UNDP (2002) reports increased land fragmentation.

inequality in Latin America (the Gini coefficients using consumption and income data are 0.47 and 0.57, respectively).

The exclusionary labor and educational politics of the government are closely connected with land expansion. The World Bank (2003a) and UNDP (2000) claim that land politics in the past were partially designed to create a low-wage labor force by reducing the agricultural land available to the indigenous. Because insufficient cheap labor, in particular for coffee, was considered to be the main barrier to an expansion of export crops, the elite actively sought to create and maintain poverty during that period. The expropriation of indigenous communal lands helped to create rural underemployment by forcing families into marginal areas, or leaving them without access to sufficient land. Insofar, Guatemala's agricultural sector developed essentially on the backs of indigenous and campesino workers. According to UNDP (2000), an increasing share of the indigenous and campesino population was forced into numerous forms of mandatory labor in conjunction with mass land expropriations.

In 1873, the *Contribución de Caminos* decreed that all able male citizens were obliged to provide free labor for public projects to build roads or to pay a commutation fee. While this free work applied to all male citizens, in practice only the indigenous and campesino population was forced to perform it. In 1877, Guatemala instituted its *mandamiento* forced-labor system in which villages were required to supply crews of up to 60 people for periods of 15 to 30 days to coffee plantations. In 1934, the *Ley Contra Vagancia* obliged landless peasants to work at least 150 days per year on plantations. Proof of service was required in the workers' personal workbooks.

Moreover, indentured labor was also common. Under this system, advances were given to workers in anticipation of a certain amount of work in the future. Debts were then deducted from the worker's harvest or required in cash. Such debts commonly built up to such high levels that the plantation owners essentially controlled the workers. Debts were monitored by local public authorities who were authorized to arrest any defaulters, as evidenced by debt recordings in the personal workbooks that the indigenous peasants were required to keep. Lovell (1988) finds that coercive labor laws did not register in a uniform way across the country. However, many of the indigenous and campesinos did loose their lands and were forced into these mandatory forms of labor.

These forced labor laws remained in effect until the middle of the 20th century. After the democratic revolution in 1944, the Agrarian Reform Law of 1952 finally prohibited all forms of servitude and slavery. Regarding agricultural land, according to Luján (2000), the law had a moderate redistributional character. However, the agrarian reform was abandoned with a military and Central Intelligence Agency (CIA) backed *coup d'état* in 1954. At that time a decree was issued that permitted a reintroduction of a semi-feudal system under which landowners could avail themselves of a cheap labor force by providing subsistence plots on their plantations in exchange for labor during the harvest period. In some parts of the country, this practice still continues today, and minimum labor standards are often not enforced. In consequence, the economy that resulted provided little incentives for workers or firms to accumulate human capital.

Low schooling is also an outcome of a discriminatory education system. As evidenced in UNDP (2000) and World Bank (2003a), education in Guatemala was traditionally reserved for the citizens, a status not fully extended to woman and the indigenous until 1945. Because the education system systematically excluded the indigenous, virtually the entire indigenous and campesino population remained illiterate until the early 20th century. Making the educational policy part of a broader strategy of political exclusion, illiteracy was then used as a pretext for ineligibility for voting.

3. Directed and Spontaneous Colonization

Colonization policies had the most severe impact on forest cover loss. Land colonization was concentrated in the northern lowlands, particularly in the Petén.[51] It began shortly after the military coup in 1954, which both dismantled the previous agrarian reform and initiated government-promoted land colonization. In early 1960, within the context of a growing agro-export economy, high population growth rates and increasing land scarcity, the government decided to open the northern lowlands to colonization and development. Katz (2000) documents that the opening of the agricultural frontier, particularly in the Petén, was an easy way for the military governments to increase agricultural production, and to provide an escape for land-hungry peasants, while not compromising the Government's anti-resdistributional policies.

The Petén is Guatemala's northernmost department and compromises $^1/_3$ of the national land mass or about 36,000 km^2 of originally low-altitude moist tropical forest ecosystems. The Petén ecosystem is characterized by the fact that most nutrients are stored in the vegetation, and these nutrients are continually recycled

51 Land colonization was also important in the *Franja Transversal del Norte*, the region immediately below the Petén (which includes proportions of the lowlands from the Departments of Quiché, Alta Verapaz, Izabal and Huehuetenago). Despite its geographic proximity to the Petén, colonization patterns were different here. In particular, a focus was laid on small and medium farm settlement. Colonization and deforestation patterns in this region are poorly documented. Cabrera (1995), Kaimowitz (1995) and UNDP (1998) provide illustrations of a region almost entirely deforested.

between the soil and the biomass. Because of these characteristics, the elimination of the vegetative cover decreases soil fertility and the productive potential of the land. Nevertheless, the Petén still contains one of the largest remaining areas of tropical rainforest in Mesoamerica with high levels of biodiversity, as Méndez (1999) documents.

From the Spanish conquest of central Petén in 1697 until the 1960s, Guatemalans widely neglected the distant hinterland, considering it a dangerous and unsafe place. Population density and immigration was negligible.[52] Schwartz (1990) illustrates that during the Spanish colonial period the small economy of the Petén was initially based on cattle and horse ranching. The traditional cattle raising systems were based on open cattle grazing in the large areas of *natural* pasture. After a decline in ranching in the middle of the 19th century, the economy was based on agriculture and the extraction of non-timber products. There was no year-round road access from the Petén to the rest of Guatemala. The majority of the department's habitants lived in the department capital or small towns.

In 1959, the central government made an effort to colonize and develop the department and created the *Empresa Nacional de Fomento y Desarrollo de El Petén* (FYDEP). Kaimowitz (1995) describes how this state enterprise behaved as a largely autonomous regional government with nearly unlimited authority. Throughout most of its history, military officers ran the 'National Enterprise for Economic Development of the Petén.' A lack of continuity at the administrative level, pressure from metropolitan politicians, and mismanagement hindered the effective use of financial resources. Because of its historic association with previous military governments and its strong reputation for corruption, FYDEP was dissolved in the mid-1980s — Guatemala's transition to civilian rule.

According to Schwartz (1990), FYDEP began to promote colonization into the Petén by *large landholders*.[53] This decision to colonize was based at least in part on the conclusions of studies by *Latinconsult*, a consulting firm. It argued that cattle ranching would be the most appropriate land use for much of the Petén. FYDEP

---

52 Migration is poorly studied in Guatemala. A seminal contribution is Spielmann (1973). Based on census data, he reports that during 1950-1964 there was no significant migration to the Petén. Moreover, only 30 percent of all migrants moved to urban centers. Most people preferred to migrate to the southern coast plantations. Based on unpublished census data for 1994, Gellert (2000) finds that migration to metropolitan Guatemala and, in particular the Petén, has sharply increased.

53 Kaimowitz (1995) reports that initially the FYDEP sold land ranging from 2-9 U.S. dollars per hectare. A down payment was required, with the remainder to be paid over 10-20 years at zero interest. Land prices in the Petén rose rapidly. Today, depending on the land characteristics and tenure form, a hectare values approximately 60-600 U.S. dollars.

built a basic infrastructure of roads, small bridges, a modern airport, grain storage facilities, and brought electricity to most towns. FYDEP opened an all-weather dirt road from central Petén to the central highlands in 1970. Farmers in the Petén began sending maize to the south, and to a lesser extent also beans, rice and cattle.

FYDEP employed four criteria to set land prices: access to roads and markets, potential for commercial timber exploitation, soil quality, and access to water resources. FYDEP also imposed regulations on buyers to prevent land speculations and took measures to conserve the forests. However, due to its limited administrative capacity, infraction was the rule.

Three major types of people applied to purchase land made available, entrepreneurs and professionals from the large cities, politicians and military officers from various regions, and medium size ranchers from eastern Guatemala. Because there were no immediate prospects for labor-intensive industries, and agricultural intensification could not be sustained, FYDEP wanted only gradual migration flows. Therefore, FYDEP was never eager to sell land to *milperos* (maize farmers) and indigenous migrants but preferred large-scale and middle-class Ladino settlers.

However, starting in 1966, politicians frequently pressured the enterprise to sell land to thousands of land-poor settlers from the south. Ever since then, FYDEP has been unable to cope with uncontrolled spontaneous colonization. According to Schwartz (1995a; 1995b), immigration finally ran out of control when the level of violent military conflict decreased in the mid 1980s. Ever since that time, anarchic colonization processes have been taking place. Grandia et al. (2001) suggest that population growth rates may have exceeded 9 percent per year. Total population may have risen from approximately 25,000 in the 1960s to over 500,000 for the early 1990s.

The government decision to sell extensive areas of land in the Petén to major ranchers at below market prices was clearly a key factor in the rapid deforestation that occurred between the 1960s and the 1980s. Road construction together with considerations related to cattle, spurred deforestation. Expectations from rising land prices and the need to clear forestland as a way to enhance tenure security also drove deforestation. However, Kaimowitz (1995) finds that subsidized livestock credit was of marginal importance. Only a small percent of the Petén ranchers received credit. Moreover, livestock credit in the department has steadily declined as a result of both increasing real interest rates and a general decline in public agricultural loans. Since there appears to have been little private lending for livestock in the Petén, most of the investments by large and medium-size landowners was probably self-financed.

The Petén has evidently served as the country's main agricultural frontier, and as an important site for large-scale ranching. Government policies have permitted large landholders with privileged land access to reap substantial rents, which were made possible by public investment in infrastructure. It is less clear, however, to what degree logging, timber extraction operations, shifting cultivation and oil exploitation[54] were responsible for deforestation, and how all these activities are linked to one another. Due to the anarchic settlement process and scarcity of data, much remains speculative.

Colonization patterns changed, however, for the period of the late 1980s. In fact, most qualitative research agrees that since Guatemala's transition to civilian rule in 1985, and the ceasing of the military conflict, one of the greatest threats to the Petén is the migration of thousands of land-poor peasants into the region (Elías et al. 1997; FLACSO 2000; Katz 2000; Schwartz 1995b; Valenzuela de Pisano 1996; World Bank 1995a). Rural Guatemalans fleeing from land scarcity and with limited employment opportunity come to the Petén in search of agricultural production. In spite of the lack of reliable data on forest cover change in the Department over the last decades, virtually all observers agree that the changes in land use and forest cover have been dramatic.

4. *Protected Areas and Civil War Refugees*

The last phase of deforestation in Guatemala can be associated with the return of the civil war refugees during the 1990s, and the massive expansion of protected areas by environmental groups. According to the final report of the Commission for Historical Clarification (1999), the internal military conflict left 1 million persons displaced in a total population of 10 million. Reportedly, a substantial number of civil war peasants that fled to Mexico, are now returning. Cabrera (1995) argues that extensive rural migration flux combined with land-scarcity exaggerates violent conflict over land and deforestation.

Given the increased threat of invasion into the forest margins by smallholders, environmental non-governmental organizations (NGOs) together with governmental institutions have responded with the massive establishment of protected areas. According to CONAMA et al. (1999a), the majority of protected areas have been set up with increased international financing and technical support between 1986-1995. UNDP (2002) states there were 123 protected areas in 2001, covering approximately 28.6 percent of the country's total landmass. However,

---

54 Oil exploitation in the Petén started in the 1980s. Companies withdrew their activities during the civil war. Rosenfeld (1999) states that with the end of guerilla activity development of the oil industry in the Petén is proceeding. Until today, however, only few contracts have been granted. The Xan Oil Field in the *Laguna del Tigre* National Park is the most important.

CONAMA et al. (1999a) reports that the protected areas in Guatemala are not representative regarding ecosystem variability. This frequently leads to environmentalists calling for further areas. Only 13 percent of Guatemala's parks had an approved and executed administrative framework in 1997. However, this percent has recently increased. This suggests a gradual improvement in the management of the formerly 'paper parks.' UNDP (2002) estimates that in 2002, about 87 percent of the parks had such a managerial framework.

The majority of the protected areas are administrated by the *Consejo Nacional de Areas Protegidas* (CONAP), a reportedly weak public institution, which is subordinated to the *Presidencia de la República*. In some cases, NGOs or other institutions are accepted as co-administrators. According to the *area* protected by parks and their financial revenues, environmental NGOs play *de facto* the predominant role in Guatemala. In principle, most protected areas seek to combine the goals of nature conservation with improving rural livelihoods, and they are run as an Integrated Conservation and Development Project (ICDP). Despite the magnitude of the protected areas and the supposedly heavy impact they have on the land use decisions of the peasants, there is no systematic information regarding the protected areas' contribution to forest conservation and rural development. However, an extremely weak executive and local administrative capacity (J. Godoy 1998), a high administrative and wage overhead (Galindo 1999), and the disappointing results of many ICDPs in developing countries, all suggest that the conservation impact might be modest in magnitude (for a summary see Loening and Markussen 2003).

The most ambitious conservation project, created in 1990, is the Maya Biosphere Reserve in the Petén. With 16,000 km^2 it corresponds to the size of the country El Salvador and covers approximately $^1/_2$ of the Department, or about $^1/_3$ of the entire Guatemalan system of protected areas. The reserve contains three different types of management units. A core area of national parks and biological reserves has the highest level of protection. A large multiple-zone allows some forms of extractive harvesting, ranching, farming, hunting and commercial logging. A buffer zone south of the reserve has no restrictions. The reserve is run by a unique blend of local and international NGOs, international development institutions and national authorities.[55]

55 Conservation organizations promote a number of sustainable agriculture techniques to increase productivity, reduce erosion, increase labor requirements and decrease the effects of agricultural pests. In the Petén, the use of green manures is often promoted. This system most commonly involves the development of an *abonera*, a plot on which velvet beans (*frijol abono*) are planted, and which later in the year is used as a plot to grow maize. For a detailed description of such techniques in Guatemala, see *Defensores de la Naturaleza* (2001).

According to Valenzuela de Pisano (1996) and Shriar (2001), agencies have a strong focus on nature conservation and place little emphasis on the underlying socio-economic causes that lead to the immigration of peasants. A common feature of conservationists is the belief that deforestation follows subsistence-driven patterns (see for example Nations et al. 1999 and *Defensores de la Naturaleza* 2001). Consequently, extension agencies promote sustainable agriculture techniques that aim to intensify agricultural production.

B. Magnitude and Location of Forest Cover Loss

Having presented the main trends of deforestation, the next paragraphs analyze the magnitude (section 1) and location (section 2) of forest cover change in Guatemala. In addition, it provides a brief account of the country's environmental diversity (section 3). Overall, given the historical and socio-economic context, there can be little doubt that deforestation has been rapid. Despite considerable data gaps, this is confirmed by virtually all deforestation studies that have been carried out for Guatemala.

1. Magnitude of Deforestation

Figure 12 scatters data on forest cover change as a percentage of total land area from 1950-2000. The data is taken from Loening and Markussen (2003) who synthesize the results from more than 24 studies on deforestation and land use in Guatemala. It is reproduced in Appendix Two. Most studies are unpublished consultant or government reports. According to local experts, national forestry inventories were carried out in 1950 by the *Instituto Nacional Forestal* (INAFOR), 1975-1976 by Mittak (1977), 1987-1988 by Sagastume (1992), and 1998-1999 by INAB (2000). The original inventory prior to Mittak (1977) is reported to be lost. The most reliable estimate probably comes from the FAO (2001). It compares data from satellite imagery for 1987-1988 and 1998-1999.

The data is typically based on aerial photography and, for later periods, on satellite imagery. Sometimes agricultural census, socio-economic surveys or other estimates complement it. Since each author employs different methodologies and much of the data is of dubious quality, forest cover estimates vary greatly. However, the overall trend clearly suggests that forest cover change has been dramatic. In 1950 forests covered nearly 65 percent of Guatemala's total land area. Only about 26 percent remained forested in 2000. This implies an estimated loss in forest resources of approximately 60 percent for the entire period (70,451 km^2 in 1950 compared to 28,497 km^2 in 2000).

According to Figure 12, there may have been changing patterns over time in deforestation. A speculative interpretation, indicated by the dotted line, would be to assume that deforestation slowed down in the 1980s. Most likely this decrease is associated with the peak of Guatemala's internal military conflict during that period. Kaimowitz (1995; 1996) argues that the instability of the civil war discouraged deforestation activities. In particular, it reduced land prices and the number of farmers interested in purchasing land from the government. In addition, farmland was abandoned when there was internal military conflict. Especially in regions where violence was heavy, the rate of deforestation was reduced.

Figure 12. Guatemala: Forest Cover Estimates, 1950-2000
(in percent of total land area) [a/]

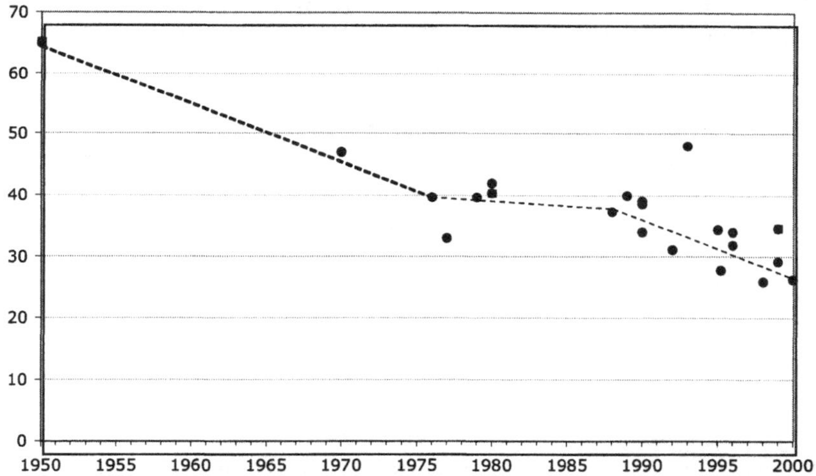

Source: Author's elaboration, based on data from Loening and Markussen (2003). a/ The dotted line is speculative and suggests a decreasing trend in deforestation patterns during a period of the civil war.

Some studies present estimates on annual forest cover *change*. The estimates analyzed in Loening and Markussen (2003) suggest annual forest cover change lies between 54,000 and 90,000 hectares. However, the data does not allow an inference about whether deforestation has increased over time. In general, environmental movements and conservation agencies tend to report higher figures than forestry institutions or the FAO. Kaimowitz (1996) claims that most estimates are too high. Annual deforestation has rather been between 50,000 and 60,000 hectares than the 80,000 or 90,000 hectares mentioned in most studies. This is empirically confirmed by the FAO (2001) using satellite imagery, and by Baumeister (2001) analyzing land use changes over the past decades. According to the FAO (2001), annual deforestation was approximately 1.7 percent between 1990 and 2000. This is comparatively high and places Guatemala among the top $^1/_3$ of all countries worldwide that are affected by the loss of forest cover.

2. Location of Deforestation

For the period 1975-1988, the latest information available at the department level is CONAMA et al. (1999a) and Elías et al. (1997). They report that deforestation is a countrywide phenomenon. In absolute terms, however, deforestation is located in the northern lowlands, particularly in the Petén. In fact, more than $^1/_2$ of the country's deforestation is reported to be in the Petén. A back of the envelope calculation from Cabrera (1995) suggests annual deforestation at approximately 39,000 hectares. Based on comparatively good quality data, Sader et al. (2001) report that in the buffer zones of the Maya Biosphere Reserve annual deforestation even exceeded 3 percent during the 1990s (see Table 19). Note that overall deforestation trends show increasing patterns, despite much of the environmentalists conservation efforts.[56] Moreover, they seem to have increased significantly in 1990, the year when the reserve was founded.

Table 19. The Petén: Annual Forest Clearing Rates in Maya Biosphere Reserve, 1986-1997 (in percent)

Area	1986-90	1990-93	1993-95	1995-97
Multiple Use Zone	0.05	0.16	0.25	0.25
Buffer Zone	0.74	2.71	3.76	3.28
Total reserve	0.04	0.23	0.33	0.36

Source: Sader et al. (2000; 2001). The time categories are taken from the source.

Other areas threatened heavily by deforestation are the eastern regions (Departments of Jalapa, Jutiapa, Chiquimula, El Progreso, Santa Rosa and Zacapa) but also the central regions (Sacatepéquez and Guatemala). Less critical are the Western Highlands (Departments of Sololá, Totonicapán, Chimaltenango and Baja Verapaz, as well as Huehuetenango, Quiché, San Marcos and Quetzaltenango). Deforestation in the highlands is usually associated with high levels of soil erosion. In fact, many of the cleared lands have been so degraded that they are no longer useful for agricultural production.

56 In a preliminary analysis for the period 1997-1999, unfortunately plagued by heavy data deficiencies, Sader et al. (2000) find that deforestation might be *lower* than in previous periods. However, *total destruction* of the reserve is probably *higher* than ever due to numerous forest fires. UNDP (2002) reports that forest fires were particularly high in 1998 but eventually have decreased over time.

3. *Environmental Diversity*

Given the poor quality of most estimates regarding forest cover change, it does not come as a big surprise that much less is known about the environmental diversity of the country. There is neither measurement for the conservation of biodiversity nor information about the evolution of species loss over time. Nations et al. (1989), UNDP (1998) and CONAMA et al. (1999b, 1999c) summarize the available evidence. Based on incomplete inventories, they claim Guatemala to be the country with one of the highest levels in species diversity in Central America. However, an objective framework to assess the biological importance of geographic areas is missing in all these estimates. UNDP (2002) lists 1170 endemic species for Guatemala and ranks the country 24th out of 25 countries with respect to forest biodiversity. Due to its natural location and its biogeographic situation, Myers et al. (2000) classify the country equally as a 'hotspot' regarding species diversity. The reasoning is essentially based on Guatemala's pronounced climatic conditions and its varied landscape. De la Cruz (1982) suggests that the country has 14 Holdridge Life Zones.

Other studies are more cautious. For example, in a World Bank priority setting report for Latin America, Dinerstein et al. (1995) identify ecoregions of comparatively high biodiversity conservation value based on final conservation status and biological distinctiveness. The regions are then classified into four broad categories. According to this scheme, experts define ecoregions in descending order as globally, regionally, bioregionally or locally outstanding. For the case of Guatemala, the report claims that the tropical forests in the Petén and cloud montane forests in the highlands are seriously threatened and of great biodiversity value, although these forests are only categorized here as bioregionally outstanding. Insofar they are classified far behind such regions as the Amazon tropical moist forests which are considered to be of global importance.

C. Direct Sources of Deforestation

Table 20 presents data for direct sources of resource degradation in the period 1993-1997. It is based on estimates from national forest experts. The estimate suggests shifting farming systems (*agricultura migratoria*) are the main deforestation factor, followed by pasture expansion, illegal logging, and firewood consumption. Commercial agriculture for export crops and other factors, such as logging activities or natural disasters, appear to be of minor importance. According to *Banco de Guatemala*, the forest sector accounts for approximately 2.5 to 2.6 percent in GDP during the 1990s.[57] UNDP (2002) claims that about 97 percent of

57 Direct information from *Banco de Guatemala, Departamento de Estadísticas Económicas, Sección de Cuentas Nacionales*. Given the lack of precise baseline

the country's forest production during that period was used for firewood production. This leaves only around 3 percent for industrial wood production and other purposes. In fact, Guatemala has a negative trade balance for wood products, principally due to the importation of paper products.

Somewhat surprising then is the low share of forest degradation attributed to firewood collection. According to the World Bank et al. (2003), 80.3 percent of all Guatemalans use firewood as their main source of energy. In particular, the rural poor continue to rely almost entirely on firewood for cooking. Income, education, access to social services and ethnicity are important determinants of fuel choice. While firewood collection is often thought to be an important source of deforestation, this issue is little studied in Guatemala. The estimate in Table 20 suggests the impact of firewood collection on forest degradation to be low.[58] However, research for other countries has ascertained equally that most deforestation is caused by clearing for agriculture or logging, and not by wood collection. For example, Heltberg (2001) finds that the impact of firewood collection for the case of rural India is highly localized. Much wood is not collected from forested land. Firewood collection causes forest degradation only in certain places, particularly in areas of high population density, around cities, and on fragile and sloping lands.

Commercial agriculture and licensed logging, though occasionally opening up penetration roads and enabling farmers to move deeper into the woods, seem to be of marginal importance (World Bank 1995a). However, illegal and selective logging, especially in the Petén, has been reported to be a direct source of deforestation. Due to the secrecy involved, evidence on this topic is merely narrative. Schwartz (1990; 1995a) reports clandestine sawmills operating in Petén and Mexico that use Petén wood and employ workers from Guatemala, Mexico and Belize. In addition, there is a substantial number of independent small-scale loggers reported who combine woodcutting with other income-producing activities, such as the extraction of shate, chicle latex and *pimienta gorda*, or hunting. According to the FAO (1999), radical environmental movements may have unintentionally spurred these clandestine activities. Because of the their emphasis on strict

---

information, in particular for firewood energy consumption, a responsible statistician suggested that the reliability of this number might be weak. Personal communication with Jorge Minera, July 20, 2001.

58 See Schwartz (1995a) for a contrary argument. Katz (2000) reports that the average Guatemalan rural household may use the equivalent of 2 or 3 trees per month for firewood purposes, or approximately 25-30 trees per year. Of that, approximately $^1/_2$ come from felled trees.

preservation, conservation groups have made it difficult for companies to obtain licenses to harvest trees and non-timber products.

Table 20. Guatemala: Direct Sources of Deforestation, 1993-1997
(in 1,000 hectares and percent)

Direct source	Annual deforestation	Percent
Migratory agriculture	64.37	78.5
Pasture expansion	8.20	10.0
Illegal logging	4.10	5.0
Firewood consumption	2.46	3.0
Forest fires	1.64	2.0
Natural factors	0.82	1.0
Commercial agriculture	0.41	0.5

Source: MAGA, PAFG and INAB (1998).

The main controversy on the direct sources of deforestation in Guatemala concerns whether agricultural expansion comes mainly from migratory agriculture farming systems or large-scale pasture expansion. Since pasture expansion has been particularly high in the Petén, in two influential studies Kaimowitz (1995; 1996) argues that large-scale livestock expansion has favored the conversion of forest cover here rather than land clearing by small farmers. Moreover, Kaimowitz (1995) claims that large-scale pasture expansion may even have protected certain forests from land clearing by small farmers.

Other studies are more cautious and simply refer to pasture expansion and small farmer's land clearing without quantifying effects (see for example Schwartz 1990; 1995a). Much of the uncertainty is due to the lack of reliable data on land use changes over time, the anarchic situation in the Petén, and changing deforestation patterns over time. The issue is further complicated by the fact that agricultural encroachment and pasture expansion often go hand in hand. Forest areas are typically converted by farmers and then later used for cattle systems. In addition, with the exception perhaps of farmers with prime agricultural land, the first thing that almost any small farmer in Guatemala does when accumulating money is to purchase cattle.

As pointed out in Table 21, pure pasture expansion in the Petén accounted for less than 10 percent, and mixed crops and pasture were 30 percent of total forest cover loss. If none of this mixed use category were pasture, livestock expansion would have presented less than 10 percent of total forest cover loss. If all of it were pasture, livestock expansion would have presented more than 38 percent. However, the available evidence gradually suggests that large-scale pasture expansion is becoming less important than it was in earlier periods. Already in 1981, a study from the Central Bank reported that many ranches in the Petén had failed or were not profitable. *Banco de Guatemala* (1981) argues this was due to inadequate road access, water supply problems, unacceptable low stocking rates, inexperienced management, inadequate knowledge of cattle ranching and the use of methods that work in the south coast of Guatemala but not in the Petén. Moreover, the study claimed the returns to ranching per unit of hectare were lower than agriculture and, hence, not particularly attractive.

Table 21. The Petén: Land Use Change, 1987-1993
(in1,000 hectares and percent)

Category	Land use change	Percent
Pasture	36	8.5
Grasslands and natural pasture	10	2.4
Mixed use (agriculture and pasture)	127	30.0
Abandoned agricultural land	111	26.2
Agricultural land with residual forests	140	33.1
Inundated land areas	-1	-0.2
Forests	*-423*	*-100.0*

Source: World Bank (1995a) and own calculations.

Figure 13, based on information from the Economic Commission of Latin America (CEPAL) Macroeconomics Database, shows the evolution of aggregate cattle population in Guatemala for the period 1980-2001. About 10 percent of total livestock is located in the Petén. Since no disaggregated time series data for the Petén is available, some care should be taken when interpreting Figure 13. However, the figure clearly suggests that cattle population was almost stagnant during the 1980s, and has continually decreased since the mid-1990s.

Therefore, livestock expansion and associated forest clearing may have become much less important during the past decades than in earlier periods. In addition, Kaimowitz (1996) argues that after the mid 1970s international conditions for beef exports continually worsened due to the restrictive European Community, U.S. and Mexican import regulations. As expected for a low-income country, the domestic demand for beef in Guatemala is traditionally low.

This finding is consistent with the data on land use change for Guatemala 1979-1999 presented in Table 22. The estimate suggests that deforestation is almost entirely associated with the expansion of other land area combined with open forests. Baumeister (2001) claims this category to be associated with agricultural expansion and shifting cultivation.[59] Finally, empirical case studies from Grunberg et al. (2000) as well as Sader et al. (2001) support the view that during the 1990s smallholders encroachment along river and road corridors has become the single most important factor associated with forest cover loss in northern Guatemala.

Figure 13. Guatemala: Cattle Population and Milk Production, 1980-2001 (in million head and million liters)

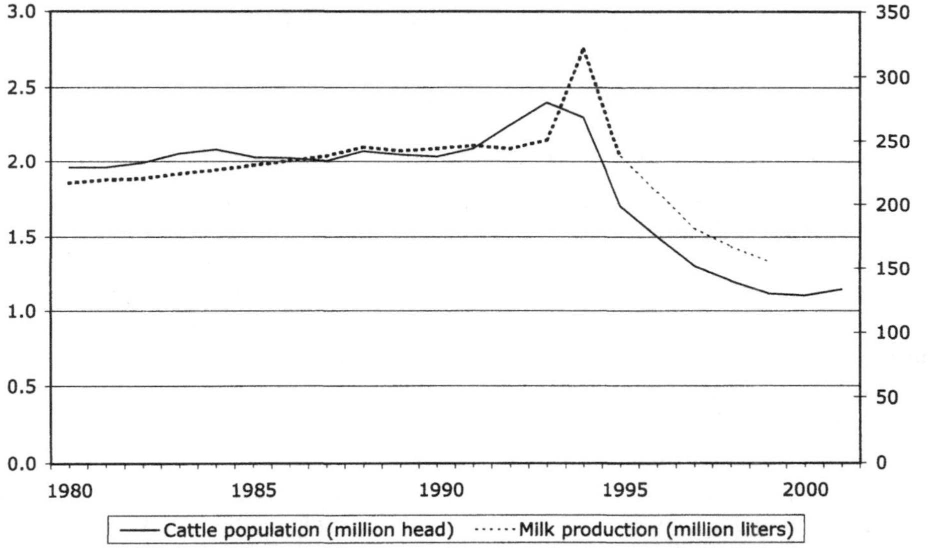

Source: CEPAL (2003), based on data from *Banco de Guatemala* and the National Statistics Institute (INE). The left axis refers to the amount of cattle population.

To summarize, the decline of large-scale pasture expansion, the negligible importance of commercial farming and logging, and the unsuitability for cultivation of the remaining land area (CONAMA et al. 1999a) within the context of continuing high deforestation indicate that smallholders' migratory agriculture (shifting cultivation) is the main direct source of deforestation in Guatemala during the 1990s.

59 The estimate from Baumeister (2001) is based on satellite imaginary, but partly also on socio-economic data. Regarding the measurement of pasture expansion, survey and census data can lead to biases if ranchers have incentives to report less cattle.

Table 22. Guatemala: Land Use Change, 1979-1999
(in 1,000 hectares and percent)

Category	1979	1999	Change	Change in percent
Agricultural land	1,310	1,490	180	15.7
Other agricultural land area combined with open forests	3,766	4,638	872	76.0
Pasture	1,334	1,400	66	5.8
Other land	156	185	29	2.5
Forests	*4,323*	*3,176*	*-1,147*	*-100.0*

Source: Baumeister (2001) and own calculations.

D. Underlying Determinants of Deforestation: A Review

This section analyzes some of the underlying economic parameters of land use decisions in Guatemala for the period 1990-2001 as they are identified in the literature. The *number* of deforestation studies and consulting reports sharply contrasts with the *analytical* work on this subject. For example, in co-operation with national forest institutions, the FAO (1999) synthesized more than 35 studies and reports on deforestation for Guatemala, and conducted targeted interviews to help overcome information constraints. Overall, the report remains inconclusive. The FAO asserts that there is no general agreement on the causal structure of deforestation in Guatemala.

However, a closer look here at selected deforestation studies does reveal some important findings. Appendix Two presents a schematic overview of the methodologies, respective research focus, and results of the reviewed studies. The following paragraphs present the findings on the following parameters of deforestation: poverty, population growth and migration (section 1), road construction and soil conditions (section 2), agricultural intensification (section 3), and property rights (section 4). Much of the analysis is qualitative and focuses on the Maya Biosphere Reserve in the Petén.

1. Poverty, Population Growth and Migration

The relationship between poverty and deforestation is rarely addressed explicitly. However, some studies do refer to the country's broader socio-economic context. In line with the previous historical overview, it is argued that the root causes of high migration are inequality of land distribution and the unfavorable socio-economic conditions that prevail in most parts of the country (Elías et al. 1997; Valenzuela de Pisano 1996; Schwartz 1990, 1995a, 1995b; World Bank 1995a). In a descriptive analysis, based on unpublished 1994 census data, Gellert

(2000) essentially qualifies rural migration as a survival strategy of the poor. However, Bilsborrow (1992) identifies severe research gaps regarding the exact underlying causes of rural migration, the origin, and the socio-economic characteristics of migrants.

Broadly speaking, despite much data uncertainty, the single greatest consistent finding of qualitative research is that natural population growth and rural migration flows are key parameters for environmental degradation and forest decline (Bilsborrow 1992; Elías et al. 1997; FLACSO 2000; Katz 2000; Nations et al. 1999; Schwartz 1990; Southgate and Basterrechea 1993; Valenzuela de Pisano 1996; World Bank 1995a). Equally, a consultant report from Chemonics International et al. (2000) finds deforestation on the Maya Biosphere Reserve in the Petén essentially due to a high natural population growth and migrants from other areas of the country.

Empirically, however, only Grunberg et al. (2000) have addressed the deforestation-population nexus. In a spatial regression for the buffer zone of the Maya Biosphere Reserve in the Petén, Grunberg et al. find that population growth and deforestation show a significant relationship for the period 1986-1999. However, the analysis is plagued by serious deficiencies.[60] In particular, spatial and temporal auto-correlation problems and the low quality of the population data in the Petén limit the reliability of the analysis. Moreover, the regression makes no reference to the potential endogeneity of the variable with respect to infrastructure, soil conditions or socio-economic factors.

2. *Soil Conditions and Road Construction*

In line with spatial regression analysis for other countries, Grunberg et al. (2000) find that well draining soil types are more likely to be deforested than poorly draining soil types in the Maya Biosphere Reserve of the Petén. In addition, over time, the deforestation rate increases on well draining soils while remaining close to zero on poorly draining soils. As expected, perennial roads are good indicators for deforestation threats in Grunberg's et al. simulation model. Equally, Sader et al. (2001) report that forest cover change in the Maya Biosphere Reserve

---

60 Population estimates for the Petén vary greatly. At the low end, the National Statistics Institute (INE) reports a population growth rate of 4.1 percent. Grandia (2000) argues that this figure does not account adequately for migration. Also, natural population growth is higher in the Petén than elsewhere. At the high end, according to a survey conducted by a consulting firm, there is an estimated annual growth of 9.5 percent. Virtually every institution seems to manage differing statistics falling in between these two estimates.

essentially occurs along river and road corridors. Also, Rosenfeld (1999) finds that spontaneous colonization processes are indirectly promoted by the road and pipeline construction undertaken by oil exploitation activities. Finally, in his voluminous study of the historical colonization processes for the Petén, Schwartz (1990) remarks that with the opening of an all-weather road from the Petén to the rest of the country in 1970, deforestation and spontaneous encroachment increased.

3. Agricultural Productivity

Agricultural intensification is actively promoted by conservation agencies as an effective tool to reduce deforestation in the Petén and elsewhere in the country. However, the very limited evidence for Guatemala does not support this as an effective strategy. In a qualitative analysis, Shriar (2001) finds that extension agencies are frustrated by the lack of interest smallholders have for such practices in the Maya Biosphere Reserve. He argues that agricultural intensification involves high opportunity costs of labor, and this seems to make such techniques unattractive to most peasants. Moreover, unfavorable market conditions — except for maize — and other factors, such as fear of snakes and vandalism, limit farmers' interest in applying agricultural intensification techniques. Equally, Chemonics International et al. (2000) report no evidence that the promotion of such techniques does contribute to conserving the forest cover in the Petén.

An empirical case study for the *Sierra de la Minas Biosphere Reserve* (which includes proportions of the Departments of Izabal and Alta Verapaz, as well as Baja Verapaz, El Progreso and Zacapa) *Defensores de la Naturaleza* (2001) find that the adoption of agricultural intensification techniques significantly increases farmers' demand for agricultural land use. The study is located in core areas of the second largest biosphere reserve in Guatemala (2,400 km^2) and uses survey data from 1998 for approximately 150 Q'eqchi' households. Overall, the study finds that farmers who use sustainable agriculture techniques put their saved labor to use in ways that increase deforestation, for example by increasing the amount of area for planting maize or by establishing cash crops in forest areas. *Defensores de la Naturaleza* (2001) suggests that the effect is due to the open access situation, where farmers lack the incentive to be efficient in land use.[61]

---

61 *Defensores de la Naturaleza* (2001) argue that intensification techniques are still a good instrument for forest conservation because of a number of positive externalities, such as improvements of rural livelihoods, local participation, the reduction of forest fires etc. Given that such techniques proved to have the *exact* opposite effect on forest conservation, this argumentation seems puzzling.

4. *Property Rights*

Regarding the effects of land tenure and property rights on natural resource exploitation, the available evidence is entirely qualitative. The most comprehensive analysis comes from Katz (2000) and is based on a study by the World Bank (1995a). For the Petén, a key finding is that insecure private land tenure regimes have encouraged resource-mining activities because using the land is a necessary mechanism for establishing property rights. Moreover, in accordance with the observations from the previous paragraph, uncertainty over property rights frequently lead farmers to produce crops with short-growing cycles. Consequently, conservation NGO movement activities geared towards the adoption of sustainable agriculture are frustrated by smallholders' lack of interest. Because of their limited size, communal land tenure regimes only play a minor role in the Petén.

In stark contrast to the Petén are the Western Highlands of Guatemala. They cover approximately 18 percent of Guatemala's territory and are home for more than 30 percent of the national population. Just as the Petén, the Western Highlands are ecologically diverse. They also constitute the principal watershed for most rivers in Guatemala. The fact that deforestation has been relatively low despite the high level of poverty among the predominantly indigenous smallholders, the high population density, and the lack of property rights in terms of legally registered titles has stimulated numerous debates. The World Bank (1995a), Elías et al. (1997) and more pronounced Katz (2000) argue that the social capital of the indigenous fosters a sense of ownership and respect for boundaries that can partially substitute for legal property rights.[62] Hence, deforestation is reduced because smallholders have incentives for conserving their resources. Moreover, there is no 'race for property rights' like in the Petén, where the migratory nature of population has prevented the creation of social capital. By contrast, in the Western Highlands, the social capital base has allowed a series of common property regimes and communal owned forests to be established.

5. *Summing-Up*

Most of the reviewed studies concentrate on a particular issue, location or time period. In particular, regarding evidence about the socio-economic parameters of

62 The basic idea behind the notion of social capital is that relationships among individuals give rise to something valuable. This intangible value can then be drawn upon to improve individual and collective well-being. Social capital may have its foundations in ethnicity, religion, shared history or other group membership. It is manifested in collective knowledge, including environmental knowledge, respect for group rules and norms, and the creation and maintenance of self-governing institutions (see Katz 2000).

deforestation and land use in protected areas, such as in the Maya Biosphere Reserve, it is hard to generalize the findings to other settings. Research has a strong focus on anthropological, sociological and nature conservation issues, and is almost entirely qualitative. Hence, many of the conclusions and policy recommendations tend to be speculative. In fact, Grunberg et al. (2000) and *Defensores de la Naturaleza* (2001) are the only papers that empirically address some of the underlying factors of deforestation. There is no research regarding such important parameters as credit expansion, non-farm employment and, of course, human capital endowment.

In general, most of the research implicitly refers to a subsistence-based explanation of land use. Ironically, in particular regarding the effects of agricultural intensification and property rights, the available evidence supports the analytical relevance of a market-based explanation. The next section takes a closer look at the empirical determinants of deforestation and land use in Guatemala. The studies reviewed here may serve as valuable input in the final formulation of the hypotheses concerning the effects of economic parameters on deforestation.

IV. Empirical Evidence on Deforestation and Land Use in Guatemala

Despite the considerable attention devoted to deforestation, the impact of different economic parameters on the process or the manner in which these various factors interact is poorly understood. This is certainly true for Guatemala where scant *empirical* research exists and the qualitative findings are *not* open for generalization. The following paragraphs try to remedy this by quantifying the effects of selected variables on deforestation and land use decisions and validating some of the hypotheses derived from the qualitative analysis. A particular focus will be laid on the role of education and non-farm employment.[63]

In order to empirically address these issues, the next paragraphs are organized as follows. Section A presents the conceptual framework. The subsequent regression analyses display the results, with a descending level of aggregation, from various regressions based on three distinct data sets. Section B is a regional-level analysis. Section C is a countrywide household-level analysis. Section D finally examines land use determinants for Guatemala's main agricultural frontier region: The Petén.

A. Conceptual Framework

The conceptual framework of the following analysis is based on the land-rent approach. As explained in Chapter II, the basic idea is straightforward. To recapitulate, there is a potential rent attached to the use of each plot of land. Land rent can be defined as the gross value of production minus all costs of production. The model then simply predicts that land will be devoted to the activity yielding the highest rent. While land rent by itself is not directly observable, it is possible to perceive land use patterns and key determinants of prices and productivity. Chomitz and Gray (1996) as well as Deininger and Minten (2002) show that land use can be empirically analyzed in a linear regression model. Consequently, in such a model, a vector of variables that affect either prices or agricultural productivity determines agricultural land use.

---

63 There are manifold definitions regarding *non-farm* employment. Throughout this study, the term refers to all activities in the *non-agricultural* sectors, i.e. all economic activities in rural areas except agriculture, livestock and hunting. As such, it does *not* include *farm wages*, for example, temporary occupations at large coffee plantations. In the analysis for the Petén, however, temporary farm wages are included into the analysis as a *separate* variable. In addition, notice that due to data limitations no distinction can be made between the different types of non-farm activities, i.e. distinguishing low-productivity and comparatively high productivity jobs.

Table 23. Expected Signs of Selected Variables on Deforestation and Land Use

Variables	Empirical proxy used [a/]			Expected sign
	Countrywide		The Petén	
	Regional	Household	Household	
Favorable physical-geographic characteristics	N.D.	Departmental dummies	Municipal dummies	+
Insecure property rights	N.D. [b/]	N.D.	Dummy squatter plot	(+)
Informal land tenure regimes	N.D.	Dummy indigenous	Dummy indigenous	(–)
Higher soil degradation	N.D.	Years living at farm	Years owning plot	+
Better availability of direct assistance	N.D.	Dummy technical assistance	Dummy green manures	(+)
Higher capital equipment	N.D.	Number of rooms	Number of rooms	+
Higher distance costs	N.D.	Time to get firewood	Distance to plot	–
	N.D.	Time to next service point	N.D.	–
Higher opportunity costs of labor [c/]	Rural non-farm employment	Dummy rural non-farm employment	Dummy rural non-farm employment	–
	N.D.	N.D.	Dummy temporary farm wage	–
Population	Department's population	Household size	Household size	(+)
More education	Years of schooling in department	Education of household head	Education of household head	(–)

Source: Author's elaboration. a/ For definitions and details on the construction of the variables, see Appendix Two. Brackets indicate a potentially uncertain outcome. N.D. = no data available. b/ Partly proxied by *microfinca* variable, see text. c/ Rural-non farm employment refers to engagement predominantly in non-agricultural occupations. The relevant unit is the working population in the regional level analysis, and employment of the household head in the household level analyses.

A list of selected variables used in the subsequent regression analysis and the expected signs are provided in Table 23. At the household level, some variables are proxied. For instance, departmental or municipal dummies may to some degree substitute physical-geographic characteristics. Following Deininger and Minten (2002), ethnicity may hold as a proxy for informal land tenure regimes.[64] As evidenced in the previous sections, the expected signs concord with selected empirical research for other settings, and the tentative qualitative outcome for Guatemala. However, both for theoretical and empirical reasoning, it is rather difficult to predict the sign for education, property rights and technical assistance.

(1) Education. The impact of education on agricultural land use is not a priori clear. On the one hand, education could reduce deforestation via its impact on wage income, certain types of rural non-farm activities, and population growth. Other factors, such as the appreciation for non-timber uses of forests, could also play a role. On the other hand, education could increase agricultural productivity and may boost deforestation. Nevertheless, in rural Guatemala productivity effects may be negligible. As evidenced by the ENCOVI (2000), average education of rural household heads is about 2 years. To show significant effects on agricultural productivity, Phillips and Marble (1986) find that — for the case of Guatemala — farmers require at least 4 years of education. Taken together, this gradually suggests that increased education could be associated with reduced land use and deforestation in rural Guatemala.

(2) Property rights. Low levels of formal or informal tenure security could be associated with higher levels of deforestation if people deforest to establish property rights. However, if agricultural use provides high returns, then more secure property rights that guarantee the ability to continue agricultural cultivation could just as well lead to increased deforestation. Most analytical and empirical research on the relationship between property rights and deforestation find it difficult to determine an unambiguous sign for the variable (Jaramillo and Kelly 1997; Kaimowitz and Angelsen 2002). For the case of Guatemala, however, qualitative studies from the World Bank (1995a) and Katz (2000) suggest that both informal and formal land tenure regimes have a potential to reduce deforestation.

64 Of course, this is admittedly rough. Ethnicity could be correlated with many other factors, such as cultural attitudes, small-scale farm practices and location-specific factors. In addition, Guatemala has a pronounced cultural diversity. Following Katz (2000), however, the approximation is found to be reasonable. In particular, the proxy applies to traditional *indigenous* communal land tenure forms in the Western Highlands.

Tentatively then, higher levels of tenure security can be expected to reduce deforestation here.

(3) Technical assistance. The direct impact of technical assistance, for example via the implementation of sustainable agriculture practices, depends on the underlying analytical framework. According to a market-based explanation, measures that aim to directly increase farmers' productivity could increase deforestation and the demand for additional agricultural land. This outcome is gradually supported by limited location-specific qualitative and empirical research for Guatemala. Nevertheless, it should be remembered that most analytical and empirical models make ambiguous predictions for this variable.

B. Regional Determinants of Forest Cover Change

The availability and quality of data limit the analysis of deforestation at the regional (departmental) level. Thus, care should be taken when interpreting the results. The analysis includes all 21 Departments but excludes the metropolitan district. Given the limitations of the number of explanatory variables, the econometric model is rather simple and assumes a log-linear relationship between the variables. However, the results are found to be robust. Using a logarithmic or linear specification does not bias the sign or significance of the variables. The regressions are based on the following equation:

$$(33) \qquad \Delta \log DEF_i = c + \beta_{ij} \cdot X_{ij} + \gamma \cdot DUMMY_{Petén} + u_i$$

where $\Delta \log DEF_i$ is deforestation per capita in region i, X_{ij} a vector of the explanatory variables j, β_{ij} the corresponding coefficient, γ the coefficient of the dummy variable, and u_i the error term. Variables to be tested include total land area of *microfincas*, the departmental share of extreme rural poverty, the departmental share of the working population primarily employed in the non-agricultural sectors (here referred to as non-farm employment), average education of the working population (urban and rural), and a dummy for the Petén. The high significance and the positive sign of the dummy indicate that exogenous factors, not captured by the variables, impact on forest cover loss in this Department. Maize yield as a proxy for agricultural productivity, the indigenous share of the department population, and road density were found to be insignificant. Consequently, these variables are excluded from the analysis.

A brief description of the variables and sources can be found in Table 24. Forest cover change for 1975-1988 has been calculated from Mittak (1977) and Sagastume (1992). The comparison here is based on unpublished calculations by Juventino Gálvez from Rafael Landívar University at Guatemala-City. The data has been thoroughly revised and includes all open and closed forest categories except for some minor or not clearly determined categories. Recently, the INAB (2000) elaborated a forest inventory for 1999. Unfortunately, no comparison could be made because of the difference in methodologies used.

Table 24. Guatemala: Annotations and Descriptive Statistics for Regional Deforestation Analysis, 1975-1988

Variable	Source	Observations	Mean	S.D.
Deforestation per thousand habitants (km^2)	Mittak (1977), Sagastume (1992) and CENSO (1981)	Revised data, based on an unpublished comparison by Juventino Gálvez	2.73	4.11
Microfinca land area (km^2)	SEGEPLAN and MAGA (1984)	Based on the 1979 Agricultural Census	25.6	21.9
Rural extreme poverty (share)	World Bank (1995b)	Based on ENS (1989)	0.72	0.16
Rural non-farm employment (share)	UNDP (1999)	Based on CENSO (1994)	0.21	0.13
Mean years of schooling	World Bank (1995c)	Based on ENS (1989)	2.44	0.74

Source: Author's calculations. S.D. = standard deviation.

Disaggregated socio-economic data for the period 1977-1988 is hard to come by. Therefore, the census and survey data relies largely on secondary sources. The descriptive statistics in Table 24 point out that the mean education for rural and urban population is only about 2 years. Also, extreme rural poverty is high.[65] On average, only about 21 percent of the entire rural workforce find non-agricultural employment. A shortcoming is that employment data refers to 1994. However, the overall trends presented in UNDP (1999) suggest that changes over time have been negligible in the composition of the rural workforce.

Despite the few explanatory variables and the data quality, the regressions in Table 25 show a reasonable fit. The adjusted R^2 is between 0.62 and 0.72 for the different estimations. All equations include the total area of so-called *microfincas*, that is, farms with less than 0.7 hectares of agricultural land. Despite its

65 Calculations of extreme poverty rates by the World Bank (1995b) are based on a person's average minimum caloric requirement (2,172 Kcal/day) and an adjustment to account for 'wasted food.' The full poverty line equals the extreme poverty line plus an allowance for non-food consumption. Notice that World Bank (2003a) and UNDP (2000) revisions reduced slightly the estimates due to data inconsistencies.

significance, the interpretation of the negative sign is ambiguous. In most parts of the country *microfincas* are insufficient to support a family. Therefore, it is hypothesized that the *microfinca* variable holds as a proxy for a different distribution of property rights in the country. For example, *microfinca* land area is relatively higher in regions affected by moderate deforestation such as the Western Highlands, but very low in the Petén or Jutiapa. In this sense, more area dedicated to *microfincas* could indicate higher levels of tenure security. This, in turn, could result in decreasing levels of per capita deforestation. An alternative interpretation is that the variable could also proxy for the level of diversification between agricultural and non-agricultural income sources.

Table 25. Guatemala: Determinants of Deforestation in Regional Model, 1975-1988

	Dependent variable: deforestation per capita (km^2) [a/]			
Explanatory variables	(1)	(2)	(3)	(4)
Constant	-0.710	1.801**	3.058**	3.127**
	(-0.76)	(4.31)	(3.41)	(4.12)
Microfinca land area (km^2)	-0.047**	-0.035**	-0.049**	-0.044**
	(-5.70)	(-5.63)	(-5.10)	(-5.78)
Rural extreme poverty (share)	2.793⁺	...	...	...
	(2.08)			
Rural non-farm employment (share)	...	-3.732*	...	-2.892**
		(-2.76)		(-3.66)
Mean years of schooling	...	...	-0.711*	-0.523*
			(-2.46)	(-2.17)
Dummy Petén	1.797**	1.421**	1.782**	1.417**
	(6.36)	(4.20)	(6.72)	(5.76)
Adjusted R^2	0.621	0.668	0.652	0.722
F-statistic	11.93	14.42	13.49	13.98
S.E. of regression	0.811	0.759	0.777	0.694
N	21	21	21	21

Huber/White heteroskedasticity-consistent t-statistics in parenthesis.

⁺ significant at 10%, * significant at 5%, ** significant at 1%.

Source: Author's calculations. a/ Estimated by OLS.

Regarding poverty, column (1) suggests that there is a relationship between per capita deforestation and *extreme* rural poverty. However, the significance of the variable is only moderate. The positive sign of the coefficient indicates that increasing levels of extreme rural poverty are associated with higher per capita deforestation. Poverty does not enter explicitly in the land rent approach. Therefore, in column (2) the poverty variable is replaced with the share of the rural workforce employed in non-farm activities. The negative sign indicates that an increased participation of the rural workforce in non-agricultural activities is equally associated with lower levels of per capita deforestation. Given the sign and significance, employment outside agriculture seems to have a higher predictive power than the poverty variable on its own. As evidenced in column (3), schooling is found to have a significant deforestation reducing effect.

Finally, in column (4) both non-farm activities and schooling are used as explanatory variables. The inclusion of both variables increases the R^2. Since higher levels of schooling are expected to be partly associated with better access to certain types of non-farm activities, the inclusion of both variables into the same equation is somewhat critical. However, at the departmental level, the potential endogeneity of non-farm employment with respect to schooling seems to be of minor importance. That is, the separate regressions for both variables in column (2) and (3) show only moderate deviations both in sign and significance than the results presented in column (4). An explanation for this could be that schooling impacts equally on other factors, such as fertility and rural-urban migration. On the other hand, non-farm activities may also be determined by other factors than exclusively by schooling. For instance, access to rural infrastructure and geographic characteristics could be important. The omission of these factors suggests that the OLS estimates presented in Table 25 could be biased.

Overall, the analysis at the regional level confirms the initial hypotheses postulating a deforestation reducing effect of schooling and employment outside agriculture. However, it is plagued with several deficiencies. First, with only 21 observations and the limited numbers of explanatory variables, the analysis is rather scarce. Second, the regressions are based on poor-quality data and completely omit physical-geographic variables. Finally, deforestation from 1975-1986 was affected by the civil war. Hence, distinct deforestation patterns during this period could bias the estimate. All this could limit the reliability of the results in terms of policy conclusions. In order to overcome these constraints, the next section takes a look at household determinants of land use in Guatemala.

C. Household Determinants of Land Use in Guatemala

At the household level, there is no data available regarding forest cover change. However, deforestation may be examined indirectly by factors that explain the size of agricultural plots. Hence, the key assumption in the following analysis is that agricultural expansion has been the principal direct source of deforestation in

Guatemala.[66] The analysis is based on the *Encuesta Nacional de Condiciones de Vida* or ENCOVI (2000). The Living Standard Measurement Survey (LSMS) is currently the country's most comprehensive data source at the household level. It was originally designed for the World Bank's (2003a) poverty assessment. In fact, the survey is the first data source since the 1979 agricultural census that provides reliable countrywide household data on agricultural land use. Guatemala has a poor tradition in collecting statistics and has manifold data gaps, as a result of the three-decades of civil war and the former taboo on such topics as poverty, social equity and agricultural land use in government circles, along with inadequate staffing and insufficient financial resources.

Table 26. Guatemala: Descriptive Statistics for Analysis of Agricultural Land Use, 2000 (per rural household)

Variables (N = 2264)	Mean	S.D.
Cultivated land area (hectares)	0.85	3.20
Firewood time (minutes) [a/]	60.3	64.0
Service point time (minutes) [a/]	37.0	55.7
Number of rooms	1.70	0.94
Years living at farm	13.6	12.9
Weekly worked hours household head	34.9	17.6
Age household head (years)	44.1	14.6
Education household head (years)	1.91	2.51
Household size (persons)	6.07	2.64
Dummy rural non-farm employment	0.21	0.41
Dummy indigenous	0.57	0.50
Dummy technical assistance	0.04	0.19
Dummy female head	0.07	0.25
Dummy piped water	0.56	0.50
Dummy basic sanitation	0.05	0.21
Dummy electricity	0.51	0.50

Source: Author's calculations based on ENCOVI (2000) survey data. S.D. = standard deviation. a/ Distance measures.

A brief look at the descriptive statistics in Table 26 reveals more or less stagnant patterns of development in rural Guatemala. In particular, over the past

66 Recall that it has been argued before that agricultural expansion is likely the main direct source of deforestation.

decade, non-farm employment has remained at approximately 21 percent.[67] Mean education of rural household heads is less than 2 years. Likewise, access to basic infrastructure services is very limited. More than 40 percent of rural households have no access to electricity and piped water. The time to collect firewood is assumed to proxy the distance to the agricultural plot. On average, the ENCOVI (2000) suggest a travelling distance of about one-hour to the plot. Market access is proxied by the distance to the next service point. By definition, service points include markets, churches, various administrative units, bus stations, public telephones or banks.

Despite Guatemala being a physically diverse country with many isolated areas, the average walking distance to market of about 40 minutes suggest there is market access for most households. The average cultivated land area is less than 1 hectare, and 57 percent of the population is indigenous. As such, the land use data may slightly over-sample indigenous households. Edwards (2002) reports that, according to the 1994 census, the indigenous account for about 42 percent of the total population. This number is based on a *self-identifying* question. Earlier census data and unofficial estimates frequently report higher values. However, this is due to the distinct classification criteria. The interviewer here *observes* ethnicity.

Explanatory variables include distance measures, the number of rooms as a proxy for the capital equipment of the household, years living at the farms as a proxy for soil degradation, weekly work hours of the household head, education of this head, and various dummies for non-farm employment, ethnicity, female head, technical assistance and basic social infrastructure. Table 26 provides a list of the variables together with descriptive statistics. A detailed overview of the construction of the respective variables can be found in Appendix Two.

A major challenge was the construction of the dependent variable. The ENCOVI (2000) employs a vast combination of metric, U.S. and old Spanish measures. This results in more than 18 different land measures. Physical-geographic variables are proxied by 21 departmental dummies D_k. For space limitations, these variables are not reported. Most of the departmental dummies are highly significant. In fact, they explain about 40 percent of the variance in the regressions. The regression analysis is based on the following equation:

$$(34) \qquad \log AREA_i = c + \beta_j \cdot X_{ij} + \gamma_k \cdot D_k + u_i$$

where log AREA is the natural logarithm of the cultivated agricultural land area for household i, X_{ij} represents a vector of explanatory variables j, β_{ij} the

67 This figures refers to *primary* employment of household head in the non-agricultural sectors.

corresponding explanatory variables, and u_i is the error term.[68] A semi-logarithmic form is the preferred econometric specification. While other specifications lead to similar results, the fit of the model reduces significantly. Overall, the regressions have an R^2 between 0.47 and 0.49. For a household survey on rural land use with more than 2000 observations, this is acceptable. The results can be summarized as follows:

(1) Education. Column (1) in Table 27 reveals a significant deforestation-reducing effect of the household head's education level. Since the regressions are estimated in log-linear form, the estimate suggest that 1 additional year of schooling implies a reduction of about 7 percent in cultivated land area. In other words, a household head with complete primary education (6 years) would exhibit a reduced demand for agricultural land of more than $^1/_3$ compared to his counterpart with no formal education. This is a strong effect.

(2) Distance costs. As expected, increased distance cost is associated with a reduction of cultivated land area. Somewhat surprisingly, however, the quantitative effect is rather small. An explanation would be that *milpa* (maize) farmers care relatively little about the distance to market or the costs associated with walking to their plots.

(3) Soil degradation and capital equipment. The variable that proxies for soil degradation does not enter significantly into the regressions. This is perhaps because years living at the farm is only weakly associated with soil degradation. Or, soil degradation exhibits spatially different patterns, which are not captured by the variable. By contrast, the capital equipment, as proxied by the number of rooms of the household, is highly significant.

(4) Indigenous dummy. Indigenous households have a reduced demand for agricultural land area. Since in the popular debate in Guatemala, the indigenous are often blamed for being one of the country's main deforestation agents, the negative sign here and its high significance are enlightening. An interpretation, unfortunately, is less straightforward. In line with Katz (2000), one could assume

---

68 Since 93 percent of rural households in the ENCOVI (2000) survey have access to agricultural land, selection bias is unlikely to be a problem here. The fact that such a high percentage of rural Guatemalan households is still engaged in some agricultural activity may be due to religious believes: most households prefer to plant their own maize — of limited quantity — rather than buying it from the market.

that the indigenous social capital base and hence, informal tenure regimes, imply a deforestation reducing effect. In other parts of the country, however, the indigenous could show a reduced demand for agricultural land area because of their small-scale farm practices, or because they are expelled to marginal agricultural areas with nothing left to exploit. Another reason for the reduced demand of the indigenous for agricultural land could be due to cultural attitudes, i.e. in the sense of a higher appreciation of natural resources.[69]

(5) Technical assistance and weekly worked hours. Access to technical assistance, either by NGO or government agencies, gradually suggests a deforestation augmenting-effect. This is in line with the case study from *Defensores de la Naturaleza* (2001). However, the variable is only weakly significant and not robust. Moreover, given that selection bias and endogeneity could play a role (only 4 percent of the households receive assistance), this result should be viewed with care. On the other hand, the negative sign for the 'weekly worked hours' variable suggest a moderate but significant deforestation reducing effect. That is, technological change that encourages labor-intensive farm practices could provide an avenue to reduce deforestation in Guatemala.

(6) Female-headed households, access to electricity, and non-farm employment. Female-headed households exhibit a significant negative correlation with agricultural land use. An explanation for this result is that females in rural Guatemalan household have a strong focus on certain types of non-farm activities, such as their elaborated handicrafts and their engagement in trade-related activities. Moreover, the high correlation of schooling and electricity with non-farm employment suggests these factors to be important determinants (see also Box 6). Consequently, a separate regression is run in column (2). Education and the dummies for female head as well as electricity are replaced by rural non-farm employment. In line with the evidence from the regional level analysis, non-farm employment shows a strong and significant deforestation-reducing effect. Given the endogeneity of non-farm employment, however, the true causal effect is likely to be biased here.

(7) Household size. Column (2) includes the average household size. At first sight, the effect seems to be moderate. 1 additional household member is associated

69 Lima (1995: 78-79) writes on the Maya *cosmovisión*: "*Él ha hecho el universo: la gente, los árboles, las flores, los matorrales, todas las piedras, la tierra... Por eso, para todo debe pedirse permiso a Él: se cometa una falta contra Él cuando se cortan los árboles...*" For an anthropological look at these issues see Maas (2004).

with a 5 percent increase in agricultural land use. However, the inclusion of the variable imposes several problems within the chosen framework — population cannot be considered as exogenous. To deal with this problem statistically, instrumental variable techniques (IV) are used in column (3). Instruments of household size are education, age, age-squared, and dummies for access to piped water and sanitation. These variables are highly correlated with household size but, with the exception of education, have no direct impact on agricultural land use. The estimated coefficient of household size by IV estimation alters significantly, suggesting that the earlier OLS results are biased downwards. In fact, the effect of population becomes quite important. The regression suggests that, on average, 1 additional household member increases agricultural land use by more than 10 percent.

In sum, the countrywide household level analysis on agricultural land use supports the findings of the earlier regional results. Schooling and non-farm activities exhibit a strong and significant deforestation reducing effect. However, there are various other important factors, for instance, household size and, probably, also informal land tenure regimes, as proxied by the indigenous dummy. Moreover, the provision of basic infrastructure services is essential for reduced deforestation because of their impact on certain types of non-farm activities and household size.

With respect to the spatial patterns of deforestation, however, the analysis has a serious shortcoming. Current deforestation in Guatemala occurs predominantly in the Petén. In particular regarding biodiversity loss, this makes other Departments much less relevant. In addition, one could criticize the implicit assumption of the analysis that deforestation in agricultural frontier regions follows the same logic as in other regions. This, of course, must not necessarily be the case. In order to deal with this potential critique, the next section takes a look at the empirical determinants of deforestation in the Petén.

D. Household Determinants of Land Use in the Petén

Guatemala's northern Department provides a unique opportunity to study the determinants of agricultural expansion. The data for the subsequent analysis comes from the *Encuesta de Salud y Materno Infantil* or ENSMI (1999). What makes the health survey so interesting is that, for the Petén, it includes an environmental module.[70] The module contains information on agricultural land use, natural resources, and rural migration. The environmental module was originally designed as an experimental survey, initiating a more systematic approach of data collection.

70 I would like to thank Luis Ochoa, from Macro International, and Norman Schwartz, University of Delaware, for making available the data set.

Box 6. Barriers to Rural Non-Farm Employment in Guatemala: Education, Social Infrastructure, and Gender Discrimination

For Guatemala, there are three recent studies that analyze the determinants of rural non-farm employment. Vakis (2002) finds a very close correlation between non-farm activities and rural poverty. Essentially, this is because households can diversify their sources of income, which allows them to augment their incomes and to minimize the effect of exogenous shocks on farm activities. In addition, the non-agricultural sector offers landless households another option for generating incomes instead of engaging in resource-mining activities, i.e. deforestation. A regression analysis on the probability of entering into non-agricultural occupations based on ENCOVI (2000) data indicates that human capital, such as education and the ability to speak Spanish, constitute key factors to participating in comparatively 'high-income' non-farm activities. In addition, access to basic social infrastructure, such as piped water, sanitation and connection to electricity, increase significantly the probability of being employed in the non-farm sector.

Using 1997 household survey data for 6 Guatemalan Departments, Pagán (2002) essentially confirms these results. However, while focussing on gender differences in rural labor market decisions, his results suggest that external constraints explain most of the observed gender gaps. He argues that low human capital endowment is only one structural factor that prevents a higher participation of woman in rural non-farm activities. From a public policy perspective, the reduction of several other forms of gender-related discrimination, such as customer discrimination, better credit access, and the reduction of within-family gender barriers, would be a key issue.

Finally, with both quantitative and qualitative methods, Johannsen (2003) analyzes the Guatemalan rural non-agricultural sector. Based on ENEI (2002) survey data, she confirms the pronounced gender gaps, and the importance of basic social infrastructure in remote areas. In addition, she argues that the non-agricultural sector represents an increasingly important source of income and employment, with the potential for several additional positive functions, such as risk reduction, gender equality, and natural resource conservation. Education has a positive influence on the probability of being employed outside agriculture — albeit with a quantitatively smaller influence than in previous studies. This could be for two reasons. First, Johannsen only focuses on the rural working population and makes no distinction between the different productivity levels of non-agricultural employment. Second, having a pilot character, the ENEI survey is suspected to have a sampling error. An interesting finding is finally the pronounced difference between indigenous ethnic groups, which, according to Johannsen, raises questions about a possible cultural determinant connected to non-agricultural activities.

Table 27. Guatemala: Determinants of Agricultural Land Use, 2000

	Dependent variable: log of cultivated land area (hectares)		
	OLS	OLS	IV
Explanatory variables [a/]	(1)	(2)	(3)
Constant	-1.891**	-2.352**	-2.649**
	(-8.66)	(-9.13)	(-8.20)
Years living at farm	0.002	0.003	0.003
	(0.69)	(0.95)	(0.94)
Weekly worked hours household head	-0.005*	-0.004⁺	-0.003
	(-2.36)	(-1.80)	(-1.43)
Firewood time (minutes)	-0.001⁺	-0.001⁺	-0.001
	(-1.75)	(-1.66)	(-1.28)
Service point time (minutes)	-0.002**	-0.003**	-0.002**
	(-3.14)	(-4.32)	(-3.94)
Number of rooms	0.189**	0.145**	0.118**
	(4.57)	(3.43)	(2.71)
Dummy indigenous	-0.340**	-0.279**	-0.292**
	(-3.38)	(-2.61)	(-2.72)
Dummy technical assistance	0.395⁺	0.349	0.261
	(1.66)	(1.36)	(0.97)
Dummy female head	-0.435**	...	...
	(-3.06)		
Dummy electricity	-0.378**	...	...
	(-4.48)		
Education household head (years)	-0.069**	...	...
	(-4.40)		
Dummy rural non-farm employment	...	-0.340**	-0.331**
		(-2.98)	(-2.82)
Household size (persons) [b/]	...	0.045**	0.111**
		(2.93)	(2.69)
Adjusted R^2	0.496	0.480	0.473
F-statistic	72.88	70.78	68.50
S.E. of regression	1.170	1.188	1.205
N	2264	2264	2264

Huber/White heteroskedasticity-consistent t-statistics in parenthesis.

⁺ significant at 10%, * significant at 5%, ** significant at 1%.

a/ The explanatory variables include 21 departmental dummies, of which 15 are statistically significant at 5% or better. Binary variables equal 1 if response is yes.

b/ Household size is instrumentalized by education of household head, age, age squared, and dummies for access to piped water and basic sanitation.

Source: Author's calculations based on ENCOVI (2000) survey data.

For an agricultural frontier region, the number of observations in the survey is quite large. With more than 600 complete observations, it slightly exceeds the household-level analyses from Pichón (1997) and Godoy and Contreras (2001). This makes the analysis of the survey a worthwhile objective, with implications that could be relevant beyond the Petén region.

Before proceeding with the regression analysis, it is interesting to take a look at some descriptive results of the survey. The subsequent paragraphs draw on a descriptive analysis presented by Grandia et al. (2001). One of the most interesting findings here refers to immigration. Many of the migrants are relatively young families. Migration increased sharply in the 1970s and reached its height during the early 1990s. While Ladino migration decreased over time, indigenous migration increased.[71] The overwhelming part of the population in the Petén, however, is Ladino and not indigenous. Migrants come predominately from the north and northeast of Guatemala (part of the so-called poverty-belt), and to a lesser extent also from the southwest. The Departments are, in descending order: Alta Verapaz, Izabal, Jutiapa, Escuintla, Santa Rosa and Chiquimula.

Table 28. The Petén: Reasons for Migration, 1999 (in percent)

Principal reason to migrate	to the Petén	inside the Petén
Land scarcity	65.4	48.4
Family	17.8	15.8
Finding non-farm employment	4.7	6.1
Better access to social services	1.4	5.1
Violence	1.4	2.4
Other	9.3	22.2

Source: Grandia et al. (2001).

As evidenced in Table 28, the main reason to come to the Petén is land-scarcity. In addition, the survey indicates that land-scarcity is more pronounced for the indigenous than for the Ladino population. Once having arrived in the Department, families move several times. In order to find suitable plots, this moving generally occurs from the Department's south to its north. This *could* be an indication that land-scarcity is nowadays becoming a problem even within the

71 Recall that this finding is consistent with the qualitative results in Chapter III, suggesting that smallholder's encroachment and poverty-induced rural migration to the Petén increased over time.

Petén, and that deforestation is increasingly due to internal migration rather than immigration.

The main source of income for approximately $^2/_3$ of the population is agriculture. The predominant crop is slash-and-burn-cultivated maize. Only about 16 percent of the households have livestock, mostly in very small quantities. Agricultural diversification plays a minor role. While almost all newly arrived migrants practice shifting cultivation, there is a tendency to abandon these activities over time in favor of alternative crops or non-farm work. An important finding is that agricultural production is generally *not* subsistence-oriented. That is, only about 25 percent of the households use the produced maize exclusively for family consumption.

Another striking result refers to the self-evaluation of the 'quality of life.' Table 29 indicates that the overwhelming part of migrants feel they are better off in the Petén. Nevertheless, while migration seems to pay off in some sense, poverty still remains an issue. The environmental module itself does not provide information on this regard. However, World Bank (2003a) estimates based on the ENCOVI (2000) reveal that about 68 percent of the Petén's population is poor, compared to the national average of 56 percent. However, extreme poverty is about 13 percent, and lower than the national average of about 16 percent. The ENSMI (1999) also indicates that in the Petén about 46 percent of all children under 5 suffer from chronic malnutrition, which is in line with the 'national average' (but places Guatemala last in the Latin American context).

Table 29. The Petén: Self-Evaluation of 'Quality of Life', 1999
(in percent)

Migrants area of origin	Self-evaluation of the quality of life			
	Better	Worse	Same	Missing
Urban	75.1	4.5	19.1	1.3
Rural	78.8	2.7	18.0	0.5
Total	77.2	3.4	18.5	0.9

Source: Grandia et al. (2001).

Compared to the country-wide data, the descriptive statistics in Table 30 point out several differences of land use in the Petén. In particular, the average plot extension is quite large. This reflects historic colonization patterns of large landholders in the Petén. Also, a few very large farms bias the mean value. On the other hand, Grandia et al. (2001) as well as Cabrera (1995) observe that climatic and physical-geographic soil characteristics require a much larger amount of land to support a family than in the rest of the country.

On average, households own their plots for about 8 years, compared to about 14 years in other parts of the country. This is an indication that much of the colonization-related deforestation of the Department has taken place over the past decade. Moreover, employment outside agriculture and access to basic infrastructure services are limited. On the other hand, access to agricultural assistance seems to be more common in the Petén. About 40 percent of the households in the sample use sustainable agriculture techniques (green manures) as promoted by various NGOs. Most other variables are in line with the national data. That is, walking distance to the respective plot, household size, the age of household head, and mean education are almost identical to the national average.

Table 30. The Petén: Descriptive Statistics for Analysis of Agricultural Land Use, 1999 (per rural household)

Variables (N = 621)	Mean	S.D.
Extension of plot (hectares)	24.4	27.5
Distance to plot (minutes)	65.2	62.6
Number of sleeping rooms	1.39	0.73
Years owning first plot	8.20	7.41
Age household head (years)	43.1	14.7
Household size (persons)	6.03	2.72
Education household head (years)	1.92	2.55
Dummy rural non-farm employment [a/]	0.14	0.35
Dummy temporary farm wage [b/]	0.34	0.47
Dummy born in the Petén	0.20	0.40
Dummy indigenous	0.27	0.44
Dummy squatter plot	0.18	0.38
Dummy green manures	0.39	0.49
Dummy piped water	0.32	0.47
Dummy basic sanitation	0.06	0.23

Source: Author's calculations based on Environmental Module ENSMI (1999) survey data. S.D. = standard deviation. a/ Household head primarily engaged in non-agricultural activities. b/ Household head temporarily works on large farms.

Regarding the determinants of land use, the following regression analysis is based on the same formula and uses roughly the same set of variables as the previous section. An overview of the construction of the variables can be found in Appendix Two. Unfortunately, there is no data on the weekly-worked hours of the household head (to measure labor-intensive work). In addition, the dummies for electricity and female-headed households are omitted because of their insignificant

Table 31. The Petén: Determinants of Agricultural Land Use, 1999

	Dependent variable: log of plot extension (hectares)		
	OLS	OLS	IV
Explanatory variables [a/]	(1)	(2)	(3)
Constant	4.080**	3.950**	3.623**
	(17.9)	(16.7)	(11.7)
Distance to plot (minutes)	-0.014**	-0.014**	-0.014**
	(-2.86)	(-2.73)	(-2.82)
Distance squared	1.12E-04**	1.10E-04**	1.09E-04**
	(2.98)	(2.84)	(2.88)
Distance cubic	-2.13E-07**	-2.05E-07**	-1.99E-07**
	(-2.76)	(-2.58)	(-2.60)
Years owning first plot	0.068**	0.065**	0.064**
	(7.11)	(6.88)	(6.62)
Number of rooms	0.239**	0.243**	0.202*
	(3.00)	(2.99)	(2.30)
Dummy born in the Petén	-0.557**	-0.406*	-0.365⁺
	(-2.77)	(-2.20)	(-1.92)
Dummy indigenous	-0.318*	-0.373*	-0.394*
	(-2.06)	(-2.37)	(-2.42)
Dummy green manures	0.296*	0.274*	0.262*
	(2.25)	(2.12)	(2.00)
Dummy squatter plot	0.500**	0.469**	0.423**
	(3.52)	(3.24)	(2.78)
Dummy temporary farm wage [b/]	-0.257⁺	-0.301*	-0.307*
	(-1.86)	(-2.22)	(-2.25)
Education household head (years)	-0.180*	...	...
	(-1.97)		
Education squared	0.062**	...	...
	(2.90)		
Education cubic	-0.004**	...	...
	(-3.23)		
Dummy rural non-farm employment [c/]	...	-0.467*	-0.491*
		(-2.21)	(-2.30)
Household size (persons) [d/]	...	0.034⁺	0.104*
		(1.57)	(2.09)
Adjusted R^2	0.639	0.640	0.628
F-statistic	46.85	49.41	47.67
S.E. of regression	1.408	1.407	1.420
N	621	621	621

Huber/White heteroskedasticity-consistent t-statistics in parenthesis.

⁺ significant at 10%, * significant at 5 %, ** significant at 1%.

a/ The explanatory variables include 11 municipal and regional dummies, of which 8 are statistically significant at 5% or better. Binary variables equal 1 if response is yes. b/ Household head temporarily works on large farms. c/ Household head primarily engaged in non-agricultural activities. d/ Household size is instrumentalized by education of household head, age, age squared, and dummies for access to piped water and basic sanitation.

Source: Author's calculations based on Environmental Module ENSMI (1999) survey data.

impact on land use. The regressions also include three new variables. First, they incorporate a dummy for temporary wages on larger farms, as an alternative measure for the opportunity costs of labor. Second, the missing security of property rights is proxied by a squatter plot dummy (so-called *arragadas*). Finally, they include a variable on the migration status of the household. In line with the previous regressions, physical-geographic variables and other factors are proxied by 11 municipal and sectoral dummies. For space limitations, they are not included in Table 31. As expected, these variables are highly significant. They alone explain about 55 percent of the variance in the regressions. Overall, the regressions have an R^2 between 0.63 and 0.64, which for household survey data is a good result.

At first sight, the results for the Petén are similar to the countrywide estimates. Columns (1) to (3) of Table 31 report the regression results. In particular, higher opportunity costs of labor, both regarding temporary farm wages *and* non-farm employment, sharply reduce deforestation. The number of rooms as a proxy for the capital endowment has a highly significant and positive sign. Indigenous people show a reduced demand for agricultural land use. Property rights are also quite important. Unsafe tenure forms in the forms of so-called *arragadas* (squatter plots) increase the demand for additional land. Household size shows a positive correlation with agricultural land use. Using IV techniques alters the coefficient. Interestingly, the variable's elasticity here is almost similar to the countrywide regressions: one additional household member leads to an increase in land by about 10 percent. Non-migrants show a decreased demand for additional land, which could be due to their higher involvement in non-farm activities, better education, or higher appreciation of forest resources.

The main differences of empirical land use determinants in the Petén compared to countrywide trends refer to three issues. First, the variable that proxies for soil degradation has a strong impact on deforestation. Second, there is evidence of a non-linear impact on agricultural land use for distance costs. Third, also education seems to exhibit a non-linear effect. Figures 14 and 15 visualize these effects, respectively.

(1) Soil degradation. The variable 'years owning the first plot' is highly significant and suggests a strong deforestation-increasing effect, 1 additional year of owning the plot is associated with a 7 percent increase in the demand for agricultural land use. Therefore, in principle, agricultural practices that reduce *soil degradation* should be regarded as important policy instruments to reduce deforestation. Nevertheless, the current promotion of *green manures* in the Petén, as proxied by the dummy variable, exhibits a significant and robust deforestation-increasing effect. This is in line with the result from the previous section and the qualitative studies for the Petén, such as Shriar (2001) and Chemonics International

Figure 14. The Petén: Plot Extension versus Distance, 1999

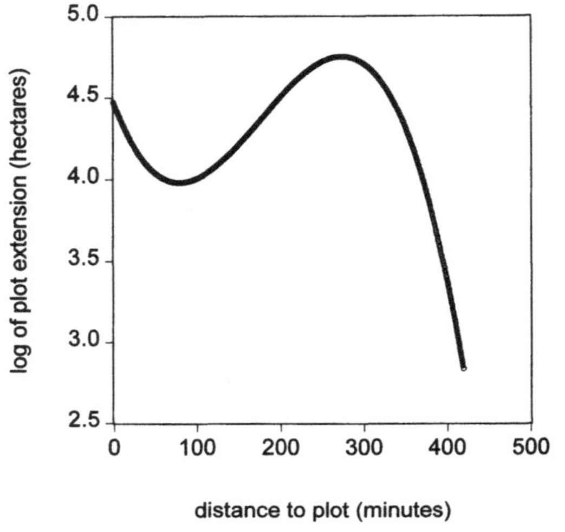

Source: Author' calculations based on Table 31, column 1, see text.

Figure 15. The Petén: Plot Extension versus Education, 1999

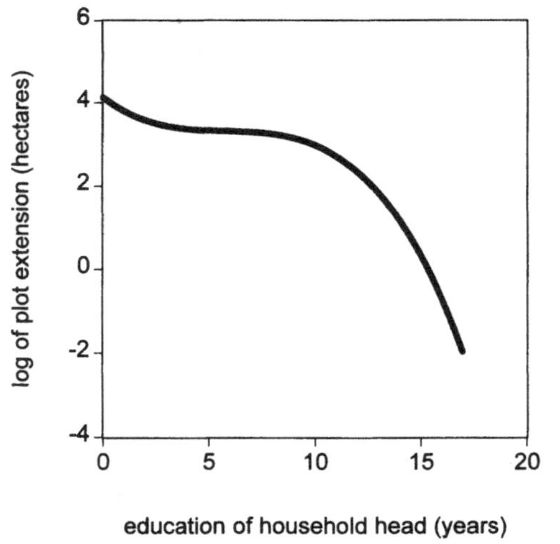

Source: Author' calculations based on Table 31, column 1, see text.

et al. (2000). It supports the assumption of a market-based approach in terms of incentives for agricultural land expansion through productivity increases. In other words, at present, the promotion of sustainable agriculture techniques seems to be having the exact opposite effect on agricultural land use practices than the one desired by extension agencies. Policymakers should closely analyze this finding.

(2) Distance. Distance costs exhibit a non-linear effect on agricultural land use. Fixing all other variables at their sample median values, Figure 14 visualizes the cubic effect of distance costs on plot extension. With a walking distance up to approximately 90 minutes, the average plot extension decreases. About 79 percent of all observation fall into this category. However, with up to about 5 hours of walking distance, the demand for agricultural land use increases (20 percent of all observations) but eventually falls again (the remaining 1 percent). There are two potential explanations for this phenomenon. On the one hand, contrary to the von Thünen approach, the lack of an adequate transportation infrastructure in the Petén could require a larger amount of cultivated land area in order to compensate for higher transport costs for very remote plots. On the other hand, one should take into account the Petén's historic colonization patterns. Much of the land has been obtained by absentee landowners for speculative rather than agricultural purposes. Consequently, these landowners may care less about distance costs than pure agriculturists do. In any case, the result is in line with the finding of Chomitz and Gray (1996). For southern Belize, they also find a non-linear effect of distance costs on the probability of agricultural land use.

(3) Education. A somewhat surprising finding is that also education exhibits a non-linear effect on agricultural land use in the Petén. Holding the other variables at their sample median values, the cubic effect is evidenced in Figure 15. Up to 3 years of basic education reduces the demand for agricultural land use. About 78 percent of all households in the sample fall into this category. From 4 up to about 9 years of schooling, the education variable essentially shows no decreasing effect on land use (about 19 percent of all observations). After that, the demand for agricultural land use is sharply reduced (the remaining 2 percent). The non-linear effect is in line with the empirical findings from Godoy et al. (1998).

On one side, this result could reflect the conflicting effects of schooling on land use regarding the opportunity costs of labor and agricultural productivity. On the other side, the cubic effect could be explained by the Petén's historic colonization process. In other words, earlier migrants who often bought large plots of land are relatively better educated than the wave of land-poor peasant that came to the Petén in later periods. Table 32 provides some tentative support for this interpretation. It indicates that native *Peteneros* and migrants that came to the Péten prior to 1966 have comparatively high levels of education. Migrants that came to the Petén after 1966 show relatively low levels of schooling. In particular the indigenous are predominately illiterate.[72]

Table 32. The Petén: Education Profile of Adult Population, 1999 (in percent)

Education level	Native *Peteneros*	First generation migrants [a/]	Ladino migrants [b/]	Indigenous migrants [c/]
No schooling	21.6	27.6	47.3	68.8
Primary incomplete	39.1	44.1	38.9	29.6
Primary complete	18.9	10.7	6.8	1.4
Secondary and more	20.4	17.6	7.0	0.2

a/ Migrants that came to the Petén prior to 1966. b/ Migrants that came to the Petén after 1966. c/ Ethnicity according to mother tongue. Source: Author's calculations based on Environmental Module ENSMI (1999) survey data.

Table 33. The Petén: Attitudes towards Use of Forest Resources by Education Level, 1999 (in percent)

Attitude	No schooling	Primary incomplete	Primary complete	Secondary and more	Total
Conservation	46.3	46.3	54.5	71.2	49.0
Tourism	5.4	6.7	16.7	12.6	7.3
Agriculture	33.0	31.6	15.0	11.8	29.3
Cattle	15.0	15.1	9.8	2.9	13.7
Missing values	0.3	0.3	4.0	1.5	0.7

Source: Author's calculations based on Environmental Module ENSMI (1999) survey data.

Another channel by which education could impact on deforestation and agricultural land use is the appreciation of individuals for biodiverse forest resources. Although this issue is sometimes mentioned in the literature, such as in Deininger and Minten (2002), it has rarely been addressed empirically due to the

72 In this regard, sample selection bias could be an issue for the Petén. However, a regression analysis on different forms of the population's migration status (according to the classification in Table 32) with Heckman's two-step estimator yielded similar results as the OLS method, but with insignificant results for the selection term. Nonetheless, further research may deepen the analysis.

lack of adequate data. However, the Environmental Module of the ENSMI (1999) includes descriptive questions about the attitudes towards the use of forest resources in the Petén.

Regarding education, Table 33 clearly indicates that attitudes about use of forest resources are linked with the respective schooling level. While about 15 percent of the interviewed would deforest for livestock production, only 3 percent with secondary education would do so. In a similar way, preferences for agricultural use decline with increasing levels of education. Moreover, positive attitudes towards conservation and the use of forest for tourism as a resource rise with higher schooling levels.

Summing up, household-level data for Guatemala's main agricultural frontier region supports the earlier findings. Along with manifold other important factors, such as property rights, in particular higher opportunity costs of labor (non-agricultural employment *and* temporary farm wages) reduce the demand for agricultural land use. Moreover, positive attitudes towards conservation and the sustainable use of forest resources sharply increase with higher education levels. Basic schooling up to 3 years generally shows a significant deforestation-reducing effect. Nevertheless, there is evidence of a non-linear effect of schooling on deforestation. It is unclear why education has different thresholds. One could hypothesize that schooling has two different effects on agricultural land use. At low levels, an increase in basic education may be associated with better access to certain types of non-farm employment. At higher levels, a productivity effect could prevail, leading to greater clearing but eventually to decline. However, given that at the national level there is no evidence for such an effect, the results are probably best explained by the Petén historic colonization of large and relatively educated landholders.

V. Conclusion

This study has addressed some of the fundamental causes of deforestation and habitat loss in Guatemala. A conceptual analysis reveals that the effect and magnitude of changes in economic parameters, which are commonly believed to be associated with deforestation, are often inconclusive. Therefore, in order to achieve policy-relevant conclusions, empirical analyses are important. A review of selected empirical studies gradually suggests a view that market links do matter in forest margins. *Some* studies have swept away the conventional wisdom of earlier years that small-scale farmers are driven by subsistence needs as a special case. In this regard, the empirical factors, which are associated with habitat loss in Guatemala, seem to have much in common with other countries in Latin America. This makes Guatemala an interesting case study and, to some degree, the results may have implications for other settings as well.

The socio-economic causes that led to a decline in forest cover, and spurred habitat fragmentation, are multifaceted and complex. However, at the risk of oversimplification, the available evidence supports a view that after a period of large-scale agricultural and pasture expansion, smallholder's encroachment has become the single most important direct source of deforestation. A major pull factor was the government-sponsored opening up of previously inaccessible forest areas in northern Guatemala and the Petén. For Guatemala's main agricultural frontier, with high levels of biodiversity, the findings of this study suggest that land conversion and degradation is associated with persistent rural poverty and land scarcity in immigrants' areas of origin. In addition, there is evidence that most of the Petén's migrants do not follow subsistence-oriented agricultural patterns, and that resource mining in the Petén improves individuals' livelihoods. Insofar, it is fair to argue that rural poverty alleviation is *the* key issue for tackling the overwhelming majority of the deforestation and biodiversity loss in Guatemala. Much, if not most, of the deforestation is a side effect of non-agricultural policies.

What is the role of human capital in this regard? From a historical point of view, agricultural expansion during the 19th and early 20th century was highly correlated with discriminatory educational and labor polices. These past policies, in turn, have repercussions until today, not only in terms of income growth and the persistence of rural poverty, but also on deforestation. The regression analyses suggest that higher levels of education are significantly associated with less forest clearing, and a lower demand for agricultural land. This is an important finding. Since educational reforms in Guatemala are already in place, schooling could reduce forest clearing in a potentially more progressive way than via the financing of new programs to conserve tropical forests.[73] The main channel of a

73 For a critique of such programs in Guatemala, see Loening and Markussen (2003).

deforestation-reducing effect of schooling most likely operates by enhancing the probability of being employed in the non-farm sectors that indeed require skills obtained by formal education. However, other factors, such as a higher appreciation of biodiverse natural resources, lower fertility and increased rural-to-urban migration, could equally play a role.

While schooling and rural non-farm employment has the potential to reduce pressure on the forests, this study equally shows that education cannot be regarded as a panacea. Obviously, the development of a human capital base can take a long time, and many other parameters are associated with deforestation in Guatemala. Qualitatively important factors are related to the land tenure regime, access to social infrastructure — in particular electricity, but also water and sanitation — and ethnicity. The fact that indigenous households show a reduced demand for agricultural land could mainly be due to the indigenous peoples' social capital base in the sense of communal tenure regimes, as well as a higher appreciation of natural resources, and other factors.

Contrary to common beliefs, agricultural intensification programs in Guatemala seem to increase the demand for additional land. These results call into question some of the current conservation practices promoted by non-governmental organizations and bilateral donors. In addition, the empirical proxy variables used for capital equipment suggest that credit expansion *could* equally go hand in hand with increased deforestation. Since increased agricultural productivity and better access to both credit and the road network are important ingredients of poverty alleviation programs at the present time, the findings presented here point out an unpleasant conflict between poverty alleviation programs and natural resource conservation practices.

Access to richer data and more sophisticated empirical methods may allow the strengthening or clarification of some of these findings, which still have serious limitations. For example, it would be particularly interesting to analyze the role of different types of non-farm employment, i.e. to differentiate between low-productivity and comparatively 'high-productivity' non-farm jobs. Such a distinction may lead to more conclusive policy-conclusions. In addition, the spatial phenomena of deforestation should be taken into account. For the future, Guatemala offers good conditions for deepening the analysis: an improvement of current digital forest cover maps and soil inventories by the *Universidad del Valle* is underway. Recent improvements in the official survey data may soon make it possible to estimate a spatially explicit deforestation model that takes into account the socio-economic determinants of deforestation. An interesting task would be to take explicitly into account plot-specific biodiversity values, such as proposed in Deininger and Minten (2002).

Regarding education, future research may strengthen the findings presented here by exploring in more detail the causal relationship and magnitude. An important topic would be analyzing the applicability of the current educational programs in the agricultural frontier context, and the role environmental education could play. Finally, it seems that communal tenure regimes are an issue. Strengthening communal forms of resource management and their integration into the formal land tenure structure could provide a potentially inexpensive and more timely alternative than traditional land titling approaches. More research on this topic would be worthwhile as well.

Part Three

Community-Managed Schools and the Decentralization of Education in Guatemala: The Experience of PRONADE

Parts One and Two have shown that education constitutes an important consideration for Guatemala. While more schooling is obviously not the panacea to solve all the country's oppressing social and economic problems, it does have a strong potential to enhance economic growth and it is, among other factors, an important element in slowing down habitat loss. The existing empirical evidence shows that basic primary education is of particular interest. Also, the conservation of the country's natural resources is tightly linked to the human capital stock of Guatemala's *rural* economy. Quantifying the potential benefits of schooling is a challenging task. Nevertheless, from a policy perspective, it is equally important to examine how a developing country like Guatemala can successfully improve both the access to and quality of its rural primary education system.

Such an inquiry proves more difficult than it may seem to be at first glance. Glewwe (2002) claims that, until recently, many economists and international organizations have said relatively little about what governments in developing countries could actually do to raise educational levels and to improve the quality of schooling. Similarly, Lockheed and Vespor (1991) argue that the Ministries of Education in developing countries are often not sure what to do to improve their schools. This lack of vision for improvement does not imply that the education system in developing countries is already operating effectively.[74] On the contrary, low enrollment figures along with dropout rates and frequent repetitions suggest that the schooling system in these countries does not work very effectively. Quite often, institutional lack of capacity and high levels of centralization hamper the process of educational reforms. With its ethnic fragmentation and the added burdens from its past — exclusionary policies and a damaging civil war — Guatemala is no exception here. Indeed, it constitutes a most complicated case.

However, after the civil war ended in 1996, Guatemala notably increased the primary school enrollment of children in poor and remote areas. How has this been possible? Part Three shows that by contracting directly with local communities, Guatemala has employed a unique model of education decentralization that has helped to increase primary enrollment. As such, despite serious shortcomings in

74 An anecdotal observation for Guatemala should be mentioned. In one occasion, in an interview with two directors of the Ministry of Education, there was both much enthusiasm but also a lack of commitment to be felt. For example, one director said that basing decisions on education data is irrelevant to him. Another one was proud to present his office, showing technical equipment to digitize Guatemalan movie material from the 1940s.

this decentralization approach, Guatemala presents an interesting case for studying educational reform processes under very difficult circumstances. Other countries may not, of course, be directly able to replicate Guatemala's model. Nevertheless, the country shows that it is possible to blow up small innovations into a nationwide program designed to overcome some of the pitfalls of public educational services — even for the poorest households living in remote areas.

"Es obligación del Estado proporcionar y facilitar educación a sus habitantes sin discriminación alguna..."

Constitución Política de la República de Guatemala, 1985

I. Introduction

Within the context of education reforms, commonly used arguments in favor of decentralization and community participation include the need to increase the efficiency of the education system, the need to improve the quality of education, and the need to increase parental and community participation.[75] Maintaining large central bureaucracies diverts resources away from educational inputs, and creates cumbersome and unnecessary requirements while stifling the initiative of those who are most critical to ensuring school success, namely teachers, principals, and parents. Proposals for greater community participation in making school decisions and for controlling financial resources are usually presented as strategies to improve the efficiency, quality and accountability of the education system.[76] However, despite a number of compelling arguments supporting school-based management, there is relatively little empirical evidence documenting its merits in developing countries.

The IDB (2000) claims that excessive centralization and lack of school autonomy have historically plagued the Latin American educational process. Consequently, efforts to decentralize the education sector and encourage a higher degree of community participation are not new. Uemura (1999) reports that since the late 1980s several countries, including Bolivia, the Dominican Republic and Honduras, have made an effort in this direction. El Salvador has been promoting expansion and decentralization since 1991 with the program *Educación con Participación de la Comunidad* (EDUCO) in response to their problem of low

75 I have greatly benefited from interviews and discussions with Miriam Casteñada and Alvaro Fortín (PRONADE), Antje Begemann (International Project Consult and PRONADE), Yetilú de Baessa (*Universidad del Valle*), Jorge Lavarreda (*Centro de Investigaciones Económicas* — CIEN), Mathias Abram (German Technical Cooperation — GTZ), Fernando Rubio (Juárez and Associates Incorporation — MEDIR Project), Edgar Pineda and Evelyn de Segura (Ministry of Education), Edda Fabian (*Asociación de Investigaciones y Estudios Sociales* — ASIES) and Isabel Günther (University of Goettingen).

76 Of course, there are also arguments that do not favor decentralization. For example, communities may not be prepared to assume greater responsibilities. In addition, if decentralization is not part of a broader reform package, accompanied by a transfer of corresponding financial resources, unresolved educational problems may simply be passed on to the local level, see IDB (2000).

school coverage in rural areas. Jiminez and Sawada (1999) report that the program is characterized by the active participation of the local communities in the organization and daily management of the schools. Their results, one of the few empirical evaluations of community-managed school programs, suggest that the EDUCO model has been fairly successful in delivering educational services to children in rural areas. In addition, teacher and student absenteeism has decreased, and students in the EDUCO program perform at a level comparable to students enrolled in traditional schools.

Learning from El Salvador's positive experience with community participation, Guatemala has endorsed since 1996 its own *Programa Nacional de Autogestión para el Desarrollo Educativo* (PRONADE). This program has a decentralizing strategy whose main objectives are to increase access to and quality of rural primary education. It is also designed to stimulate local parental and community participation in the school administration.

This study traces the origins of PRONADE, describes the structure and implementation procedures and interprets findings from evaluations of the program. In addition, a rough empirical analysis of student achievement is provided. The overall intention of the study is to find those lessons to be learned that might be useful to strengthen the program in the future. Since the experience of PRONADE is largely undocumented, this study may prove relevant for the design of similar programs in other developing countries. The study concludes that PRONADE has enhanced community and parental participation in rural schools, while significantly contributing to the expansion of educational services into rural and indigenous communities. Nevertheless, it is less clear if PRONADE has improved student achievement given the lack of bilingual teaching practices. In this vein, the quality of the program remains questionable. Despite these reservations, however, one should take into account that without PRONADE schools many of these children would probably have been illiterate.

The study is divided into five chapters. Chapter II provides the economic and social context of Guatemala at the time PRONADE emerged. Chapter III describes the structure of PRONADE, its key actors, and the implementation structure. Chapter IV summarizes the achievements of the program and outlines some of the critical issues continuing to face PRONADE. Chapter V is the conclusion.

II. The Context

This chapter traces the origins of the *Programa Nacional de Autogestión para el Desarrollo Educativo* (PRONADE) — Guatemala's key strategy to increase primary school enrollment in rural areas. Section A gives the reader a brief overview of key problems in the Guatemalan education sector. Despite some recent progress, limited access to primary education service still remains a problem in many rural areas. Section B describes the education system prior to the Peace Accords. Section C argues that PRONADE emerged as a response to both the lack of access to primary education and to the high levels of educational centralization prevalent throughout the country. Section D covers some aspects of the country's recent progress in expanding primary school enrollment, which can partly be attributed to PRONADE.

A. Key Problems of Guatemala's Education Sector

According to preliminary data from the 2003 census, Guatemala is a country of about 12 million people with a young and rapidly growing population. About 64 percent of the population is less than 25 years of age. The annual population growth rate is 2.7 percent. The country is divided into 22 Departments. The Department of Guatemala accounts for more than 20 percent of total population. Two out of 3 Guatemalans live in rural areas, and 4 out of every 10 Guatemalans belong to an indigenous group. The majority of the indigenous population resides in over 19,000 rural communities scattered throughout the country. Most of these communities are relatively small consisting of less than 200 people. Guatemala is also home to a rich variety of ethnic and linguistic communities. The main languages spoken in the country include Spanish, which serves as the official language, 21 Mayan languages, as well as Xinca and Garífuna languages.

The World Bank's (2003a) poverty assessment reveals that Guatemala is a country of social and economic contrasts, especially between urban and rural areas. Indicators of social and economic development tend to be located in urban centers, thus attesting to the influence these centers have over the allocation of national public resources. Delivery of basic social services, including primary education, remains often unavailable or beyond the financial reach of the rural and indigenous people.

Lack of school coverage in many of the rural areas has resulted in very high adult illiteracy rates. Based on household survey data the United Nations Development Programme (UNDP 2003a) estimates that of the 2.2 million of illiterate adults, 77 percent live in rural areas and 61 percent are from indigenous groups. In urban areas, 11 percent of adults over 15 years of age are illiterate. The percentage is 31 percent in rural areas. Similarly, while 25 percent of women in urban areas are illiterate, in rural areas 50 percent are illiterate. In the Departments of Alta and Baja Verapaz as well as in El Quiché, the percentage of illiterate women reaches 88 percent and 81 percent, respectively. Average years of schooling is only 4.3 years at the national level. This compares with more than 5 years in the Department of Guatemala, and approximately 2 years in rural Guatemala.

B. Education System prior to Peace Accords

The Peace Accords signed in 1996 brought the needs of the indigenous and under-served populations of the country to the head of the national development agenda. A renewed interest in education ensued. Universal primary school coverage for the first three years was declared a national objective. The *Acuerdos de Paz* (1998) set the benchmark for a nationwide development agenda and insist on carrying out an extensive overhaul of the education system. The main objective until now remains to increase access to schooling for rural and indigenous people, as well as to modernize and decentralize the education system. The agenda seeks not only to make primary education available to all Guatemalan children, but also to foster democratic values, and to incorporate the ethnic, cultural and linguistic diversity of the country into the education curriculum.

Prior to the Peace Accords, according to the World Bank's (1995c) education study, the indicators for educational access in Guatemala were very unfavorable. Compared to the Latin American average, the data for Guatemala revealed low student enrollment rates and poor indicators of efficiency. In 1994, the net enrollment rate for primary education was 69 percent, the repetition rate reached 16 percent, and the dropout rate stood at 8 percent annually. Educational attainment was low, but it was particularly low for rural and indigenous groups. While the non-indigenous rural population completed on average 2.4 years of schooling, indigenous groups completed only 1.3 years. Net school enrollment rates were lowest in geographical areas with high concentrations of indigenous children. The number of primary school age children outside the school system was estimated at 415,000 in rural areas and 122,000 in urban areas. These figures indicate that during the mid-1990s close to 50 percent of the children living in rural areas and close to 20 percent of children in urban areas were not enrolled in school.

Public investment in education was also low. In 1994, the Guatemalan government budgeted only 1.3 percent of GDP for the education sector compared to an average of 3.6 percent in the Latin American region during that time. The allocation by sectors showed that only 51 percent of the budget was allocated to primary education, but as much as 16 percent to higher education, 10 percent to secondary education, 11 percent to administration, and 12 percent for other purposes. At the primary level, the inequitable distribution of resources was favoring the urban areas.

The World Bank (1995c) assessed the administrative structure of the Ministry of Education (MINEDUC) as highly centralized and often making decisions without integrating local concerns. The education system lacked flexibility and was hampered by the lack of administrative and financial capacity. Overall, the Ministry of Education's project implementation capacity was considered to be weak. In addition, measuring learning achievement was not feasible given the absence of a national student assessment system.

Valerio and Rojas (2000) argue that the centralization of teacher recruitment by the Ministry of Education contributed to the inefficiency of the system, and hindered its ability to reach beyond urban areas. A single salary schedule, which guaranteed salary increases every 5 years regardless of teachers' classroom performance, did not create incentives to improve teaching practices. Similarly, incentives to attract teachers to work in rural areas did not exist. Fadul (1996) reports that teacher development was considered to be inadequate, especially among teachers who catered to the needs of bilingual children in rural areas. School supervision was equally troublesome with school supervision posts allocated according to length of service — seniority determining advancement — rather than educational level, background or expertise. Supervisors were usually hampered by the lack of transport, low budget allocations and outdated per diem ceilings for operational travel.

C. Searching for Successful Education Delivery Models: Origins of PRONADE

Against this background, the Commission for Education Reform, a temporary task force established under the Ministry of Education, was given the task of realizing the objectives stated under the Peace Accords. The Commission searched for an education delivery model that would be effective in increasing access to the first 3 years of primary education in rural areas.[77] The Commission for Education Reform (1999) highlighted the importance of a program specifically set out to increase rural access to primary education.

PRONADE became an appealing program for at least three reasons. First, the program had been implemented as a pilot project since 1993 and had thus already been tested in communities. Although a formal evaluation was lacking, it appeared to be successful. Second, in order to increase schooling rapidly, communities would need to be actively involved, making the decentralized nature of the program

77 In writing this section, I have benefited from the interviews with PRONADE staff and other informants listed in the introduction of this study. Key references also include MINEDUC (2003; 1999) and *Comisión Consultiva para la Reforma Educativa* (1999).

attractive. Third, according to Valerio and Rojas (2000), PRONADE's objectives — emphasizing decentralization, community participation and indigenous inclusiveness — were in line with the Peace Accords as well as with the 'strategic' direction of the Guatemalan government during that time.

Box 7. Other Educational Models for Guatemala: Multi-Grade and Bilingual Education Methodologies

Besides PRONADE, Guatemala has implemented various other educational models for disadvantaged rural and indigenous children. Anderson (2001) reports that, in the past 10 years, the two most important models have been multi-grade teaching and bilingual education methodology. With the assistance of the United States Agency for International Development (USAID) the first schools of both models began operating in the early 1990s. There are also various pilots combining these two methodologies.

The multi-grade education model — known as New Multi-grade School or *Nueva Escuela Unitaria* (NEU) — is children-centered, based on learning principles that stress collaborative learning, peer teaching, the use of self-instructional guides, and participation in student government. In the classrooms of NEU schools, children of various ages play together and cooperate on lessons and projects sitting at common tables instead of individual desks. The principle of self-directed learning that prevails in New Multi-grade Schools allows students to work at their own pace and develop time-management skills. Collaborative projects help students develop communication skills, and the incorporation of cultural themes into those projects means that what the students are learning is relevant to their lives. A pilot evaluation from Chesterfield (1994) made a positive assessment of student achievement in NEU schools.

To address the specific needs of the indigenous students, Guatemala also began a process of creating bilingual schools in Departments with a high concentration of Mayan population. These school are managed by the Ministry of Education's Directorate General of Bilingual and Intercultural Education. The *Dirección General de Educación Bilingüe Intercultural* (DIGEBI) is located outside the Ministry. Due to chronic under-funding it operates in a run-down office environment. One of the main tasks of DIGEBI is to supply bilingual schools with books. However, de facto most schools do not have bilingual textbooks. Moreover, while teachers do *speak* an indigenous language, they are frequently *illiterate* in indigenous languages, and are as such not adequately trained to provide formal bilingual education to the children.

PRONADE originally began in 1993 with the objective of administering two government funds that had been specifically established to increase access to education in rural areas. The available funds were expected to finance community organizations offering educational support services.

Supporters of PRONADE argue that the program is originated as a solution to the problem of insufficient school coverage in rural areas. In 1993, the first school emerged as a small pilot program. Within months, the program expanded to a dozen other schools in communities nearby. CIEN (1999) reports that in these early stages the program was called *Saq'bé*, a Kaqchikel word that translates into 'path of light.'

When a new government administration (Ramiro de León Carpio) came into office in 1993, it established PRONADE within the Ministry of Education. Basically, PRONADE continued administering the two funds, although legal challenges and funding shortages delayed its broader implementation. Full implementation of the program did not take place until 1994 when the Social Investment Fund provided financing for a pilot program in additional 45 *comunidades*. With the financing of the Social Investment Fund, the program expanded rapidly, covering about 200 communities within two years.

In an effort to increase PRONADE's effectiveness, another government administration (Álvaro Arzú Irigoyen) coming into office in 1996, built on a major re-vitalization of the program. All school infrastructure matters were delegated to the Social Investment Fund. Authority over administrative and non-infrastructure matters was given to PRONADE's Implementation Unit. According to MINEDUC (1999), other important features included the creation of a legal framework for community participation, the establishment of a trust fund within the Ministry of Public Finance (MFP) to channel PRONADE's budget, and the incorporation of NGO-led experience into the program. In 1997, the Ministry of Education gained the authority to recognize the legal status of the local Education Committees. These are key elements of PRONADE and administer the local school program (see Chapter III).

As other Latin American countries, Guatemala has experimented with a number of education reform proposals and various pilot programs over the years.[78] According to the World Bank (1997), some staff from the Ministry of Education first perceived PRONADE as 'yet another program' designed to increase access to education in rural areas. They expressed their doubts about the mode of delivery and predicted that the program would be short-lived. Despite such skepticism, PRONADE succeeded in drawing public attention of the pilot program to the

78 For the period 1990-2000, *Foro Interuniversitario* (2000) list more than 60 proposals for education reform. IDESAC (2001) includes a bibliography list of about 150 contributions to the Guatemalan education reform process, including numerous descriptions of pilot programs.

public. In late 1996, PRONADE was officially selected as Guatemala's strategy to increase educational access in rural areas. With the support of the German Development Bank (KfW), the World Bank and the Inter-American Development Bank (IDB) the program expanded across the country.

D. Education System after Peace Accords

Has Guatemala made substantial progress in its education system since the signing of the Peace Accords? Edwards (2002) finds a persistently large education gap between the non-poor and the poor, as well as between the Ladino and indigenous population. In 2000, the primary gross enrollment ratio reached 99 percent and primary net enrollment 79 percent. For primary education, the gross enrollment rate of the non-poor is 110 percent and net enrollment 90 percent, compared to the corresponding figures of 93 percent and 72 percent of the poor (see Table 34).

Table 34. Guatemala: School Enrollment by Ethnicity and Level of Poverty, 2000 (in percent)

School level	Total a/	Non-poor	Poor b/	Ladinos	Indigenous c/
Gross enrollment ratios					
Preprimary	26	42	18	30	21
Primary	99	110	93	103	94
Secondary	31	54	14	41	19
Tertiary	20	38	2	29	8
Net enrollment ratios					
Preprimary	23	39	16	28	18
Primary	79	90	72	84	72
Secondary	25	44	10	33	14
Tertiary	9	16	1	13	3

Source: Edwards (2002). a/ Due to the reliance on household survey data, the numbers here differ slightly from the Ministry of Education's official data. b/ The poverty line refers to a person's average minimum caloric requirement (estimated at 2,172 kcal/day) and adjustments for 'wasted-food' as well as for non-food consumption, see World Bank (2003a). c/ Ethnicity according to self-identification.

This persistent divide between the 'rich' and 'poor' as well as between urban and rural areas is manifested by the enrollment gap between Ladino and indigenous children. The gross enrollment rate of indigenous children is 94 percent, while that of Ladino children is 103 percent. The corresponding figures for net enrollment rate is 84 percent, and 72 percent, respectively. In secondary and tertiary education the gaps are even more pronounced. The large difference between the net and the gross ratio represents grade-by-age misalignments and indicates inefficiency.[79]

Figure 16. Guatemala: Net Enrollment, Repetition and Dropout Rates in Primary Schools, 1996-2001 (in percent)

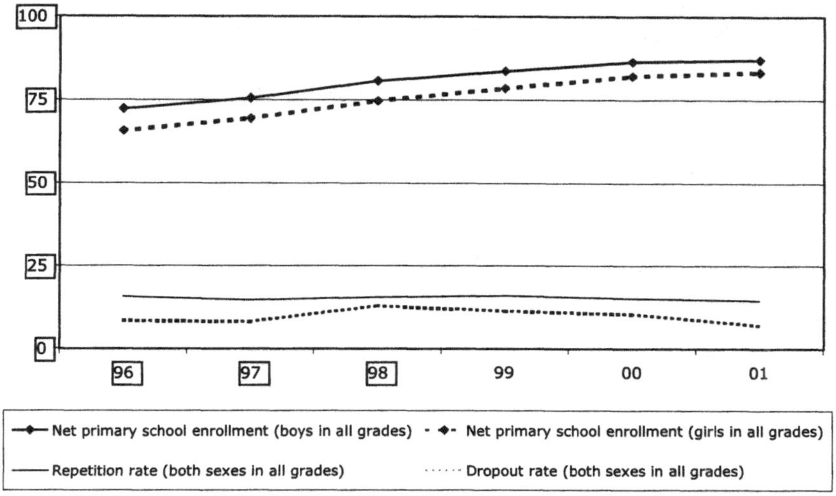

Source: UNDP (2002) based on data from the Ministry of Education.

Nevertheless, Figure 16 shows that Guatemala has made substantial progress in expanding educational coverage.[80] Within only 5 years primary net enrollment grew by about 15 percent for boys, and 18 percent for girls, respectively. According to CIEN (2000b) it is plausible to argue that the increased enrollment rates can be attributed to the massive expansion of PRONADE schools in rural Guatemala (subject to Chapter IV). The expansion was also made possible by

79 When students repeat grades, gross enrollment ratios inflate. Recall that the primary *gross* enrollment ratio is defined as the ratio of *all* enrolled primary students to the population of the age group 7-12. By contrast, the primary *net* enrollment ratio is defined as the ratio of primary students in the designated *age group* to the total population of this age group. Consequently, net enrollment ratios understate enrollment if there are over-age children in the class.

80 Using additional indicators, equally Anderson (2001) as well as Marqués and Bannon (2003) come to the conclusion that Guatemala has shown considerable progress.

increased public educational expenditures. According to UNDP (2003a), as a percentage of GDP, government education expenditures rose from 1.3 percent in 1995 to 2.6 percent in 2002. As such, education expenditures are in line with the quantitative targets set by the Peace Accords from 1996. In absolute terms, however, they still represent a modest figure compared to other Latin American countries.

Figure 16 shows that dropout and repetition rates have remained constant at relatively high levels. Equally, UNDP (2003a) reports that lack of assistance to primary schooling remains of concern. Table 35 suggests that, on average, about 16 percent of all Guatemalan children did not attend school in 2002. Non-assistance is particularly pronounced for rural and indigenous areas. Taken together, these numbers *suggest* low efficiency and low quality of the education system.[81] Can this be confirmed empirically?

Table 35. Guatemala: Primary School Children Absenteeism, 2000-2002 (in percent)

Characteristics [a/]	2000	2002
Sex		
Girls	20.5	19.3
Boys	15.4	13.1
Area		
Urban	11.1	10.8
Rural	21.3	18.9
Ethnic group		
K'iche'	24.3	20.9
Q'eqchi	37.9	18.0
Kaqchikel	20.1	22.5
Mam	19.9	21.6
Ladino	13.0	10.5
Total	17.8	16.2

Source: UNDP (2003a) based on household survey data. a/ For the age group 7-12 years.

In 1997, the Ministry of Education launched a National Program of Evaluation of School Achievements (PRONERE) to monitor and measure quality of schooling.

81 Educational quality is here defined as the extent to which children learn basic skills and knowledge necessary to function in society and utilize these skills in their life. For a discussion see IDB (2000).

The evaluations were carried out on 3rd an 6th graders in reading and mathematics. The data, however, has never been made available to the public. CIEN (2002) summarizes the evidence and finds that student achievement in Guatemala is generally low. Test competence is barely sufficient to answer $^1/_2$ of the test items in reading — and less than $^1/_2$ in mathematics. Moreover, quality improvements over time are found to be negligible.

The variations within groups and between groups are large. In reading, the most prominent difference in average test scores is between Ladinos and indigenous students. Indigenous children score more than 1 standard deviation below the Ladino students. Urban school students perform significantly above rural school students. The differences between rural and urban test scores, however, are not too pronounced and rather show that *both* urban and rural schools perform unsatisfactory. In mathematics, the difference between Ladino and indigenous student test scores is narrower than in reading. This indicates that indigenous students are not inherently low performers, but are likely to suffer from linguistic barriers.

Bratsberg and Terrell (2002) carried out an interesting study that allowed them to compare the quality of the Guatemalan education system with that of other countries. Using data from the U.S. census, they estimate country-specific returns to education among male immigrants in the U.S. labor market. Since immigrants are competing in the same market without being affected by their home countries' labor market conditions, their rates of return are useful pointers to the educational quality of their home country. Male immigrants educated in Central America registered the lowest returns among all immigrants,[82] falling behind the African immigrants in the sample. Western Europe and Japan registered the highest return. Given that the workers' characteristics and distance to home countries are controlled for, what accounts for the variations in the returns is the education quality of the home countries. The returns to education of male immigrants educated in Guatemala were only about 2 percent and well below the average returns to immigrants from Central America. Consequently, it may be inferred that the quality of Guatemala's education system during the past decades was lower than for countries with a similar level of development.

The assumed low quality of the Guatemalan education system is of serious concern. First, students who receive poor quality education learn little and *tend* to repeat classes and drop out earlier. As such, they do not stay in the system long enough to complete primary education and later enroll in secondary school. Second, enrollment expansion per se, without ensuring that children acquire basic skills in reading and mathematics, is unlikely to enhance productivity or enhance

82 Except Haiti and the Dominican Republic.

the chance to find a job in the 'high-productivity' non-farm sector. Third, public resources are used more efficiently if the number of repeaters decreases. When there are fewer repeaters in the system, more students have the chance to graduate with the same number of teachers being employed, classrooms being built, and other support services being provided.

To summarize, Guatemala's education system has shown improvements since 1996. However, the available data and qualitative assessments suggest that, particularly for the first grades of primary education, the system still suffers from limited coverage, inequities, low internal efficiency and low quality. At all levels, there are fewer females enrolled, and the indigenous females are the most disadvantaged.

According to the World Bank (2003a), the education system has, compared to other countries in the Latin America region, inadequate financing.[83] Without adequate financing, services are limited for many children, and this is of particular concern. UNDP (2003a) reports that more than 60 percent of Guatemala's population is below 15 years of age. Consequently, with a young and rapidly growing population of annually 2.7 percent, the education system has to continue to expand rapidly only to keep up with the increasing demand. In this vein, the following chapters analyze the role of the community-managed school approach.

83 Table 2 in Part One compares recent data on public spending on education in Guatemala with its Central American neighbors.

III. Objectives, Key Actors and Implementation of PRONADE

Before assessing the impact of PRONADE, the aim of this chapter is to provide an insight into the institutional structure of PRONADE. Sections A and B shed a light on the program's key objectives and its organizational structure. Section C explains the implementation process at the community level. Section D describes the transfer of funds to the Education Committees.[84]

A. Objectives and Structure

According to Valerio and Rojas (2000), PRONADE is a decentralized, community-led program that seeks to increase access to schooling and to improve the quality of primary education. A key focus is rural areas and areas dominated by indigenous communities. Rural communities with no access to education services receive financing directly from the Ministry of Education to get new schools.

Communities qualify to participate in the program if they meet at least four criteria. First, the community must find a site for the school and demonstrate the ability to and a genuine interest in managing a new school. Second, the community must be located at least 3 kilometers away from the nearest public school. Third, the community must have at least 25 primary school-age children. Fourth, the community must not have any teachers already on the official government's payroll.

Financing for the program is allocated to communities to cover teacher salaries, learning materials and school snacks, and *Instituciones de Servicios Educativos* (ISE) to cover administrative training and educational support services. The Service Institutions are NGOs that have specialized in education and community development. They are contracted by PRONADE and receive payment for their services. Financing is contingent on extensive community participation related to the school. School affairs managed by the Committees usually range from hiring teachers to setting the local school calendar. A *Comité Educativo* (COEDUCA) represents each community. The Education Committee is elected locally by the community and is composed of parents and community members.

PRONADE schools are run besides the traditional schooling system. At the national level, the program is coordinated by a relatively small Implementation Unit with a staff of less than 60, located in the capital. This unit is responsible for

84 There are few detailed descriptions available on the organizational structure of the program and the implementation processes. As a consequence, much information here comes from interviews held in July 2001 with PRONADE staff and other informants listed in the introduction of this study. References for the following paragraphs also include Valerio and Rojas (2000), CIEN (1999), MINEDUC (2003) as well as MINEDUC and PRONADE (2001).

strategic planning, financial management, monitoring, and evaluation. The unit coordinates closely with the Social Investment Fund on school infrastructure matters, and on educational policy and assessment issues with the Ministry of Education. In keeping with the decentralized nature of the program, the Implementation Unit leaves all school administration and managerial decisions in the hands of the Education Committees. The local Committees receive technical assistance and overall advice from the participating NGO-backed Educational Service Institutions.

PRONADE's main objective is to open up educational opportunities for the thousands of out-of-school children until full primary school coverage has been attained. The immediate goal is to ensure that the majority of the primary school-age children in every Department receives educational services. Priority is given to Departments that have not yet reached a minimum coverage otherwise. These are also the Departments with the highest proportion of indigenous population with over 60 percent of the population monolingual in one of the Mayan languages. Today, PRONADE provides its services to children in virtually all regions of the country.

Figure 17. Institutional Structure of PRONADE

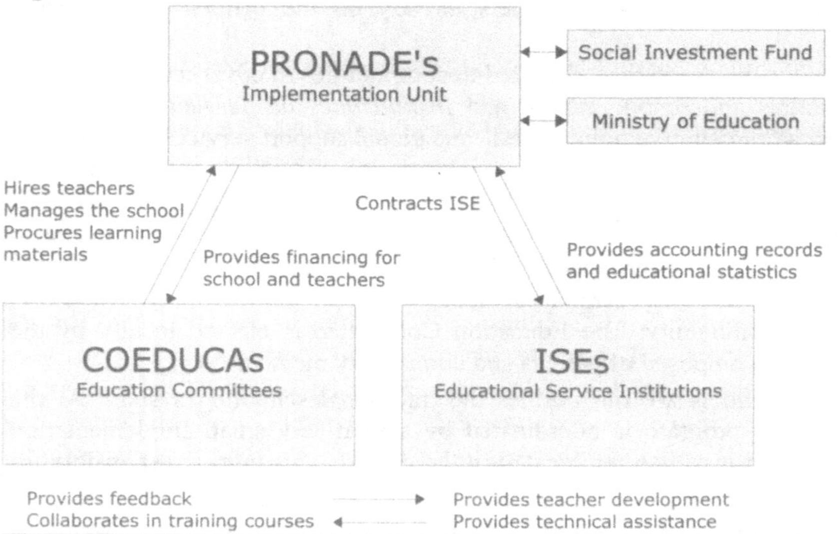

Source: Adopted from Valerio and Rojas (2000).

CIEN (1999) reports that along with achieving quantitative expansion, PRONADE claims specific *learning goals* for its students (beyond the standard curriculum). For example, with the completion of the first three years at the program, PRONADE students are expected to work well individually and as a team, respect school and private property, value their cultural identity, express ideas with confidence and self-esteem, and appreciate the country. In addition, students who live in multicultural contexts are expected to be bilingual in a Mayan language and in Spanish, value their cultural background, and respect the environment and natural resources.[85]

B. Key Actors

The implementation structure of the program is illustrated in Figure 17. There are three main actors in the implementation of PRONADE, namely the Education Committees, the Educational Service Institutions, and PRONADE's Implementation Unit. Drawing from MINEDUC (2003), the respective duties of these actors are explained in the following sections.

1. Education Committees

The *Comité Educativo* is at the heart of the implementation structure. The Committees are established as legal entities and are formally entrusted with administering the program on behalf of the community. The Committees are composed of parents and community members irrespective of their level of education.[86] They are responsible for seven key administrative functions: the contracting and paying of teacher's salaries, maintaining accounting records, monitoring teachers and student attendance, defining the school schedule and calendar within the existing national legal framework, buying and distributing school materials, monitoring school libraries, and organizing school breakfast programs. The Committees receive funds directly from Ministry of Education. Technical assistance and administrative training is provided by the Service Institutions.

2. Educational Service Institutions

PRONADE's Implementation Unit contracts the *Instituciones de Servicios Educativos*. They are NGOs and are expected to fulfill five main tasks. These include identifying educational needs in the communities, assisting the Education Committees in obtaining their legal status, providing financial and administrative training for the Committees, providing teacher development courses on multi-grade

85 There is no information available on the de facto achievements of this goal. See ASIES (1988) for a loose proposal on an environmental education strategy for Guatemala.

86 However, at least two members of the committee are required to be literate.

and bilingual classroom practices, and maintain updated information on the schools and students under their supervision.[87]

In order to qualify for a contract with PRONADE, the Educational Service Institutions must have had at least 3 years of experience in community development. In theory, the Service Institutions are required to have a legal standing, have an office in the locality, be willing to participate in staff training, have bilingual staff ready to interact with people from the local community, and to be willing and able to work with a minimum of 5 communities. MINEDUC and PRONADE (2000a) show that about 80 percent of the NGOs have already worked before on community and social development projects, and concentrate their activities in a specific geographical area of the country.

In order to receive funds from PRONADE, the Educational Service institution must respond to a call for proposals put out by PRONADE's Implementation Unit. The Service Institutions submit a proposal package that provides information about their technical strengths as well as on the estimated costs of rendering their services. PRONADE's Implementation Unit evaluates the proposals and makes funding decisions by weighing technical strength slightly above economic aspects. Once the contract is awarded, a successful NGO receives a 25 percent advance on their services and the remaining 75 percent upon signature of a contract between PRONADE and the Education Committee. CIEN (2000a) reports that on average about $^1/_3$ of the Educational Service Institution's budget comes from PRONADE resources. In 1995, there was only 1 NGO participating in the program. By 1998, the number of Educational Service Institutions had increased to 25. In 2000, the number has been reduced to 16 but eventually increased again (see Table 36). The decline in the number of the NGOs was partly due to the implementation of a more rigorous selection process.[88]

3. *Implementation Unit*

The implementation unit headquartered in the capital is responsible for seven key activities. These include outlining the general framework of the program,

---

87 According to PRONADE staff, the reliance on NGO support is a major innovation of Guatemala's community-managed school program.

88 The GTZ (2000) points out a series of problems related to the Educational Service Institutions. In particular, in 2000 there was an oligopoly of only 3 NGOs that provide their services to about 44 percent of the Education Committees. The potential for strong influence here means that there is a risk of politicizing the program. This may have contributed to Guatemala's reduced funding for PRONADE since 2001 under the Alfonso Portillo Government.

determining the geographical areas that receive support, and signing the legal covenant with the Education Committees. Other tasks involve identifying, selecting, contracting and supervising educational service institutions, monitoring and evaluating the program, transferring funds to the Education Committees, and coordination with the Ministry of Education and other institutions. PRONADE is monitored by a steering Committee composed of the Minister of Education, an executive director of the ministry, 3 councils, and 2 members from the private sector. The Implementation Unit also works closely with the Social Investment Fund in all matters regarding upgrading or building new school infrastructure facilities.

C. Implementation Process

This section provides insight into the execution of PRONADE and explains how PRONADE is implemented at the community level. The following paragraphs, as illustrated in Figure 18, refer to three specific stages. Overall, the Ministry of Education's duty is to execute the program and to ensure that education reforms are advanced. The ministry also assists with the initial general identification of communities that have little or no access to education, and provides recognition for the legal status of the Education Committees.

1. Community Identification

The first step in the process of carrying out the PRONADE goals is to identify those communities that are in need and without educational services. This is done by the educational service NGOs that receive a contract to do so from PRONADE. On average, it takes about 45 days to identify and evaluate the needs of a community. In 1996, PRONADE required only 1 contract with an NGO to carry out the three stages of the program. This changed in 1997 when PRONADE required two contracts with the educational service institutions, one for promoting community development and another for follow-up. In 1998, PRONADE decided to have three separate contracts: one contract encompasses community identification, another one entails the organization and legalization of the Education Committees, and the final one is for program follow-up.

Educational service institution may select whether to bid for one, two or all three contract phases based on their technical expertise and geographical location. Educational service institutions are granted a time frame of 45 days to identify a community, outline its needs, and submit appropriate information to PRONADE. Once PRONADE verifies the information and the needs of the community, the service institution receives an average of about 200 U.S. dollars per community identified. In order to control the identification process, PRONADE has established a ceiling on the number of communities that may be identified by an individual service institution.

Figure 18. Implementation Stages of PRONADE [a/]

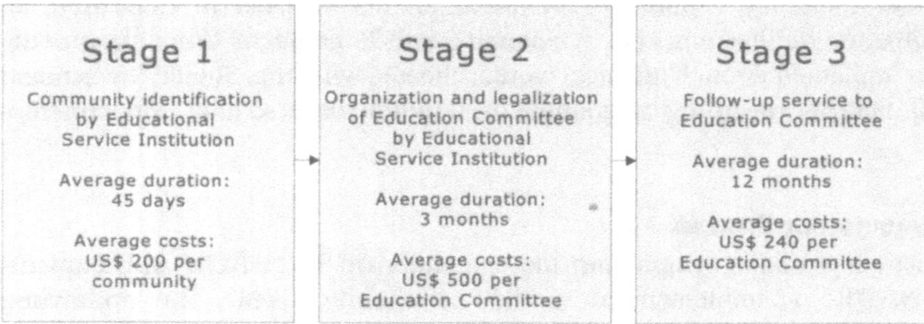

Source: Adopted from Valerio and Rojas (2000). a/ Data refers to 2000.

2. Organization of Local Education Committees

During this second stage, the Educational Service Institution enters into another contract with PRONADE to provide technical support to the communities. More specifically, the role of the Service Institutions is to ensure that the communities establish the Education Committee, elect a provisional board of directors, and obtain legal status. Once the committee is legally established, the Service Institution provides a 3-day training in administration and financial management. The average time frame for the committee to obtain legal status is about 3 months. The average unit cost for the Service Institutions is about 500 U.S. dollars per Education Committee established.

3. Follow-Up Services

The third type of contract between the Educational Service Institutions and PRONADE is a 12-month contract to provide follow-up services to the Education Committee. In order to participate in this stage, in addition to the requirements necessary to participate in stages 1 and 2, the NGO must meet several new requirements. Namely, the staff of the Service Institution must have experience in teaching and pedagogical methods, and has to be fluent in the Mayan language of the local community.

In principle, a background with pedagogical methods and a fluency in the local Mayan language are essential for providing the necessary training to teachers and representatives of the Education Committees. The committees receive a total of 9 days of training. Teachers receive 22 days of training during non-school working periods. Usually teachers are given a 10-day training course in the 1st trimester, 5 days in the 2nd trimester and 7 days in the 3rd trimester. In theory, these activities are meant to improve the quality of educational services in PRONADE schools. The NGOs are required to make periodic visits to the school to ensure effective implementation of the program and to monitor results that are, then, submitted to PRONADE's monitoring and evaluation unit. The Service Institutions receive about 250 U.S. dollars per community per month to perform these follow-up activities.

Transfers to the Education Committees are paid out every 3 months prior to rendering services. Although funds flow from PRONADE directly to the committee, the Service Institutions provide input in developing the budget and ensuring that funds are spent according to the categories established with PRONADE. The Education Committee makes all payments out of their local checking account. The Educational Service Institutions and PRONADE's financial and administrative unit is responsible for supervising this process.

Valerio and Rojas (2000) report that the Education Committees receive funds to pay for teacher salaries equivalent to about 240 U.S. dollars per teacher per month. In 2000, the Committees also receive about 40 U.S. dollars per student per year to buy school materials, teaching supplies, and to provide a daily school breakfast. In addition, PRONADE claims to supply new schools with curriculum materials, mini libraries, and other didactic materials.

D. Transfer of Funds

PRONADE established a trust fund to administer resources and streamline payments to the Education Committees and the Educational Service Institutions. Consistent with an agreement that establishes PRONADE as a legal entity, the Ministry of Public Finance is required to allocate resources to the trust fund to ensure a smooth implementation of the program. The Agreement requires the Ministry to disburse funds every 3 months to a local Guatemalan bank (*Bancafé*) according to the statements of expenditures submitted by PRONADE.

However, in practice, obtaining the funds is subject to a very bureaucratic process. CIEN (1999) as well as Valerio and Rojas (2000) report that it takes on average up to two months for the deposit to become effective. The bureaucratic process may be one reason for the frequent claims of teachers' salaries being paid late and of overdue disbursements for school materials that hamper the execution of the program.

PRONADE's Implementation Unit first requests funds from the Ministry of Education to make a single purchasing order with payment in the order of to *Bancafé*. The Ministry of Education then approves the request and sends the order to the Ministry of Public Finance. Next it submits the order to the National

Controllers Office for approval. Upon approval, the Ministry of Public Finance sends a notice to PRONADE. The program's administrative unit then presents notice to *Banco de Guatemala*. The Central Bank then issues a check payable to PRONADE's trust account with *Bancafé*. Finally, *Bancafé* deposits the approved payments in local branches to be available to the Educational Service Institutions and the Education Committees. *Bancafé* then submits payment reports to the Ministry of Public Finance, the National Controllers Office and PRONADE's administrative unit. PRONADE's administrative unit sends the Ministry of Public Finance at the end of each trimester reports on the execution of the funds.

IV. What Has PRONADE Delivered?

Much to the surprise of the staff from the Ministry of Education — which in the beginning considered local communities unable to organize and run their schools — the PRONADE project demonstrates that rural and indigenous communities can be trained to manage their schools, even with low levels of formal education. In addition, the PRONADE experience in Guatemala is proving a showcase for an offensive decentralization measure meant to be successful. Former isolated rural and indigenous communities have been empowered to administer and manage local schools. Although public resources come from the Ministry of Education, the local communities have received authority and other powers.

More specific achievements are discussed in the following paragraphs. Section A and B show that PRONADE has achieved some of its main goals: quantitative expansion, decentralization and an improved parental participation in school decisions. However, section C shows that evaluations of the quality of program have come to critical conclusions. Finally, section D includes a rough empirical analysis and discusses the quality of PRONADE's educational service.

Table 36. Expansion of PRONADE, 1995-2003

Year	Primary school children	Preschool children	Primary school teachers	Education Committees	Educational Service Institutions	Departments
1995	2,902	0	82	45	1	1
1996	67,734	0	808	327	6	13
1997	118,392	0	1,635	892	15	15
1998	179,442	8,900	3,769	1,990	25	20
1999	221,739	27,700	6,777	2,815	24	20
2000	294,041	40,900	9,305	3,437	16	21
2001	310,119	N.D.	10,091	3,423	17	21
2002	321,629	N.D.	10,560	3,419	19	21
2003	372,068	N.D.	12,023	4,119	26	21

Source: Author's elaboration based on MINEDUC and PRONADE (2000a), CIEN (2000b) and MINEDUC (2003). N.D. = no data available.

A. Quantitative Expansion

In a relatively short time period, PRONADE has moved from a small pilot program to a nationwide project. The quantitative expansion of the program can be observed in Table 36. In 2003, about 372,000 children were enrolled in primary schools of PRONADE. The program has succeeded in organizing and approving close to 4,100 Education Committees and has hired more than 12,000 primary school teachers. PRONADE Schools can be found in 21 of the 22 Departments (excluding the metropolitan department). They are concentrated in the most disadvantaged regions (Departments of Alta and Baja Verapaz, Huehuetenago, and El Quiché). These 4 departments alone represent approximately $^1/_2$ of the total number of primary school children served by the program.

UNDP (2002) reports that the net enrollment rate in primary education has substantially increased in 1995-2001. PRONADE had a significant role in increasing this expansion. To illustrate the importance of PRONADE, it is important to emphasize that, in 2001, PRONADE schools represented about $^1/_3$ of all primary school enrollment in rural areas. At the national level, PRONADE schools account for more than 14 percent of total enrollment in primary education. The quantitative success of the program, coupled with the increasing demand for preschool education, has prompted PRONADE to provide a preschool program since 1998. Preschool enrollment increased from 8,900 to almost 41,000 in 2000. As such, the preschool program accounts for more than 12 percent of total enrollment in 2000 (Figure 19).

B. Decentralization and Parental Participation

Given the notable expansion of primary schooling and the community commitment to the program, CIEN (1999; 2000b) argues that education decentralization policies have been implemented in Guatemala with relative success. Of course, this success cannot be traced to one single policy intervention, namely PRONADE, but rather to a combination of favorable conditions and policies. Among these are Guatemala's recent commitment to increase primary school enrollment in the rural areas. In addition, some regions were already familiar with their Educational Service Institution. Besides education, they were receiving support from the NGOs in various other aspects of social development. PRONADE has also enjoyed continuous 'high-level' government support. Finally, Valerio and Rojas (2000) argue that the program seems to be staffed by committed personnel that has continually been open for recommendations from evaluation studies.

Parental participation has brought benefits to the community due to the close collaboration that exists between parents, students, and teachers. The ability of the local communities to solve school problems themselves has helped to increase the importance parents attach to education and school management. MINEDUC and PRONADE (1999) report that parents and community members were initially critical of the decentralized nature of the program. However, the success the program had so far in making basic education available helped to ease the parents' discomfort. In addition, MINEDUC (1999) finds also finds that with PRONADE in place the community participates more frequently in other civic affairs. In an ethnographic study, equally Asturias et al. (2001) find that PRONADE school services contribute to strengthen local organization skills and is a source of non-farm income, for example regarding school materials, commerce, and in terms of market integration. With the knowledge gained from school-management, communities also find the motivation to improve their physical infrastructure facilities.

Figure 19. PRONADE School Enrollment, 1995-2001
(as percentage of total enrollment)

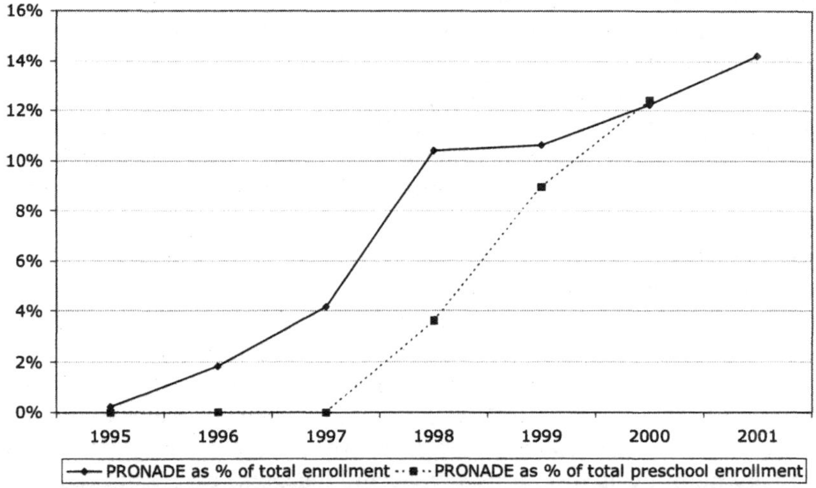

Source: Author's elaboration based on data from the Ministry of Education.

According to MINEDUC and PRONADE's (1999; 2000a) self-evaluations, the Educational Committees' members are mostly parents of school children. In general, the Committees are reported to be satisfied with their new ability to make decisions. Two of their most important activities are financial management and teacher supervision. However, these self-evaluations report that the greatest challenges the Education Committee members face is to leave work to participate in training sessions and the delay in payments to some of the Committees. These issues are focused on in the next section.

C. Mixed Results from Evaluations

Notwithstanding PRONADE's impressive quantitative expansion, little is known about its second main goal: the improvement of the educational quality in rural schools and the program's impact on students' learning achievements. The GTZ (2000) claims that not only per student costs, but also repetition and drop out rates seem to be higher in PRONADE schools than in traditional rural schools. Unfortunately, there is no reliable data that would allow comparing the internal efficiency between PRONADE and traditional rural schools.[89] However, there are three qualitative evaluation reports, which provide some insights into the functioning of the program.

1. Evaluation of the Centro de Investigaciones Económicas Nacionales

The first evaluation study was conducted by a leading Guatemalan research institution. CIEN (1999) surveyed the principal actors in the program and compared traditional rural schools with PRONADE schools. Findings from this evaluation indicate that traditional schools are more likely to offer preschool services (this finding led PRONADE to incorporate preschool services into its program). In addition, they also have a larger student population. While traditional schools have between 31 and 50 students, PRONADE schools only have between 21 and 30 students.

The CIEN (1999) evaluation claims that, somewhat surprisingly, there is no difference in the language of instruction by type of school. About $^2/_3$ of the schools both traditional and PRONADE teach in Spanish, and about $^1/_3$ teach in Spanish *and* in the local indigenous language. However, PRONADE schools have a greater percentage of teachers providing multi-grade instruction compared to traditional schools. According to the report, PRONADE teacher display a greater motivation compared to teachers in traditional schools. However, focus group interviews revealed relatively high levels of job insecurity, and teachers' distress at receiving their salary every 3 months instead of every month. Finally, only about 80 percent of PRONADE teachers have a teaching certificate: the lack of trained personnel in some departments forced PRONADE to hire untrained teachers or *promotores*.

2. Self-Evaluations from PRONADE and the Ministry of Education

In order to measure the program's progress, frequent evaluations are also carried out by MINEDUC and PRONADE (1999; 2000a). The main findings from these self-evaluations indicate that PRONADE schools offer an additional 20 minutes of instruction per day compared to similar rural schools. The report also claims that, in principle, the program ensures that students remain in school for the allotted 5 hours per day and the 180 days per year. According to the self-

89 Given that PRONADE schools typically operate under the most difficult conditions, the problem is to make the data 'comparable', as pointed out by MINEDUC and PRONADE (2000b).

evaluation, the program has an impact on parents' supervision of the teacher, the development of the school infrastructure and parental collaboration in school management. MINEDUC and PRONADE (2000a) also find that about 45 percent of parents visit the school principal once a month, compared to 27 percent for parents in traditional rural schools.

However, contrary to the CIEN (1999) evaluation, the program is found to be less adequate in using materials in the local indigenous languages and in multi-grade teaching. Only 1 percent of the surveyed schools had materials in Mayan languages. This clearly contradicts the goals of the program and questions how accountable the Educational Service Institutions are. In fact, PRONADE faces serious problems in providing adequate infrastructure facilities and in reducing student absenteeism. Unfortunately, the self-elevations do not provide data on drop-out and repetition rates. About $^1/_3$ of PRONADE schools do not have access to water, $^1/_5$ do not have access to sanitation facilities, and more than $^1/_3$ of the schools do not satisfy 'minimum requirements' for effective learning. As such, the schooling infrastructure of PRONADE is worse than in comparable rural schools.

3. *Evaluation from the German Technical Cooperation*

Equally a report from the GTZ (2000) comes to an critical assessment regarding the quality of PRONADE's education services. The report finds that only 1 out of the 16 Educational Service Institutions (in 2000) uses bilingual and multi-grade teaching techniques. The remaining 15 institutions basically rely on traditional monolingual teaching. This report also points out the severe lack of materials in most PRONADE schools and the lack of teachers trained in Mayan culture and language. The curriculum provided by most Educational Service Institutions is found to be irrelevant to the reality of most indigenous children. In addition, teachers are often forced to combine 2 or more grades into a class but without being trained to apply multi-grade teaching.

Another bottleneck is the tardy disbursements of funds for teacher salaries, school materials and educational support services. In addition, teacher's commitment seems to remain below the expectations of the program. Unlike the traditional schooling scheme, PRONADE offers no job security and no competitive social compensation structure. Parents on the Education Committees often have difficulties in full-filling the requirement of attending training sessions since they cannot afford to lose their daily income. Finally, inadequate communication between municipal education offices and PRONADE schools lead to resentments. Consequently, according to this report, it is not uncommon for municipal education officers to question PRONADE schools their eligibility status. As such, they often do not receive official textbooks and supporting materials.

To summarize, PRONADE has within the past years achieved a notable expansion of school services into remote rural areas. Critical issues are the quality of PRONADE schools, their integration into the formal educational system, the teachers' salary structure, the de facto functioning of the NGO-backed Educational Service Institutions and, in particular, their failure to include bilingual and multi-grade teaching techniques in their program. Hence, the question arises if the fast expansion has come at the expense of quality.

D. Lower Student Achievement in PRONADE Schools?

This section evaluates whether moving away from the traditional and centralized education programs towards greater community involvement has an impact on student achievement in Guatemala. The following paragraphs present results from national achievement evaluations which are then followed by a rough empirical analysis of student achievement in rural Guatemalan schools.

1. Results from National Achievement Evaluations

The Ministry of Education launched a National Assessment System to monitor students' achievement in 1997. The *Programa Nacional de Rendimiento Escolar* (PRONERE) is an effort measure educational quality and is run under the auspices of the *Universidad del Valle.* A formal in-depth evaluation of student achievement exclusively for PRONADE schools has not taken place yet. However, the tests carried out in 1999 and 2000 include a limited number of PRONADE schools in their sample. In total, the evaluations surveyed about 30,000 students, $^1/_2$ of them located in rural Guatemala. The evaluations from Baessa (2000; 2001) are based on standardized test scores for linguistic and mathematical achievements. On a scale ranging from zero to 100, on average, students succeed in about $^1/_2$ of the items. This can be interpreted as an indicator of the overall low quality of the country's schooling system.[90]

Table 37 summarizes the results for rural primary schooling in Guatemala. Two items are of interest. First, except for PRONADE, all other programs tend to perform better in 2000 than in 1999. However, the questionnaires are not fully identical for each year. Consequently, care must be taken when interpreting these achievement scores over time. Second, the standardized average test scores on language and mathematics for students enrolled in PRONADE schools are lower

---

90 Personal communication with Yetilú de Baessa, *Centro de Investigaciones Educativas, Universidad del Valle*, June 27, 2001. She indicated that there is a lack of transfer capacity. For example, students are able to master basic numerical operations but then typically fail to apply these skills to real-day problems.

than those enrolled in traditional rural schools. Baessa (2001) finds that the differences are statistically significant for reading, but insignificant for mathematics.

At first sight, the differences are not surprising given that PRONADE students presumably come from the most disadvantaged backgrounds. However, it *is* surprising that in comparison with test scores from multi-grade and bilingual schooling programs — operating under similar conditions — PRONADE students still tend to score unfavorably. When all three programs are compared, the multi-grade schools tend to outperform both the bilingual and the community-managed schools. Unfortunately, the descriptive findings from Baessa (2000; 2001) neither control for student characteristics nor for the physical and pedagogical infrastructure of the schools. Therefore, it is unclear whether average test scores are a function of these factors or if they can be attributed to the school organization. One possibility to address this issue is to estimate an education production function.

2. *Determinants of Student Achievement: A Word of Caution*

Before proceeding with this kind of analysis, a word of caution is worthwhile. In an empirical review of studies on the effects of educational inputs on students performance in developing countries, Hanushek (1995) and Velez et al. (1993) for Latin America, both authors conclude that there is no clear and robust relationship between key school inputs and student performance. Also Glewwe (2002) points out that studies of education production functions generally have yielded mixed outcomes. Due to the inherent econometric problems, results should be taken with a great deal of caution. Two of the main problems can be summarized as follows.

First, along with influences coming from measurement errors and data collection issues, the scores may be determined by exogenous choices. This is particular relevant for the present study. For example, some explanatory variables that determine achievement scores, such as the type of school, may be systematically related to unobservable characteristics, which are not random. This can bias the estimates. However, the direction of the effect remains unclear. If the important unobserved characteristics are students' motivation to learn and parents' commitment to education and these variables are positively correlated with participation in community-managed schools, empirical estimates would overestimate the role of PRONADE. However, as pointed out by Jiminez and Sawada (1999), the bias might be mitigated by the fact that community managed school explicitly target the economically and socially disadvantaged communities.

A second potential selectivity bias arises when some students are absent on the day the achievement test is administered. Students may be absent for a number of reasons. Some of these, such as illness, have nothing to do with their achievement scores. But other reasons may be tied to the school organization. A similar type of selection problem can occur when students simply are not enrolled in school. Those who do enroll may be a biased sample of children. A series of other important but omitted variables may also be present. For example, if unobserved components of a child's learning ability or unobserved school- and teacher-quality variables are positively correlated with observed school and teacher variables, the estimated impacts on the observed variables could be biased. One way to 'minimize' this kind of problem is to include a large number of variables, as is typically the case in educational production functions. However, some variables, such as teacher motivation or students ability, are difficult to measure. Moreover, in the case of Guatemala, the number of variables that are significantly correlated with achievement scores is rather limited.

Table 37. Achievement Scores for 3rd and 6th Grade in Rural Guatemala, 1999-2000

	Math computation a/		Reading comprehension a/	
Category	1999	2000	1999	2000
3rd Grade				
Traditional rural schools	42.10	47.62	52.19	62.11
	(16.9)	(...)	(18.3)	(...)
PRONADE (community-managed	39.66	38.75	46.63	46.27
schools)	(15.7)	(...)	(19.9)	(...)
NEU (multi-grade schools)	41.54	47.05	55.85	60.87
	(16.9)	(...)	(16.9)	(...)
DIGBI (bilingual schools)	37.60	39.29	45.02	43.94
	(14.8)	(...)	(15.6)	(...)
6th Grade				
Traditional rural school	52.83	58.71	44.67	51.75
	(18.5)	(18.7)	(16.5)	(16.9)
PRONADE (community-managed	46.91	49.79	36.71	36.38
schools)	(17.9)	(20.8)	(14.1)	(12.7)
NEU (multi-grade schools)	54.90	56.48	43.04	46.74
	(18.6)	(20.0)	(15.2)	(15.2)
DIGBI (bilingual schools)	46.77	50.08	35.39	37.11
	(16.5)	(19.1)	(16.6)	(13.6)

Source: Baessa (2000; 2001). a/ Standard deviations in parenthesis. The standardized test ranges from zero to 100, which is the maximum score. For details see Baessa (2001).

Altogether, the application of OLS regressions can lead to biased estimates of the impact of school quality on learning. Some problems underestimate the impacts, others overestimate them, and still others could go either way. Hanushek (1995) argues that the difficulties are so daunting that they are hard to overcome. Thus, estimates of production functions for cognitive skills should be regarded as suggestive, not definitive. For the following regressions, selection bias is likely to be a problem. Unfortunately, in terms of data availability, it seems impossible to deal with this issue empirically.[91] A future analysis that allows correcting for sample selection is needed to determine whether the differences in mean student scores between PRONADE, multi-grade, bilingual and traditional rural education programs holds for richer data sets.

3. Guatemala: Determinants of Achievement and Effect of PRONADE

With this in mind, Table 38 presents the results from a simple OLS regression on student achievement scores in language and mathematics for Guatemala. The estimate is based on the PRONERE (2000) survey for rural primary schools for the 3rd grade.[92] The selection of the variables is based on a priori considerations and is in line with similar analysis of this kind of genre, for example Jiminez and Sawada (1999). The R^2 of the regressions for reading comprehension shows a modest fit of 0.33, which is in line with similar studies of this genre. The variance explained for math achievement is even lower. The large amount of unexplained variance for both regressions can be attributed to innate ability, the health and nutritional status, and other factors not captured by the survey. Most of the 17 explanatory variables are highly significant, even after controlling for heteroskedasticity. They can be classified into 4 broad categories: school organization variables, student background, as well as physical and pedagogical inputs.

(1) School organization variables. The dummy variable that tests for the 'PRONADE effect' reveals an interesting outcome. Community-managed schools show a negative, albeit insignificant, effect on reading comprehension. By contrast,

91 The limited amount of variables does not allow correct identification of the sample selection terms for school choice. In addition, the number of observations for PRONADE school is small (N=81). Nevertheless, Glewwe (2002) finds that education studies that attempted to control for sample selection have found this kind of bias to be modest in magnitude.

92 I would like to thank the *Centro de Investigaciones Educativas, Universidad del Valle*, for making available the data set. The descriptive statistics are displayed in Appendix Three. The 3rd grade is considered most relevant in the context of this study. However, the results for the 6th grade would be similar.

PRONADE Schools seem to affect negatively and significantly math achievement. How to interpret this finding?

There are two potential explanations. First, since the results for reading comprehension are not significantly different from zero, one *may* conclude that that the PRONADE effect is not different on child learning than in traditional schools. This holds even after controlling for students' characteristics as well as for as physical and pedagogical inputs. In mathematics, however, the negative correlation may point out to the missing bilingual curriculum in most PRONADE schools. Since language skills also affect the development of complex numerical thoughts, the language barrier may prevent indigenous children from achieving higher scores. However, there are two problems with this interpretation. On the one hand, language characteristics are partly controlled for by the indigenous dummy variable. On the other hand, recall that the difference between Ladino and indigenous student math test scores is generally narrower than in reading, suggesting that the test scores are predominately affected in language achievement.

Second, an alternative interpretation would be that PRONADE's teachers' quality plays a role. In this vein, teacher quality would be more important for math than for language achievement. Unfortunately, there is no data to test this hypothesis. However, one should remember the discussion on the evaluation studies of PRONADE schools, equally pointing into this direction.

The effects for the two other school forms are rather straightforward. New Multi-grade Schools (NEU) are significantly and positively correlated with language achievement, but less so for math. This may point out that self-directed learning of children at various ages significantly strengthens comprehensive skills but has no effect on math achievement. The finding that students' achievement scores is negatively correlated with Guatemalan bilingual education (DIGEBI) points out the lack of good-quality bilingual education for most Mayan students. This is a product of the situation that bilingual textbooks and formally trained teachers are virtually unavailable in most DIGEBI schools, and that the program as a whole suffers from chronic under-funding.

(2) Student's characteristics. Another important finding here is the negative effect of the indigenous dummy variables. The effect is more pronounced for reading comprehension than for math computation. The fact that speaking an indigenous language is negatively correlated with achievement scores, and that the effect is so strong, points specifically to the importance of bilingual education. However, not only language barriers may play a role. The World Bank (2003a) finds that rural indigenous children are often affected by chronic malnutrition. In addition, given this disadvantage, children tend to enter school late: often they are physically not strong enough to walk the long distances.

Table 38. Determinants of Achievement for Primary Schooling in Rural Guatemala, 3rd Grade, 2000

	Dependent variable:			
	(1)		(2)	
Explanatory variables a/	Reading comprehension score		Math computation score	
Constant	-50.14**	(19.1)	42.41**	(15.6)
Age (years)	-0.396*	(-2.06)	0.217	(1.09)
Dummy indigenous b/	-10.16**	(-13.8)	-4.280**	(5.56)
Dummy girl	-2.256**	(-4.69)	-4.715**	(-9.17)
Television (hours/day)	1.384**	(6.53)	1.018**	(4.69)
Father's education (years)	0.306**	(2.85)	0.351**	(3.02)
Mother's education (years)	0.379**	(3.45)	0.134*	(2.33)
Father's homework assistance (hours/week)	0.141*	(2.56)	0.351**	(3.02)
Dummy repeater	-0.862+	(-1.67)	-1.860**	(-3.43)
Number of students/teacher	-0.059**	(-2.64)	-0.073**	(-3.12)
Number of books used in classroom	1.558**	(3.94)	1.107**	(2.68)
Dummy student has own books	-1.226*	(-2.26)	0.272	(0.47)
Number of sanitary/student	0.580**	(5.30)	0.333**	(2.94)
Dummy electricity (school)	4.580**	(7.47)	2.693**	(4.16)
Dummy drainage (school)	2.216**	(3.55)	2.227**	(3.43)
Dummy PRONADE (community school)	-2.244	(-1.32)	-4.835*	(-2.24)
Dummy NEU (multi-grade school)	3.063*	(1.97)	1.808	(0.96)
Dummy DIGEBI (bilingual school)	-5.879**	(-6.93)	-2.948**	(-3.27)
Adjusted R^2	0.329		0.142	
S.E. of regression	15.24		16.25	
F-statistic	64.76		19.56	
N	4221		4221	

Huber/White heteroskedasticity-consistent t-statistics in parenthesis.

+Significant at 10, * significant at 5%, ** significant at 1%.

a/ Estimated by OLS. Binary variables equal 1 if response is yes. The explanatory variables include 21 Departmental dummies, of which 16 are statistically significant at 5 percent or better. b/ Ethnicity according to the speaking of an indigenous language.

Source: Author's calculations based on PRONERE (2000) school survey data.

The other findings can be briefly outlined. The fact that girls score on average lower than boys suggests that gender discrimination plays a role in rural

Guatemala. Repetition was weekly correlated with language comprehension scores. The effect of repetition, however, was negative for math achievement. Over-aged children score worse in reading comprehension than their average aged counterparts. This suggests that attention should be given to late enrollment. Both father's and mother's education is significantly associated with higher test scores. However, only the father's assistance in homework has a significant impact on student achievement — the variable for mother's assistance had an insignificant impact on student achievement. Consequently, it was removed from the equations. The insignificance is likely to be due to the low level of adult female education in rural Guatemala.

Finally, the daily hours of watching television had a positive correlation with both language and math test scores. This strong impact suggests that the availability of television may not only be interpreted in terms of achieving cognitive skills by watching television but in particular marking the household's socio-economic status: the availability of television requires a connection to the electricity net.

(3) Physical and pedagogical inputs. The student-teacher ratio shows a negative correlation with student achievement. However, the quantitative effect is modest in magnitude. This is an interesting finding since the student-teacher ratio is often used as an additional indicator for quality of schooling. In Guatemala, however, it seems to be less irrelevant (this may also be an outcome of the suspected poor teachers' quality and their often-missing commitment). By contrast, the number of books *used* in the *classroom* is positively correlated with student achievement. The effect is more pronounced for reading comprehension than for mathematics. A puzzling finding, however, is that the *ownership* of books has a negative correlation with student achievement. Consequently, one may ask whether these books are indeed used appropriately. Finally, the availability of schooling infrastructure such as electricity (light) as well as sanitary and drainage facilities has a very strong and significant effect on student achievement.

Overall, school organizational practices, student characteristics, and physical and pedagogical inputs have an influence on achievement. It appears that PRONADE schools have no impact on student achievement regarding language, and a negative one on mathematics. This *may* be used to point out the missing bilingual education component of the program. Alternatively, PRONADE teachers may underperform when compared to the traditional system. Another finding is that physical and pedagogical inputs are quantitatively among the most important determinants for student achievement. Consequently, concentrating on just a few aspects — such as sanitation, electricity, and the availability of books — may lead to substantial improvements in student achievement in rural Guatemala. However, the results should be treated with some caution. As with most studies of this genre, the available data only explains a small amount of the variance and the equations may suffer from selectivity bias.

V. Conclusion

PRONADE has concentrated its efforts in expanding primary school and preschool enrollments. The PRONADE model has been remarkably successful in expanding educational opportunities in rural areas. Moreover, the decentralized nature of the program has been instrumental in getting families more involved in their children's schooling. It may also have generated a number of positive externalities at the community level, such as a greater participation in civic affairs, generation of non-farm income possibilities, and the strengthening of local organization skills. But has it delivered more? This study has assessed the impact of PRONADE through summarizing key findings from evaluation studies and presented an — admittedly rough and preliminary — empirical analysis student achievement.

The main findings indicate first, that the institutional structure of PRONADE has been less beneficial than originally expected. Due to administrative and financial difficulties there have been delays in payments of teacher salaries and providing teaching materials. The non-competitive salary structure, in terms of social benefits, has hampered the teachers' commitment to the program. Furthermore, a key invention of the program — the involvement of NGO-backed Educational Service Institution — has been thought to assist the local communities in school management and to provide inputs for multi-grade and bilingual training. The evidence reveals unfortunately that de facto only a few NGOs fulfill this expectation adequately. The dominance of few institutions also runs the risk of politicizing the project. Consequently, one challenge for PRONADE will be the integration of the program into Guatemala's formal education system.

Second, there is evidence that community-led schools underperform on student achievement tests when compared to traditional rural schools or bilingual and multi-grade programs. This is not surprising since PRONADE students come from the most disadvantaged backgrounds. What *is* interesting is that, after controlling for student background and for physical and pedagogical inputs, the differences disappear for reading comprehension but not for numerical computations. Regarding reading comprehension, the results suggest that community-managed schools may have no significant impact on student achievement. Here PRONADE schools appear to be comparable with the traditional system.

However, math achievement is significantly lower than in traditional rural schools. The negative correlation may point out to the missing bilingual curriculum in most community-managed schools. An alternative interpretation would be that the teacher quality plays a role. However, there is no data available to test the hypothesis that PRONADE teachers underperform when compared to the traditional system. Despite these shortcomings, however, one should take into account that without PRONADE schools it is likely that many children would not have had access to education at all.

In-depth evaluations of the program with richer data and more sophisticated methods are needed to determine the impact of the PRONADE program on student achievement, repetition and dropout rates, and also to determine the effectiveness of its teachers. In the past, one important feature of PRONADE has been its ability to receive feedback and adopt the recommendations from evaluations (see for example the CIEN 1999 evaluation). If this practice continues, evaluations of the program could prove a valuable input to improve PRONADE's schools quality.

Third, community-managed schools are not a panacea to solve the complicated issues contributing to poor educational access and quality in developing countries. For the case of rural Guatemala, the empirical results clearly indicate that other issues, many of them apparently beyond the question of school organization forms, play a role. Indeed, one of the key problems needing to be addressed is the question on how to provide a *good-quality* bilingual education for the disadvantaged indigenous children. Solving this problem has strong implications regarding the funding of such programs, teacher training, and the elaboration and distribution of school materials.

Moreover, it appears that concentrating on only a few objectives, such as a better school infrastructure in terms of sanitation and electric light, and the de facto availability of books, is at least as important as the question of school organization form. Finally, the causes for students being absent in rural Guatemala should be thoroughly researched and analyzed. In this regard, conditional cash transfer programs, offering a potentially promising way for promoting better educational outcomes, may play a role.

Concluding Remarks

In distinct parts of this study, an attempt has been made to detect how Guatemala can increase the access and quality of its educational system and, in particular, to disentangle some selected threads of the empirical relationships between economic growth, human capital formation, and biodiversity conservation in Guatemala. To conclude, some personal observations should be made.

By no means being the only driving force, human capital investment constitutes, nevertheless, a path towards enhancing future growth and slowing down the loss of biodiverse wealth. Given the manifold interactions documented here, however, one hesitates to claim that human capital alone can be the panacea. One generalization, though, makes sense. Insufficient per capita growth and current resource degradation are both correlated to a single deficiency, which is Guatemala's tremendous failure in the past to invest in broad-based human capital accumulation and other measures aiming to promote countrywide socio-economic outcomes. By remedying this immense deficit, the country's economic activities could be strengthened and become less dependent on the exploitation of natural wealth. Ultimately, as human capital accumulates, it seems that people better acquire the appreciation of biodiversity that natural resources deserve.

By the same token, failure to engage in human capital investment could perpetuate the historical disadvantage of Guatemala, hamper economic growth, impair rural livelihoods, and continue the destruction of environmental wealth. Consequently, increased funding allocated to the development of human capital for all citizens of Guatemala should be a serious commitment, if indeed the situation painted here is to improve. The elite of the country should be made to understand the advantage of living in a country where all citizens are educated and healthy. This will be the challenge for the Guatemalan society, where the affluent appear to have believed for hundreds of years that property and power is dependent on an impoverished, low-skilled class. Whether policy makers indeed move in this direction, remains to be seen.

Appendices

Appendix One

1. Augmented Dickey-Fuller Test for Unit Roots

	ADF test statistic	
Variables	Levels	First differences
log y	-2.24	-4.87**
log k	-1.85	-4.36**
log k (4 percent depreciation)	-1.76	-4.38**
log k (disaggregated estimate)	-1.33	-2.99*
log k (quality adjusted)	-2.04	-2.97*
log h	-0.23	-2.97*
log h (Barro and Lee)	-0.72	-4.76**
log h (Cohen and Soto)	-1.49	-4.54**
log primary schooling	-1.18	-3.37**
log secondary schooling	-0.07	-3.23**
log tertiary schooling	-1.35	-4.33**
log life expectancy	-2.41	-4.25**
log trade volume/GDP	-1.91	-4.21**
log terms of trade	-2.03	-5.20**
log capital imports/investment	-2.05	-4.74**
log military expenditure/GDP	-1.45	-5.17**

** (*) Rejects the hypothesis of a unit root at the 1 (5) percent significance level assuming 1 lag in the test equation, constant included. The MacKinnon critical values are –3.59 (-2.93) at the 1 (5) percent level.

2. Primary Time Series Data Sources

Variables	Abbreviation	Source
Gross domestic product (GDP) (in 1958 Quetzals)	Y	*Banco de Guatemala.*
Capital stock (in 1958 Quetzals)	K	Perpetual inventory estimates, see text.
Gross fixed capital formation (in 1958 Quetzals)	I	*Banco de Guatemala.* Aggregated data is for 1950-2002, disaggregated information applies to 1970-2002.
Annual rental rates	$v_{i,t}$	Calculations are based on Morán and Valle (2002) data set for implicit price estimates, and *Banco de Guatemala* for disaggregated gross fixed capital formation and real interest rates.
Physical capital quality index	zq	Estimated, see text.
Imports (in 1958 Quetzals)	IM	*Banco de Guatemala.*
Imported capital goods (in 1958 Quetzals)	IM_{cap}	*Banco de Guatemala.*
Exports (in 1958 Quetzals)	EX	*Banco de Guatemala.*
Commodity terms of trade (1970=100)	ToT	CEPAL and CIEN (*Centro de Investigaciones Económicas Nacionales*).
Military expenditure (in 1958 Quetzals)	MIL_{exp}	Ministry of Defense expenditures are calculated from *Banco de Guatemala*, as reported in *Memorias de Labores del Banco Central*. The data compares favorably with information from the Stockholm International Peace Research Institute (SIPRI).
Life expectancy at birth (years)		World Bank (2002).
Average schooling (years)	h	Perpetual inventory estimates, see text.
Participation of primary, secondary and tertiary education in labor force	hr_{pri} hr_{sec} hr_{ter}	Perpetual inventory estimates, see text.
Population statistics (15 and 20 year old, 15-64 year old)	L15 L20 L15-64	CEPAL and CELADE (2000).

Continued on following page.

Variables	Abbreviation	Source
Labor force, total	L	Derived from the number of private contributors to the IGSS, see text. Data for 1960-2002 is taken from *Banco de Guatemala* (2003). Data for 1955-1959 is obtained directly from IGSS. Missing values for 1950-1954 were derived from SEGEPLAN (1978).
Labor quality index	hq	Author's calculations, see text. The weights are taken from Table 6, columns 2, 4 and 6.
Primary and secondary gross enrollment ratios	PRI SEC	For 1960-1990 UNESCO estimates as reported in World Bank (2002). For 1991-2002 *Ministerio de Educación* (various years) and UNDP (2002). Primary gross enrollment ratios are that of *nivel primaria*. Secondary gross enrollment ratios are that of *nivel básico*. Missing values were completed with information provided in UNESCO (various), Mitchell (1998) and *Ministerio de Educación* and SEGEPLAN (1980).
Tertiary gross enrollment ratio	TER	For 1960-1987 UNESCO estimates as reported in World Bank (2002). Missing values were either interpolated or completed with information provided in Mitchell (1998), UNESCO (1966) and UNESCO (various). For 1988-2002 ratio of students at San Carlos University (USAC) to the number of persons aged 20-24, as reported in Global Info Group (1999) and UNDP (2003a).

3. Time Series Data Used in Growth Regressions, 1950-2003

Years	Y	I	$K_{d=0.05}$	IM	EX	IM_{cap}	Mil_{exp}	ToT	zq	hq	IGSS	L	$hr_{no\ school}$	hr_{pri}	hr_{sec}	hr_{ter}	h
	thousand of 1958 Quetzals							Indices (1970=100)			workers		percent				
1950	722344	81670	1086913	104911	91487	18124	5822	166.0	NA	NA	NA	947442	72.3	24.9	2.3	0.5	1.249
1951	732525	79933	1112501	94472	82006	16018	5725	164.3	NA	NA	NA	917001	70.8	26.1	2.7	0.4	1.315
1952	747724	68940	1125815	84967	91236	12812	6751	165.0	NA	NA	NA	886560	69.5	27.2	3.0	0.3	1.374
1953	775292	67590	1137115	95080	93898	15428	6543	169.1	NA	NA	NA	856118	68.3	28.2	3.3	0.2	1.430
1954	789610	67039	1147298	105768	87010	16300	6760	183.8	NA	NA	NA	825677	67.2	29.1	3.5	0.2	1.483
1955	809107	90420	1180353	121559	97153	23842	8196	181.3	NA	NA	198809	795236	66.1	30.0	3.7	0.2	1.534
1956	882711	142481	1263816	153196	105121	41275	8592	190.2	NA	NA	203572	814288	65.2	30.7	3.9	0.2	1.583
1957	932494	154221	1354847	167210	111078	39731	9310	182.1	NA	NA	236038	944152	64.6	31.2	4.0	0.2	1.618
1958	976055	136315	1423419	164338	121675	36581	9308	153.1	NA	NA	255548	1022192	64.1	31.5	4.1	0.3	1.647
1959	1024223	125518	1477766	163049	145950	35063	9950	142.7	NA	NA	255022	1020088	63.7	31.8	4.3	0.3	1.677
1960	1049199	107812	1511690	165231	152978	33094	9358	124.7	NA	NA	264100	1056400	63.3	32.0	4.4	0.3	1.704
1961	1094267	113473	1549578	152933	156614	31847	9413	113.2	NA	NA	269065	1076260	62.8	32.2	4.6	0.4	1.736
1962	1132984	108678	1580778	164752	162587	35528	9128	114.0	NA	NA	264884	1059536	62.2	32.5	4.8	0.4	1.778
1963	1241064	128805	1630544	213401	223030	46771	11196	117.1	NA	NA	274838	1099352	61.5	32.9	5.1	0.5	1.823
1964	1298557	157790	1706807	234186	214386	57591	9995	123.8	NA	NA	322289	1289156	60.9	33.3	5.3	0.5	1.866
1965	1355156	166770	1788236	246955	242406	54065	14526	111.2	NA	NA	345519	1382076	60.2	33.7	5.6	0.5	1.910
1966	1429923	165886	1864710	251070	297952	52302	15204	103.4	NA	NA	366946	1467784	59.5	34.2	5.8	0.5	1.948
1967	1488609	184262	1955737	267088	278854	53353	16653	99.5	NA	NA	367401	1469604	58.6	35.0	5.9	0.6	1.996
1968	1619203	209430	2067380	277748	313712	62055	15778	97.2	NA	NA	395808	1583232	57.5	35.9	6.0	0.6	2.046
1969	1695892	212709	2176720	271794	353881	59445	15462	100.4	NA	NA	446540	1786160	56.5	36.9	6.0	0.7	2.095
1970	1792754	209627	2277511	293287	346035	61002	27023	100.0	100.0	100.0	448276	1793104	55.3	38.0	6.1	0.7	2.148
1971	1892832	227404	2391040	312071	360376	73122	17643	97.0	99.9	103.3	442842	1771368	53.8	39.2	6.3	0.8	2.225
1972	2031552	226112	2497600	294733	412085	63183	18850	122.6	99.6	106.0	448378	1793512	52.5	40.1	6.6	0.9	2.302
1973	2169378	251898	2624618	324212	451602	69372	17478	109.3	99.1	108.2	468863	1875452	51.3	40.8	6.9	0.9	2.376
1974	2307675	247192	2740579	370700	481581	69703	19051	94.0	98.2	109.9	539792	2159168	50.4	41.2	7.3	1.0	2.442
1975	2352750	270567	2874117	352057	497495	82220	25618	93.3	98.1	111.6	520696	2082784	49.5	41.7	7.7	1.1	2.514
1976	2526537	371393	3101804	457126	530257	123898	27376	105.6	97.3	113.3	577920	2311680	48.5	42.0	8.3	1.2	2.595
1977	2723844	405798	3352512	499819	563254	122124	33697	135.3	95.6	114.8	708815	2835260	47.6	42.3	8.8	1.3	2.673
1978	2859913	435653	3620539	521600	562663	136120	35004	124.4	91.5	116.3	769045	3076180	46.6	42.5	9.4	1.4	2.756
1979	2994650	413362	3852874	482783	619160	109077	39651	112.2	88.0	118.1	756171	3024684	45.6	42.8	10.2	1.5	2.851
1980	3106877	372592	4032822	441194	651135	77301	42822	98.3	85.7	120.0	755542	3022168	44.4	43.0	11.0	1.6	2.956
1981	3127560	401472	4232654	423061	557408	72579	47199	89.0	84.5	122.3	591019	2364076	43.0	43.4	11.9	1.8	3.078
1982	3016573	357665	4378686	334288	510171	58520	56717	82.8	82.8	123.1	609144	2436576	42.5	43.4	12.3	1.8	3.131
1983	2939604	258193	4417945	267857	454693	27213	59962	84.5	82.8	124.3	583548	2334192	41.7	43.7	12.7	1.9	3.190
1984	2953546	234936	4431984	287205	440184	32933	63903	89.0	80.9	128.2	594936	2379744	40.0	45.0	13.1	1.9	3.284
1985	2936062	220153	4430537	250278	454017	32763	58511	80.7	79.8	131.6	631654	2526616	38.4	46.2	13.4	2.0	3.370
1986	2940175	228558	4437568	213598	390455	38735	48044	96.9	76.7	134.4	660444	2641776	37.0	47.1	14.0	2.0	3.460
1987	3044395	266133	4481822	315784	413999	74773	49471	86.4	75.7	135.6	678995	2715980	36.2	47.2	14.6	2.1	3.530
1988	3162873	299826	4557557	327741	437307	72815	49156	85.5	74.3	137.5	779560	3118240	35.1	47.5	15.3	2.1	3.617
1989	3287594	318903	4648582	346883	495427	74471	47291	84.3	73.8	139.3	788367	3153468	34.0	47.7	16.2	2.1	3.714
1990	3389552	286160	4702313	344322	527782	66684	40645	86.8	73.5	135.9	785753	3143012	35.4	46.8	15.0	2.8	3.665
1991	3513627	296816	4764013	369249	502024	70072	41812	94.7	73.1	132.3	786903	3147612	36.7	45.5	14.4	3.3	3.633
1992	3683616	385212	4911025	505961	543886	124052	45730	96.6	72.4	130.0	795708	3182832	37.5	44.5	14.3	3.6	3.635
1993	3828260	411831	5077304	527335	596287	136596	41296	90.8	72.5	128.4	823239	3292956	38.0	43.6	14.6	3.9	3.654
1994	3982682	401038	5224477	553498	616330	124076	43001	103.4	73.7	129.8	830324	3321296	37.1	44.0	14.8	4.1	3.727
1995	4179767	435901	5399154	595513	693745	135417	41367	116.4	75.6	129.9	855596	3422384	36.9	43.8	15.1	4.2	3.771
1996	4303395	427259	5556456	554652	754005	121748	35309	106.8	77.8	130.1	852243	3408972	36.7	43.8	15.2	4.3	3.792
1997	4491199	523411	5802044	662824	815100	160200	33365	115.5	78.9	131.3	844407	3377628	36.0	44.1	15.5	4.4	3.842
1998	4715468	614623	6126565	825223	834616	216859	34002	114.9	79.2	133.9	887228	3548912	34.8	45.1	15.6	4.5	3.912
1999	4896875	650313	6470550	831098	873042	238777	33065	106.2	78.5	140.3	893126	3572504	31.7	47.3	16.2	4.7	4.085
2000	5073597	593028	6740050	881261	906365	217171	41519	103.2	78.4	148.4	908122	3632488	27.6	49.6	17.8	5.0	4.363
2001	5191941	603899	7006946	942247	870201	201074	48695	101.0	77.7	152.9	927768	3711072	25.0	50.5	19.4	5.1	4.576
2002 p/	5308677	634792	7291391	1004538	811532	230673	36132	99.6	77.5	156.5	953052	3812208	22.7	50.8	21.3	5.2	4.784
2003 e/	5434976	631332	7558153	1028370	822463	NA	NA	NA	NA	NA	NA	NA	NA	NA	NA	NA	NA

p/ preliminary.
e/ estimated.

4. Central America and Mexico: Sources of Growth, 1961-2000 (in percent)

Data Adjusted for Quality of Labor [a/]

Country and time period	GDP growth	Contribution of Capital	Contribution of Labor	Contribution of TFP	Country and time period	GDP growth	Contribution of Capital	Contribution of Labor	Contribution of TFP
Guatemala		(0.33)	(0.67)		*El Salvador*		(0.42)	(0.58)	
1961-70	5.5	1.4	5.0	-0.9	1961-70	5.6	2.8	2.9	0.0
1971-80	5.7	2.0	5.0	-1.3	1971-80	2.3	3.0	1.8	-2.6
1981-90	0.9	0.5	1.4	-1.0	1981-90	-0.4	0.7	1.9	-3.0
1991-00	4.1	1.2	1.6	1.3	1991-00	4.6	2.0	2.3	0.3
Nicaragua		(N.A.)	(N.A.)		*Honduras*		(N.A.)	(N.A.)	
1961-70	6.8	2.9	3.0	0.9	1961-70	4.8	2.0	2.3	0.5
1971-80	0.4	1.8	2.5	-3.9	1971-80	5.4	2.2	2.9	0.3
1981-90	-1.4	0.8	2.4	-4.7	1981-90	2.4	1.1	3.9	-2.6
1991-00	3.3	0.7	3.2	-0.6	1991-00	3.2	1.8	2.9	-1.5
Costa Rica		(0.26)	(0.74)		*Mexico*		(0.41)	(0.59)	
1961-70	6.1	1.9	3.3	0.9	1961-70	6.7	3.3	2.7	0.7
1971-80	5.6	2.4	4.5	-1.3	1971-80	6.7	3.5	3.1	0.2
1981-90	2.4	1.0	2.9	-1.5	1981-90	1.8	1.7	3.5	-3.4
1991-00	5.3	1.5	2.4	1.4	1991-00	3.5	1.6	1.9	0.1

Source: Author's calculations for Guatemala. Loayza et al. (2002) for Central America and Mexico — data here refers to the growth accounting exercise 2 (adjustments for changes in the quality of labor associated with increases in educational attainment). a/ Factor shares are in brackets. Discrepancies are due to rounding.

5. Guatemala and Chile: Sources of Growth, 1971-2000 (in percent)

Data Adjusted for Quality of Capital and Labor [a/]

Country and time period	GDP growth	Contribution of			Country and time period	GDP growth	Contribution of		
		Capital	Labor	TFP			Capital	Labor	TFP
Guatemala		(0.33)	(0.67)		*Chile*		(0.44)	(0.56)	
1971-75	5.6	1.5	3.6	0.5	1971-75	-2.0	1.1	0.3	-3.5
1976-80	5.7	1.5	6.4	-2.1	1976-80	6.8	0.7	3.4	2.7
1981-85	-1.1	0.2	-0.7	-0.5	1981-85	-0.1	1.5	2.2	-3.8
1986-90	2.9	-0.1	3.5	-0.4	1986-90	6.5	1.9	3.7	0.9
1991-95	4.3	1.1	0.6	2.6	1991-95	7.5	4.1	1.9	1.4
1996-00	4.0	1.8	2.6	-0.4	1996-00	...	...	...	...

Source: Author's calculations for Guatemala. Roldós (1997) for Chile. a/ Factor shares are in brackets. Discrepancies are due to rounding.

Appendix Two

1. Data Used in Regional Deforestation Model, 1975-1988

Departament	Forest cover		Population	Microfinca land area	Rural extreme poverty	Rural non-farm employment	Maize yield	Mean years of schooling
	1976-77	1987-88	1981	1979	1989	1994	1986-87	1989
	km^2		thousand	km^2	share of total population	share of econ. act. population	qq/mz	years
El Progreso	560	262	81	3.5	0.510	0.275	0.048	3.2
Sacatepéquez	147	100	121	15.4	0.369	0.554	0.123	3.6
Chimaltenango	680	552	230	37.8	0.757	0.149	0.186	2.8
Escuintla	306	181	335	14.7	0.604	0.303	0.265	2.7
Santa Rosa	510	210	194	14.7	0.651	0.152	0.197	3.1
Sololá	211	158	154	32.2	0.791	0.206	0.160	2.0
Totonicapán	368	322	204	55.3	0.806	0.592	0.226	1.5
Quetzaltenango	420	327	367	56.7	0.671	0.239	0.431	3.4
Suchitepéquez	262	142	238	21.0	0.642	0.233	0.229	2.6
Retalhuleu	200	12	151	18.9	0.557	0.214	0.284	2.8
San Marcos	806	515	472	67.2	0.819	0.137	0.227	1.9
Huehuetenango	2030	1919	431	62.3	0.947	0.146	0.164	1.8
El Quiché	3370	3267	328	58.8	0.878	0.178	0.124	1.1
Baja Verapaz	1310	972	116	7.7	0.941	0.143	0.135	2.3
Alta Verapaz	4218	1943	322	29.4	0.907	0.106	0.120	1.0
El Petén	21760	19385	132	2.1	0.681	0.069	0.197	2.6
Izabal	2993	2253	195	6.3	0.399	0.234	0.124	2.9
Zacapa	770	461	169	4.2	0.670	0.237	0.043	3.3
Chiquimula	971	208	116	11.2	0.902	0.113	0.040	1.7
Jalapa	945	197	136	7.0	0.748	0.096	0.034	2.3
Jutiapa	370	55	251	10.5	0.725	0.117	0.059	2.6

Source: See Table 24. Data for maize yield not used in the regressions due to insignificance. 1 quintal (qq) = 45.4 kg or 100 lbs. 1 manzana (mz) = 0.7 hectares.

2. ENCOVI (2000) Survey Variables

Variable	Code	Annotation
Cultivated agricultural land area (hectares) in rural Guatemala	area = 2 tcuerda p16b02a p16b02b	1 *acre* = 0.44 hectares 1 *caballería* = 45.08 hectares 1 *manzana* = 0.7 hectares 1 *tarea* ≈ 0.007 hectares 1 *cuerda* (25 *varas*) = 0.044 hectares all other *cuerdas* ≈ 0.05 hectares
Firewood time (minutes)	p01a41a p01a41c p01a41d	p01a41c*60 + p01a41d zero if p01a41a = 0
Service point time (minutes)	p01e04a p01e04b	p01e04a*60 + p01e04b (service points are markets, churches, administrative units, bus stations, public telephones or banks)
Number of rooms	p01a07	
Years living at farm	p01c09	
Weekly worked hours of household head	p10p04 p10b05 p10b08 p10c05 p10c06 p10c09	p10p04*p10b05*p10b08/52 + p10c05*p10c06*p10c09/52 (average weekly worked hours in first job and second job)
Age of household head (years)	edad	
Education household head (years)	p07b27a p07b27b	No education and preschool = 0 adult and primary = b07b27b secondary = 6 + b027b27b tertiary = 12 + b07b27b post-graduate = 15 + b07b27b
Household size (persons)	thogar	Number of persons living in household
Dummy rural non-farm employment	p10b02 = 1	1 = first job of household head in non-agricultural occupation
Dummy indigenous	p05b05 ≤ 7	1 = household head indigenous (self-identification)
Dummy technical assistance	p16f01 = 1	1 = household head received agricultural assistance
Dummy female head	p05a02 = 1 sexo = 1	1 = female household head
Dummy piped water	p01a05a = 1	1 = connection to piped water
Dummy basic sanitation	p01a05b = 1	1 = connection to sanitation
Dummy electricity	p01a05c = 1	1 = connection to electricity
Departmental dummies	p10b29	21 regional dummies with residence derived from place of first work, base = Department of Guatemala

3. Environmental Module ENSMI (1999) Survey Variables

Variable	Code	Annotation
Extension of plot (hectares)	p940$1 p940$2 p940$3	Cultivated land area of first, second and third parcel in hectares (1 *manzana* = 0.7 hectares)
Distance to plot (minutes)	p944h$1 p944m$1	Travel time to first parcel in minutes: p944h$1*60 + p944m$1
Number of rooms	hv216 (ENSMI) [a/]	Number of sleeping rooms
Years owning first plot	p940a$1	
Age of household head (years)	hv220 (ENSMI)	
Household size (persons)	qhmember	Number of persons living in household
Education household head (years)	p900du p900dn missing values from hv108 (ENSMI)	No education = 0 alphabetized = 3 primary = p900dn secondary = 6+ p900dn tertiary = 12 + p900dn
Dummy rural non-farm employment	p928 ≠ 61	1 = primarily non-agricultural income source of household head
Dummy temporary farm work	p923 = 1	1 = household head has temporarily worked on large farms during past 12 months
Dummy born in the Petén	p902 = 1	1 = household head born in the Petén
Dummy indigenous	qhidib > 1	1 = household head indigenous (mother-tongue indigenous)
Dummy squatter plot (*arragada*)	p939$1 = 7	1 = squatter plot without formal, transitorily or communal title
Dummy green manures	p965 = 1	1 = use of green manures (*abonos verdes*)
Dummy piped water	p978 = 1 missing values = 0	1 = access to piped water
Dummy basic sanitation	hv205 (ENSMI) = 21 or 31	1 = connection to sanitation
Municipal dummies	qhmpio qhsecc	11 regional dummies: municipality 3, section 6; municipality 4, sections 2, 3 and 4; municipality 5, sections 3, 4, 14 and 15; municipality 8, section 7; municipality 9 section 3, and municipality 12, section 9

a/ ENSMI in parenthesis signifies that the variable does not come from the Environmental *Module* of the ENSMI (1999) but from the larger health *survey* ENSMI (1999).

4. Guatemala's Land Distribution: Number of Farms, 1950-2000
(in 1,000 farms)

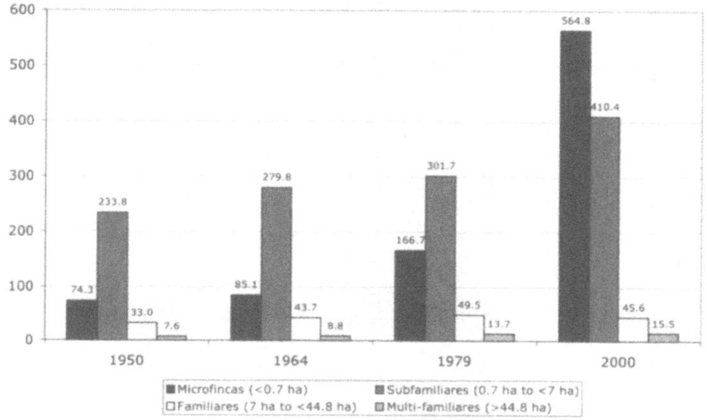

Source: Author's calculations based on data from SEGEPLAN and MAGA (1984) for 1950-1979, and UNDP (2002) for 2000.

5. Guatemala's Land Distribution: Farm Area, 1950-2000
(in million hectares)

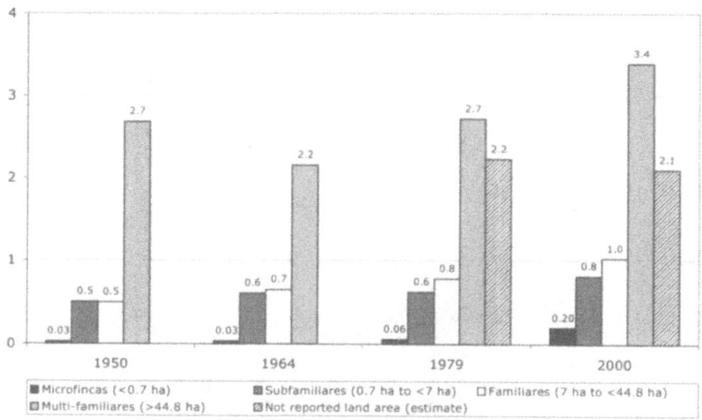

Source: Author's calculations, based on data from SEGEPLAN and MAGA (1984) for 1950-1979, and UNDP (2002) for 2000. The right balk (estimate) for 1979 and 2000 quantifies the 'missing' agricultural land not reported in census data when compared to the land use data from Baumeister (2001).

6. Guatemala: Synopsis of Deforestation Studies

Study	Methodology, research focus and time period	Area	Key results
Bilsborrow (1992)	*Qualitative:* explores underlying causal structure	Countrywide The Petén	(a) Population growth and rural migration are associated with environmental degradation; (b) research gaps related to migrant's origin areas and underlying causes of migration to the agricultural frontier
Cabrera (1995)	*Qualitative:* historical overview from Mayan civilization until the mid 1990s	Countrywide	For recent deforestation: (a) agricultural expansion as main direct source; (b) social tensions due to the large-scale promotion of protected areas; (c) massive pressure on forests due to the return of civil war migrants; (b) hypothesizes on the importance of rural non-farm employment
Defensores de la Naturaleza (2001)	*Empirical:* assess the impact of agricultural intensification on land use in 1998	Sierra de las Minas Biosphere Reserve	(a) Agricultural intensification practices increase the demand for agricultural land use; (b) open access provides no incentive for being efficient in land use and increasing agricultural productivity
Elías et al. (1997)	*Qualitative:* multidisciplinary overview to the potential underlying causes until the mid 1990s	Countrywide The Petén Western Highlands	(a) Socio-economic imbalances of Guatemala's export-led growth model and limited non-agricultural employment opportunities increase rural migration; (b) rural migration flows as key determinant of deforestation in the Petén; (c) managed colonization replaced by spontaneous colonization in the Petén; (d) population growth and poverty associated with environmental degradation in Western Highlands
FAO (1999)	*Qualitative:* synthesizes results mainly from local studies between 1979-1999, targeted interviews	Countrywide	(a) No general agreement on the causes of deforestation during the past decades; (b) agricultural and pasture expansion as main direct sources of deforestation; (c) literature with a focus on poverty, population and productivity issues during the 1990s, pasture expansion more important during the 1980s
FLACSO (2000)	*Qualitative:* multidisciplinary collection of recent studies (some are mentioned here)	The Petén	Mixed evidence to be divided into four categories: (a) socio-economic causes of deforestation; (b) 2 empirical contributions; (c) personal and institutional experiences; (d) proposals for future investigations

Continued on following page.

Study	Methodology, research focus and time period	Area	Key results
Grunberg et al. (2000)	*Empirical:* spatial regression 1986-1999 and simulations of deforestation scenarios	Maya Biosphere Reserve, Buffer Zone	(a) Soil quality, (b) distance to road and (c) human settlement as key indicators for deforestation trends; (d) little impact of wage labor
Kaimowitz (1996)	*Qualitative:* analyzes underlying causes of livestock expansion from 1979 until mid 1990s	Central America The Petén	(a) Favorable markets for livestock products, subsidized credits and road construction spur deforestation; (b) land tenure politics give incentives for deforestation; (c) limited technological change in livestock production; (d) forest policies reduce timber values; (e) political violence reduces deforestation in the 1980s
Kaimowitz (1995)	*Qualitative:* analyzes how land tenure politics have influenced land use from the 1960s until the mid 1990s; targeted interviews	The Petén Northern Transversal	(a) Pasture expansion as main determinant of deforestation; (b) land sold below market prices to privileged people; (c) subsidized credits and road construction increased land prices; (d) pasture expansion limited land clearing by small farmers; (e) inadequate land tenure politics gave incentives for deforestation; (f) political violence reduces deforestation in the 1980s; (g) Northern Transversal strip shows less favorable patterns for pasture expansion; (h) natural resource management by the government remains ineffective
Katz (2000), based on World Bank (1995a)	*Qualitative:* explores impact of land tenure regimes on deforestation	The Petén Western Highlands	(a) Social capital can substitute for well-defined property rights if it fosters a sense of ownership and respect for boundaries, as in the Western Highlands; (b) absence of property rights and social capital can lead to resource mining, as in the Petén
Nations et al. (1999)	*Qualitative:* multidisciplinary collection of environmentalist's studies, some deforestation studies	Maya Biosphere Reserve, the Petén	*Mixed evidence:* authors emphasize the role of (a) population growth; (b) extraction and illegal logging activities; (c) oil exploitation and road construction; (d) the need for increased female participation in conservation projects and (d) ecotourism. *Policy recommendations:* (a) tackle direct sources of deforestation; (b) promote agricultural intensification and credit expansion; (c) strengthen resource tenure; (d) promote local participation and ecotourism

Continued on following page.

Study	Methodology, research focus and time period	Area	Key results
Sader et al. (2001)	*Empirical:* estimates of forest cover change 1986-1997	Maya Biosphere Reserve	*Empirical finding:* (a) Annual forest clearing rates for the Maya Biosphere Reserve and its buffer zones increased over time; *Qualitative findings:* (b) smallholder encroachment plays a significant role; (c) agricultural expansion is particularly high in the buffer zone; (d) essentially all change occurs along road or river corridors
Schwartz (1987; 1990; 1995a; 1995b)	*Qualitative: anthropological* analysis beginning in the 18th century	The Petén	(a) Describes the history of socio-economic patterns in post-conquest Petén in relation to the regional ecology: low levels of socio-economic development in the Petén endured with continuity; (b) describes the colonization process beginning in the 1960s: rapid deforestation due to shifting cultivation, ranching, extraction activities and logging; (c) indigenous repression and unequal distribution of wealth as underlying root causes for migration to the Petén
Shriar (2001) based on Ph.D. dissertation	*Qualitative:* assess the impact of agricultural intensification around 1999	Maya Biosphere Reserve Buffer Zone, The Petén	(a) Labor intensive agricultural intensification programs carried out by development organizations and NGOs are unattractive for most farmers; (b) environmentalists place little or no emphasis on underlying socio-economic structure of land use decisions
Southgate and Basterrechea (1993)	*Qualitative:* overview of the potential underlying causes	Countrywide	*Speculative:* (a) Population growth and rural migration; (b) inappropriate property regimes; (c) inadequate human capital formation; (d) weak agricultural research base
Valenzuela de Pisano (1996)	*Qualitative:* historical overview and two case studies	Countrywide The Petén Sierra de la Minas Biosphere Reserve	(a) Deforestation until the 1970s is due to the expansion of export crops; (b) social imbalances and planned migration opens the agricultural frontier in the Petén; (c) population growth and subsistence agriculture as main determinants of deforestation; (d) development institutions and NGOs are inefficient because they neglect the underlying causal structure of deforestation. *Policy recommendations:* (a) land redistribution; (b) technological change; (c) agricultural and socio-economic research; (d) environmental education; (e) international cooperation efforts

Continued on following page.

Study	Methodology, research focus and time period	Area	Key results
World Bank (1995a)	*Qualitative:* explores impact of land tenure regimes on deforestation	The Petén Northern Transversal Western Highlands	(a) Describes deforestation patterns; (b) population growth, rural migration, limited technology, skewed land distribution and poverty in origin areas are determinants of deforestation; (c) pasture expansion and logging is also important in the Petén; (d) unclear land tenure regimes incentive shifting cultivation practices; (e) however, in the Western Highlands unclear land tenure regimes are substituted by informal rules. *Policy recommendations:* (a) land tenure and institutional reforms; (b) agricultural research; (c) rural development; (d) technical assistance

Source: Author's elaboration.

7. Guatemala: Forest Cover Estimates, 1950-2000

Year	Forest cover (percent of total area)	Forest cover (km^2)	Annual deforestation (hectares)	Source
1950	65.0	70,451	...	INAFOR (1982)
1950	65.2	71,000	...	OAS (1991)
1970	47.0	51,000	...	Leonard (1987)
1975-76	39.7	43,750	...	Mittak (1977)
1977	33.0	36,100	...	INAFOR (1982)
1950-77	...	...	63,700	INAFOR (1982)
1979	39.7	43,230	...	Baumeister (2001)
1980	42.0	45,500	...	Wilkie (1993)
1980	40.4	44,000	...	CONAMA (1999b)
1982	...	...	60,000	Nations und Komer (1983)
1983	...	...	60,000	Leonard (1987)
1981-85	...	...	90,000	WRI (1996)
1987-88	37.3	40,650	...	Sagastume (1992)
1989	...	...	70,000	Kaimowitz (1996)
1989	40.0	43,754	55,600	Escobar et al. (1989)
1981-90	...	...	81,000	FAO (2002)
1990	...	...	60,000-90,000	PAFG (1996)
1990	33.9	37,000	90,000	Utting (1993)
1990	38.6	42,000	...	FAO (2002)

Continued on following page.

Years	Forest cover (percent of total area)	Forest cover (km^2)	Annual deforestation (hectares)	Source
1990	39.1	42,253	...	FAO (2002)
1991	...	...	90,000	Merlet et al. (1992)
1992	31.1	33,900	...	PAFG (1996)
1992	31.1	33,902	...	CONAMA et al. (1999b)
1977-92	...	...	65,900	CONAMA et al. (1999b)
1993	48.0	52,710	...	WRI (1996)
1993	...	...	90,000	Wilkie (1993)
1995	34.4	38,410	...	FAO (2002)
1996	34.0	37,500	...	PAFG (1996)
1996	31.9	34,801	82,000	CCAD (1998)
1996	28.1	30,620	...	López (1998)
1997	...	...	90,000	CONAP (1997)
1997	...	...	82,000	FAO (2002)
1998	26.0	28,982	...	CONAMA et al. (1999b)
1999	29.2	31,760		Baumeister (2001)
1979-99	...	...	57,350	Baumeister (2001)
1998-99	34.6	37,727	...	INAB (2000)
2000	26.3	28,497	...	FAO (2001)
1990-2000	...	...	53,743	FAO (2001)

Source: Loening and Markussen (2003).

Appendix Three

1. Descriptive Statistics for Primary Schooling Achievement in Rural Guatemala, 3rd Grade, 2000

Variables (N = 4421) [a/]	Mean	S.D.
Reading comprehension score	58.4	18.6
Math comprehension score	46.4	17.2
Age (years)	10.7	1.48
Dummy indigenous	0.69	0.46
Dummy girl	0.47	0.50
Television (hours/day)	1.31	1.19
Father's education (years)	2.57	2.79
Mother's education (years)	2.01	2.49
Father's homework assistance (hours/week)	3.75	5.27
Dummy repeater	0.53	0.50
Number of students/teacher	34.9	11.9
Number of books used in classroom	0.80	0.65
Dummy student has own books	0.30	0.46
Number of sanitary/student	0.05	0.29
Dummy electricity (school)	0.21	0.41
Dummy drainage (school)	0.77	0.42
Dummy PRONADE (community school)	0.02	0.14
Dummy NEU (multi-grade school)	0.02	0.14
Dummy DIGEBI (bilingual school)	0.16	0.37

Source: Author's calculations based on PRONERE (2000) data. S.D. = standard deviation. a/ Binary variables equal 1 if response is yes.

2. PRONERE (2000) School Survey Variables

Variable	Code
Reading comprehension score	etotmat
Math comprehension score	etotlec
Age (years)	edad
Dummy indigenous (speaks Maya)	hablamaya = 1
Dummy girl	sexo = 2
Television (hours/day)	horastv
Father's education (years)	gradpapa
Mother's education (years)	gradmama
Father's homework assistance (hours/week)	asispap
Dummy repeater	vecesrep > 0
Number of students/teacher	alumaest
Number of books used in classroom	librocan
Dummy student has own books	libroprop
Number of toilets/student (school)	cuansan/cuanalumn
Dummy electricity (school)	luz = 2
Dummy drainage (school)	drenaje = 2
Dummy PRONADE (community school)	programa = 3
Dummy NEU (multi-grade school)	programa = 4
Dummy DIGEBI (bilingual school)	programa = 5

References

Acuerdos de Paz (Peace Accords) (1998), 3rd edition, edited by the Instituto de Investigaciones Económicas y Sociales at the Universidad Rafael Landívar, Ministerio de Educación, Secretaría de la Paz and the Swedish Government, Guatemala.

Agesa, R. U. (2000), "The Incentive for Rural to Urban Migration: A Re-Examination of the Harris-Todaro Model", *Applied Economic Letters*, Vol. 7, No. 2, pp. 107-110.

Andersen, L. E. (1997), "Modeling the Relationship Between Government Policy, Economic Growth, and Deforestation in the Brazilian Amazon", *Working Paper* 1997/2, Department of Economics, University of Aarhus.

Anderson, L. E. (2001), "Guatemala: The Education Sector", *Technical Paper* 2, Guatemala Poverty Assessment Program, Washington D.C., World Bank, mimeo.

Angelsen, A. (1995), "Shifting Cultivation and Deforestation: A Study from Indonesia", *World Development*, Vol. 23, No. 10, pp. 1713-1729.

Angelsen, A. (1999), "Agricultural expansion and deforestation: modelling the impact of population, market forces and property rights", *Journal of Development Economics*, Vol. 58, pp. 185-218.

Angelsen, A., E. F. Shitindi and J. Aarrestad (1999), "Why Do Farmers Expand Their Land into Forests? Theories and Evidence from Tanzania", *Environment and Development Economics*, Vol. 4, No. 3, pp. 313-331.

Angelsen, A., D. van Soest, D. Kaimowitz et al. (2001), "Technological Change and Deforestation: a Theoretical Overview", in A. Angelsen and D. Kaimowitz (eds.), *Agricultural Technologies and Tropical Deforestation*, New York and Jakarta, CABI Publishing and Center for International Forestry Research.

Arrhenius, O. (1921), "Species and Area", *Journal of Ecology*, Vol. 9, pp. 95-99.

ASIES (Asociación de Investigación y Estudios Sociales) (1988), *Educación ambiental en Guatemala: una propuesta*, Guatemala.

Asturias, L., I. Mejía de Rodas, J. P. Rodas et al. (2001), *Diseño de un estudio etnográfico piloto sobre la influencia de PRONADE en el desarrollo local*, consultant report to the Ministerio de Educación and the Programa Nacional de Autogestión para el Desarrollo Educativo, January, Guatemala, mimeo.

Auty, R. M. (2001), "Introduction and Overview", in R. M. Auty (ed.), *Resource Abundance and Economic Development*, Oxford, Oxford University Press, pp. 3-15.

Baessa, Y. et al. (2000), *Informe de resultados del Programa Nacional de Rendimiento Escolar 1999*, Centro de Investigaciones Educativas, Universidad del Valle, and Ministerio de Educación, Guatemala, mimeo.

Baessa, Y. et al. (2001), *Análisis adicionales de resultados del Programa Nacional de Evaluación del Rendimiento Escolar 2000*, Centro de Investigaciones Educativas, Universidad del Valle, and Ministerio de Educación, Guatemala, mimeo.

Bailén, J. M. (2001), *Economic Growth in Guatemala*, Washington, D.C., Appendix I of the Article IV Consultation, International Monetary Fund, pp. 85-88, mimeo.

Banco de Guatemala (1981), "Establecimiento de una empresa ganadera en Petén", *Informe Económico*, Vol. 28, pp. 21-70.

Banco de Guatemala (2003), *Empleos y salarios: estadísticas del Instituto Guatemalteco de Seguridad Social, años 1960-2002*, Departamento de Estadísticas Económicas, Sección de Análisis de Mercado y Comercio Exterior, Guatemala, mimeo.

Banerjee, A., J. Dolado, J. Galbraith and D. F. Hendry (1993), *Cointegration, Error-Correction, and the Econometric Analysis of Non-Stationary Data*, Oxford, Oxford University Press.

Banerjee, A., J. J. Dolado and R. Mestre (1998), "Error-correction mechanism test for cointegration in a single-equation framework", *Journal of Time Series Analysis*, Vol. 19, No. 3, pp. 267-283.

Barbier, E. B. (2001), "The Economics of Tropical Deforestation and Land Use: An Introduction to the Special Issue", *Land Economics*, Vol. 77, No. 2, pp. 155-171.

Barbier, E. B. and J. C. Burgess (1996), "Economic Analysis of Deforestation in Mexico", *Environment and Development Economics*, Vol. 1, No. 2, pp. 203-239.

Barbier, E. B. and J. C. Burgess (2002), "The Economics of Tropical Deforestation", in N. Hanley and C. Roberts (eds.), *Issues in Environmental Economics*, Oxford, Blackwell.

Barro, R. J. (1998), "Notes on Growth Accounting", *NBER Working Paper* 6654, Cambridge.

Barro, R. J. (2001), "Human Capital and Growth", *American Economic Review*, Vol. 91, No. 2, pp. 12-17.

Barro, R. J. and J.-W. Lee (2001), "International data on educational attainment: updates and implications", *Oxford Economic Papers*, Vol. 53, Bd. 3, pp. 541-563.

Barro, R. J. and X. Sala-i-Martin (1995), *Economic Growth*, New York, McGraw-Hill.

Bassanini, A. and S. Scarpetta (2001), "Does Human Capital Matters for Growth in OECD Countries? Evidence from Pooled Meangroup Estimates" *OECD Working Paper*, ECO/WKP 2001/8.

Baumeister, E. (2001), "Formas de acceso a la tierra y al agua en Guatemala", *Cuadernos del Desarrollo Humano* 4, Guatemala, Sistema de las Naciones Unidas en Guatemala.

Benhabib, J. and M. Spiegel (1994), "The role of human capital in economic development: evidence from aggregate cross-country data", Journal of Monetary Economics, Vol. 34, pp. 143-173.

Benhabib, J. and M. Spiegel (2003), "Human capital and technology diffusion", *Working Paper* 2003-02, Federal Reserve Bank of San Francisco.

Bils, M. and P. Klenow (2000), "Does Schooling Cause Growth?", *American Economic Review*, Vol. 90, No. 5, pp. 1160-1183.

Bilsborrow, R. E. (1992), "Rural Poverty, Migration, and the Environment in Developing Countries: Three Case Studies", *World Bank Policy Research Working Paper 1017.*

Birdsall, N., T. Pinckney and R. Sabot (2001), "Natural Resources, Human Capital, and Growth", in R. M. Auty (ed.), *Resource Abundance and Economic Development*, Oxford, Oxford University Press, pp. 57-75.

Bluffstone, R. A. (1995), "The Effect of Labor Market Performance on Deforestation in Developing Countries under Open Access: An Example from Rural Nepal", *Journal of Environmental Economics and Management*, Vol. 29, pp. 42-63.

Boisvert, V. and A. Caron (2002), "The Convention on Biological Diversity: An Institutionalist Perspective on the Debates", *Journal of Economic Issues,* Vol. 36, No. 1, pp. 151-166.

Bosworth, B. P., S. M. Collins and Y. Chen (1996), "Accounting for Differences in Economic Growth" in Kohsaka, A. (ed.), *Structural Adjustment and Economic Reform: East Asia, Latin America, and Central and Eastern Europe*, IDE International Joint Research Project Series, No. 1, pp. 47-120.

Bratsberg, B. and D. Terrell (2002), "School Quality and Returns to Education of US Immigrants", *Economic Inquiry*, Vol. 20, No. 2, pp. 177-198.

Brühl, T. (2002), "Bisherige Erfolge und Misserfolge der Biodiversitätskonvention", *Gutachten im Auftrag der Enquete-Kommission 'Globalisierung der Weltwirtschaft — Herausforderungen und Antworten'*, February, Institut für vergleichende Politikwissenschaft und Internationale Beziehungen, Johann Wolfgang Goethe-University of Frankfurt.

Cabrera, C. (1995), "Síntesis histórica de la deforestación en Guatemala: perspectivas para un nuevo siglo", *Tikalia* (Guatemala), Vol. 15 (July-December), pp. 83-101.

Card, D. (1999), "The Causal Effect of Education on Earnings", in O. Ashenfelter and D. Card (eds.), *Handbook of Labor Economics*, Vol. 3a, Amsterdam, Elsevier, pp. 1801-1863.

Card, D. (2001), "Estimating the Return to Schooling: Progress on Some Persistent Econometric Problems", *Econometrica,* Vol. 69, No. 5, pp. 1127-1160.

CCAD (Comisión Centroamericana de Ambiente y Desarrollo) (1998), *Estado del ambiente y los recursos naturales en Centroamérica*, San José, Costa Rica.

CENSO (National Census) (1981), *Censos nacionales: IV habitación y IX población, características generales*, Guatemala, Dirección General de Estadística, published 1984.

CENSO (1994), *X censo nacional de Población y IX de habitación, características henerales de población y habitación*, Guatemala, Instituto Nacional de Estadística, published 1996.

CENSO (2003), *XI Censo nacional de población y X de habitación: características generales de población y habitación*, Guatemala, Instituto Nacional de Estadística, preliminary data, mimeo.

CEPAL (Comisión Económica para América Latina) and CELADE (Centro Latinoamericano de Demografía), División de Población (2000), "Guatemala: estimaciones y proyecciones de la población de ambos sexos por años calendarios y edades simples 1950-2050*", Boletín Demográfico*, No. 66.

CEPAL (2003), Macroeconomic Database, http://www.cepal.org/, October 2003.

Chayanov, A. K. (1925/1966), *The Theory of Peasant Economy*, Homewood, Irwin.

Chemonics International, BIOFOR Consortium, and International Resource Group EPIQ ICQ (2000), *Guatemala: Assessment and Analysis of Progress toward SO5 Goals in the Maya Biosphere Reserve*, Consultant's report submitted to USAID/G-CAP, Guatemala.

Chesterfield, R. (1994), *Indicators of Democratic Behavior in NEU Schools*, consultant report to USAID, July 15, Guatemala, mimeo.

Chomitz, K. M. and D. A. Gray (1996), "Roads, Land Use, and Deforestation: A Spatial Model Applied to Belize", *World Bank Economic Review*, Vol. 10, No. 3, pp. 487-512.

Chomitz, K. M. and T. S. Thomas (2001), "Geographic Patterns of Land Use and Land Intensity in the Brazilian Amazon", *World Bank Policy Research Working Paper* 2687.

CIEN (Centro de Investigaciones Económicas Nacionales) (1999), *Análisis del impacto de la autogestión: la experiencia del PRONADE*, Guatemala.

CIEN (2000a), *Análisis de la participación de la Instituciones de Servicios Educativos*, Guatemala, mimeo.

CIEN (2000b), *El Proceso de modernización de la educación: acciones realizadas y agenda pendiente en descentralización*, Guatemala.

CIEN (2002), *Informe de progreso educativo Guatemala*, July, Guatemala.

Cohen, D. and M. Soto (2001), "Growth and human capital: Good data, good results", *Technical Paper* 179, OECD Development Centre, Paris.

Comisión Consultiva para la Reforma Educativa (Commission for Education Reform) (1999), *Plan nacional de educación de largo plazo*, preliminary version, Guatemala.

Comisión para el Esclarecimiento Histórico (Commission for Historical Clarification) (1999), *Guatemala: memoria del silencio*, Guatemala, United Nations Office for Project Services.

CONAMA et al. (Comisión Nacional de Medio Ambiente) (1999a), *Conociendo el Sistema Guatemalteco de Areas Protegidas (SIGAP)*, Estrategia Nacional para la Conservación y Uso Sostenible de la Biodiversidad, Guatemala, mimeo.

CONAMA et al. (1999b), *Las áreas silvestres de Guatemala: ¿Tienen amenazas?* Estrategia Nacional para la Conservación y Uso Sostenible de la Biodiversidad, Guatemala, mimeo.

CONAMA et al. (1999c), *La vida silvestre: uso y conservación*, Estrategia Nacional para la Conservación y Uso Sostenible de la biodiversidad, Guatemala, mimeo.

CONAP (Consejo Nacional de Áreas Protegidas) (1997), *El estado de la Reserva de la Biósfera Maya en 1996*, Guatemala, CONAP/USAID/ Fondo Peregrino, mimeo.

Connor, E. and E. McCoy (1979), "The Statistics and Biology of the Species-Area Relationship", *American Naturalist*, Vol. 113, pp. 791-833.

Contreras-Hermosilla, A. (2000), "The Underlying Causes of Forest Decline", *Occasional Paper* 30, Center for International Forestry Research, Bogor.

Culbert, T. P. (1988), *The Collapse of Ancient States and Civilizations, Tucson*, University of Arizona Press.

Dasgupta, P. (1995), "Population, Poverty, and the Local Environment", *Scientific American*, Vol. 272, No. 2, pp. 26-31.

de Ferranti, D., G. E. Perry, I. Gill et al. (2002), *Closing the Gap in Education and Technology*, Advanced Conference Edition, World Bank Latin American and Caribbean Studies, Washington D.C.

de Gregorio (1992), "Economic Growth in Latin America", *Journal of Development Economics*, Vol. 39, pp. 59-84.

de La Cruz, J. R (1982), *Clasificación de zonas de vida de Guatemala a nivel de reconocimiento*, Ministerio de Agricultura, Ganadería y Alimentación and Instituto Nacional Forestal, Guatemala, mimeo.

de La Ossa, A. (2000), "Der zentralamerikanische Integrationsprozess: Ende einer Entwicklungsalternative", Ibero-Analysen 6, Ibero-Amerikanisches Institut Preußischer Kulturbesitz, Berlin.

Defensores de la Naturaleza (2001), *Impacto de la agricultura sostenible sobre la conservación de la biodiversidad, Reserva de la Biósfera Sierra de las Minas, Guatemala*, Washington D.C., Biodiversity Support Program.

Deger, S. and S. Sen (1995), "Military Expenditures in Developing Countries", in K. Hartley and T. Sandler (eds.), *Handbook of Defense Economics*, Vol. 1, Amsterdam, Elsevier.

Deininger, K. and B. Minten (1999), "Poverty, Policies, and Deforestation: The Case of Mexico", *Economic Development and Cultural Change*, Vol. 47, No. 2, pp. 313-344.

Deininger, K. and B. Minten (2002), "Determinants of Deforestation and the Economics of Protection: An Application to Mexico", *American Journal of Agricultural Economics*, Vol. 84, No. 4, pp. 943-960.

Dietz, S. and W. N. Adger (2003), "Economic Growth, Biodiversity Loss and Conservation Effort", *CSERGE Working Paper ECM 01-03*, Centre for Social and Economic Research on the Global Environment, University of East Anglia.

Dinerstein, E., D. M. Olson, D. J. Graham et al. (1995), *A Conservation Assessment of the Terrestrial Ecoregions of Latin America and the Caribbean*, Washington, D.C., World Bank et al.

Dvorak, K. A. (1992), "Resource Management by West African Farmers and the Economics of Shifting Cultivation", *American Journal of Agricultural Economics*, Vol. 74, pp. 809-815.

Easterly, W. (2001), *The Elusive Quest for Growth: Economists' Adventures and Misadventures in the Tropics*, Cambridge, MIT Press.

Edwards, J. (2002), "Education and Poverty in Guatemala", *Guatemala Poverty Assessment Program, Technical Paper* 3, World Bank, Washington D.C., mimeo.

Edwards, S. (2000), *La situación macroecómica en Guatemala: evaluación y recomendaciones sobre política monetaria y cambiaria de Guatemala*, Banco de Guatemala.

Elías, S., G. Gellert, E. Pape et al. (1997), *Evaluación de la sostenibilidad: el caso de Guatemala*, Guatemala, Facultad Latinoamericana de Ciencias Sociales and World Wildlife Fund.

ENCOVI (Living Standard Measurement Survey) (2000), *Encuesta Nacional sobre Condiciones de Vida*, Guatemala, Instituto Nacional de Estadística, published 2002.

ENEI (Employment and Income Survey) (2002), *Encuesta Nacional de Empleo e Ingresos*, Guatemala, Instituto Nacional de Estadística, published 2002-2003 (the data here is from UNDP).

ENIGFAM (Household Income Survey) (1998), *Encuesta Nacional de Ingresos y Gastos Familiares,* Guatemala, published 2000, Instituto Nacional de Estadística.

ENS (Socio-Demographic Survey) (1989), *Encuesta Nacional Socio-Demográfica*, Guatemala, Instituto Nacional de Estadística, mimeo (the database here is from UNDP/CEPAL).

ENSMI (Health Survey) (1999), *Encuesta Nacional de Salud y Materno Infantil 1998-1999*, Guatemala, Instituto Nacional de Estadística, published 2001.

Environmental Module ENSMI (1999*), Modulo Ambiental Petén en la Encuesta Nacional de Salud y Materno Infantil 1998-1999*, Instituto Nacional de Estadística, USAID, Measure/DHS+ and Macro International Inc., mimeo (the database here is from Luis Ochoa, Measure DHS+, ORC Marco, Calverton, USA).

Escobar, J. y C. Rodríguez (1989), "Situación de los recursos forestales de Guatemala", *El primer congreso Forestal Nacional*, *Colegio de Ingenieros Agrónomos*, Guatemala, mimeo.

Fadul, S. (1996), "La formación de maestros en Guatemala", *Cuadernos de la Reforma Educativa* 9, Guatemala, Asociación de Investigación y Estudios Sociales.

FAO (Food and Agriculture Organization of the United Nations) (1999). "Annotated Bibliography Forest Cover Change Guatemala", *Forest Resources Assessment Programme, Working Paper* 13, Rome.

FAO (2001), *State of the World's Forests*, Rome.

FAO (2002), Forestry Database, http://www.fao.org, December 2002.

FLACSO (Facultad Latinoamericana de Ciencias Sociales) (2000), *Nuevas perspectivas de desarrollo sostenible en Petén*, Guatemala.

Foro Interuniversitario (2000), *Bibliografía anotada sobre reforma educativa de Guatemala,* Centro de Información y Documentación Educativa de Guatemala, Universidad Rafael Landívar et al., Guatemala.

Foster, A. D. and M. R. Rosenzweig (1996), "Technical Change and Human-capital Returns and Investments", *American Economic Review*, Vol. 86, No. 4, pp. 931-953.

Funkhouser, E. (1997), "Demand-Side and Supply-Side Explanations for Barriers to Labor Market Mobility in Developing Countries: The Case of Guatemala", *Economic Development and Cultural Change*, Vol. 45, No. 2, pp. 341-366.

Galindo, J. L. (1999), "Propuesta para una estrategia financiera del Sistema Guatemalteco de Areas Protegidas", *Documento técnico* 10, Guatemala, Presidencia de la República, Consejo Nacional de Áreas Protegidas, mimeo.

Gellert, G. (2000), "Las migraciones como estrategias de sobrevivencia de los excluidos y sus determinantes territoriales", in V. Gálvez (ed.), *Guatemala: exclusión social y estrategias para enfrentarla*, Guatemala, Facultad Latinoamericana de Ciencias Sociales, pp. 173-343.

Gemmel, N. (1996), "Evaluating the impacts of human capital stocks and accumulation on economic growth: some new evidence", *Oxford Bulletin of Economics and Statistics*, Vol. 58, pp. 9-28.

Glewwe, P. (2002), "Schools and Skills in Developing Countries: Education Policies and Socioeconomic Outcomes", *Journal of Economic Literature*, Vol. 40, pp. 436-482.

Global Info Group (1999), *En Cifras: Guatemala, perfil integral del país*, Vol. I, No. 1.1, Guatemala and Miami.

Godoy, J. (1998), *Matrices de proyectos en ejecución y un perfil conceptual: diagnóstico resumido del SIGAP*, Guatemala, consultant's report to USAID, pp. 25-27, mimeo.

Godoy, R. (2001), *Indians, Markets, and Rainforests: Theory, Methods, Analysis,* New York, Columbia University Press.

Godoy, R. and M. Contreras (2001), "A Comparative Study of Education and Tropical Deforestation among Lowland Bolivian Amerindians: Forest Values, Environmental Externality, and School Subsidies", *Economic Development and Cultural Change*, Vol. 49, No. 3, pp. 555-574.

Godoy, R., K. Wilkie, P. O'Neill et al. (1997), "Household Determinants of Deforestation by Amerindians in Honduras", *World Development*, Vol. 25, No. 6, pp. 977-987.

Godoy, R., S. Groff and K. O'Neill (1998), "The Role of Education in Neotropical Deforestation: Household Evidence from Amerindians in Honduras", *Human Ecology*, Vol. 26, No. 4, pp. 649-675.

Gómez, R. and T. Ordoñez (1991), *Programa de estabilización y ajuste estructural: un proyecto nacional de corto y mediano plazo*, Vol. 1, "Escenarios y políticas macroeconómicas", Guatemala, SEGEPLAN (Secretaría General de Planificación Económica) y GTZ (Gesellschaft für Technische Zusammenarbeit), mimeo.

Grandia, L. (2000), "¿Cuántas personas quiere usted que vivan en el Petén?" in FLACSO (2000), *Nuevas perspectivas de desarrollo sostenible en Petén*, Guatemala, pp. 137-151.

Grandia, L., N. Schwartz, A. Corzo et al. (2001), *Guatemala: salud, migración y recursos naturales en Petén, resultados del módulo ambiental en la Encuesta de Salud Materno Infantil 1999*, Guatemala, Instituto Nacional de Estadística, U.S. Agency for International Development, Measure/DHS+ and Macro International, Calverton, mimeo.

Grossman, G. and E. Helpman (1991), Innovation and Growth in the Global Economy, Cambridge, MIT Press.

Grunberg, W., D. Guertin and W. Shaw (2000), "Modeling Deforestation Risk for the Maya Biosphere Reserve, Guatemala", *Paper presented at the Twentieth Annual ESRI International User Conference*, San Diego, California, mimeo.

Grupo de Servicios de Información (1999), *Skills Development, Technology and Productivity Study*, Consultant report to the World Bank and National Competitiveness Board, July, Guatemala, mimeo.

GTZ (Gesellschaft für Technische Zusammenarbeit) (2000), "Elementos de análisis de la situación del programa PRONADE y sugerencias para el futuro", *Asesoría técnica para la autogestión educativa, Proyecto Apoyo al MINEDUC, Convenio Ministerio de Educación y Misión Técnica Alemana*, consultant report, April, Guatemala, mimeo.

Haeussler, A. (1993), *Análisis costo-beneficio de la inversión en la educación en Guatemala*, Tesis de Licenciatura, Facultad de Ciencias Económicas, Universidad Francisco Marroquín, Guatemala, mimeo.

Hanushek, E. (1995), "Interpreting Recent Research on Schooling on Developing Countries", *World Bank Research Observer*, Vol. 10, No. 2, pp. 227-246.

Harris, J. and M. Todaro (1970), "Migration, Unemployment and Development", *American Economic Review*, Vol. 60, No. 1, pp. 126-142.

Hayami, Y. and V. W. Ruttan (1985), *Agricultural Development: An International Perspective*, Baltimore, John Hopkins University Press.

Heltberg, R. (2001), "Determinants and Impact of Local Institutions for Common Resource Management", *Environment and Development Economics*, Vol. 6, No. 2, pp. 183-208.

Hendry, D. F. (1995), *Dynamic Econometrics*, Oxford, Oxford University Press.

Huffman, W. (2001), "Human Capital: Education and Agriculture", in B. L. Gardner and G. C. Rausser (eds.), *Handbook of Agricultural Economics*, Vol. 1a, Amsterdam, Elsevier, pp. 333-381.

IDB (Inter-American Development Bank) (2000), "Reforming Primary and Secondary Education in Latin America and the Caribbean: An IDB Strategy", *Sustainable Development Department, Sector Strategy and Policy Paper Series EDU-113*, Washington D.C.

IDB (2001), *Guatemala Country Paper*, Washington D.C., mimeo.

IDESAC (Instituto para el Desarrollo Económico y Social de América Central) (2001), *Bibliografías sobre reforma educativa*, Guatemala.

INAB (Instituto Nacional de Bosques) (2000), *Informe final, fase I: mapa de cobertura forestal para 1999*, Guatemala, mimeo.

INAFOR (Instituto Nacional Forestal) (1982), *Memoria de labores 1982*, Guatemala, mimeo.

Jamison, D. T. and L. I. Lau (1982), *Farmer Education and Farm Efficiency*, Baltimore, John Hopkins University Press.

Jaramillo, C. F. and T. Kelly (1997), *Deforestation and Property Rights in Latin America*, Environment Department, Inter-American Development Bank, Washington D.C.

Jenkins, H. (1995), "Education and production in the United Kingdom", *Economics Discussion Paper* 101, Nuffield College, Oxford.

Jiminez, E. and Y. Sawada (1999), "Do Community-Managed Schools Work? An Evaluation of El Salvador's EDUCO Program", *World Bank Economic Review*, Vol. 13, No. 3, pp. 415-441.

Johannsen, J. (2003), *"I'm Weaver and Farmer at the Same Time": Non-Agricultural Employment, Gender and Development in Rural Guatemala*, unpublished M.Sc. thesis, September, Institute of Rural Development, University of Goettingen.

Jones, C. I. (1995), "Time Series Tests of Endogenous Growth Models", *Quarterly Journal of Economics*, Vol. 110, No. 2, pp. 495-525.

Jones, C. I. (2003), "Growth, Capital Shares, and a New Perspective on Production Functions", Department of Economics, U.C. Berkeley, June 12, mimeo.

Kaimowitz, D. (1995), *Land Tenure, Land Markets, and Natural Resource Management in the Petén and Northern Transversal of Guatemala*, Bogor, Center for International Policy Research, mimeo.

Kaimowitz, D. (circa 1996), *Livestock and Deforestation in Central America in the 1980s and 1990s: A Policy Perspective*, Bogor, Center for International Policy Research, mimeo.

Kaimowitz, D. and A. Angelsen (1999), "Rethinking the Causes of Deforestation: Lessons from Economic Models", *World Bank Economic Review*, Vol. 14, No. 1, pp. 73-98.

Kaimowitz, D. and A. Angelsen (2002), *Economic Models of Tropical Deforestation: A Review*, Bogor, Center for International Forestry Research, third draft, mimeo.

Katz, E. (2000), "Social Capital and Natural Capital: A Comparative Analysis of Land Tenure and Natural Resource Management in Guatemala", *Land Economics*, Vol. 76, No. 1, pp. 114-132.

Klasen, S. (2002), "Low Schooling for Girls, Slower Growth for All? Cross-country Evidence on the Effect of Gender Inequality in Education and Economic Development", *World Bank Economic Review*, Vol. 16, No. 3, pp. 345-373.

Laurits R., D. Cummings and D. W. Jorgenson (1980), "Economic Growth, 1947-73: An International Comparison", in J. W. Kendrick and B. N. Vaccara (eds.), *New Developments in Productivity Measurement and Analysis*, Studies in Income and Wealth, Vol. 44, Chicago, University of Chicago Press.

Lee, J.-W. (1995), "Capital Goods Import and Long-run Growth", *Journal of Development Economics*, Vol. 48, pp. 91-110.

Leonard, H. (1987), *Natural resources and economic development in Guatemala*, New Brunswick, International Institute for Environment and Development, mimeo.

Lima, R. E. (1995), *Aproximación a la cosmovisión maya*, Instituto de Investigaciones Económicas y Sociales, Universidad Rafael Landívar, Guatemala.

Loayza, N., P. Fajnzylber and C. Calderón (2002), *Economic Growth in Latin America and the Caribbean: Stylized Facts, Explanations and Forecasts*, World Bank, Washington D.C.

Lockheed, M. E. and A. M. Vespor (1991), *Improving Primary Education in Developing Countries*, Oxford, Oxford University Press.

Loening, L. and M. Markussen (2003), "Pobreza, deforestación y sus eventuales implicaciones para la biodiversidad en Guatemala", *Economía, Sociedad y Territorio* (Mexico), Vol. 4, No. 14, pp. 297-315.

Loening, L. J. (2002), "The Impact of Education on Economic Growth in Guatemala: A Time Series Analysis Applying an Error-correction Methodology", *Discussion Paper* 87, Ibero-America Institute for Economic Research, University of Goettingen.

López, P. (1998), *Potencial de carbono y absorción de dióxido de carbono de la biomasa en pie por encima del suelo en los bosques de la República de Guatemala*, consultant report, Guatemala, mimeo.

López, R. and A. Valdés (2000), "Fighting Rural Poverty in Latin America: New Evidence and Policies" in R. López and A. Valdés (eds.), *Rural Poverty in Latin America*, New York, St. Martin's Press, pp. 1-31.

López-Cálix, J. R. (2002), "Pacto fiscal y macroeconomía del ciclo electoral en Guatemala", *Banca Central* (Guatemala), Vol. 11, pp. 79-96.

Lovell, G. W. (1988), "Resisting Conquest: Development and Guatemalan Indians", in J. M. Kirk and G. W. Schuyler (eds.), *Democracy, Development and Change*, New York, Praeger, pp. 101-107.

Lucas, R. E. (1988), "On the Mechanics of Economic Development", *Journal of Monetary Economics*, Vol. 22, pp. 3-42.

Lucas, R. E. (1990), "Why Doesn't Capital Flow from Rich to Poor Countries?" *American Economic Review*, Vol. 80, No. 2, pp. 92-96.

Lucas, R. E. (1997), "Internal Migration in Developing Countries", in M. R. Rosenzweig and O. Stark (eds.), *Handbook of Population and Family Economics*, Amsterdam, Elsevier, pp. 721-789.

Lugo, A. E., J. A. Parrotta and S. Brown (1993), "Loss in Species Caused by Tropical Deforestation and Their Recovery Through Management", *Ambio*, Vol. 22, No. 2-3, pp. 106-109.

Luján, J. (2000), *Breve historia contemporánea de Guatemala*, Mexico, Colección popular 552, Fondo de la Cultura Económica.

Maas, P. (2004), *Zur Relevanz kulturspezifischen Wissens der Q'eqchi für den Erhalt von Biodiversität im Rahmen von Naturschutzprojekten in Alta Verapaz, Guatemala*, forthcoming Ph.D. thesis, Institut für Ethnologie, University of Göttingen.

MAGA (Ministerio de Agricultura, Ganadería y Alimentación), PAFG (Plan de Acción Forestal) and INAB (Instituto Nacional de Bosques) (1998), *Proyecciones del Programa de Incentivos Forestales y necesidades de inversiones adicionales*, Guatemala, mimeo.

Mankiw, N. G., D. Romer and D. N. Weil (1992), "A Contribution to the Empirics of Economic Growth", Quarterly Journal of Economics, Vol. 107, pp. 407-437.

Marqués, J. and I. Bannon (2003), "Central America: Education Reform in a Post-Conflict Setting, Opportunities and Challenges", *CPR Working Papers* 4, World Bank, Social Development Department, Environmentally and Socially Sustainable Development Network.

Maya', Q. K. (1995), "Comentarios sobre algunos nombres de comunidades e idiomas mayas", *Boletín de Lingüística*, Universidad Rafael Landívar, Vol. 9, No. 51, pp. 1-5.

Mazumdar, D. (1988), "Rural-Urban Migration in Developing Countries", in E. S. Mills (ed.), *Handbook of Regional and Urban Economics*, Vol. 2, Amsterdam, Elsevier, pp. 1097-1028.

McArthur, R. H. and E. O. Wilson (1967), *The Theory of Island Biography*, Princeton, Princeton University Press.

Méndez, C. (1999), "How Old is the Petén Tropical Forest?" in J. D. Nations, C. J. Rader and I. Q. Neubauer (1999), *Thirteen Ways of Looking at a Tropical Forest: Guatemala's Maya Biosphere Reserve,* Washington D.C., Conservation International, pp. 31-38.

Merlet, M., G. Farrell, J.-M. Laurent et al. (1992), *Identificación de un programa regional de desarrollo sostenible en el trópico húmedo*, consultant report, Paris, Groupe de Recherche et d'Echanges Technologiques, mimeo.

Merrem, G. (2001), "Die Diskriminierung der Indianer und die soziale Ungleichheit ist schlimmer als in den letzten Jahren der Apartheid in Südafrika: Der UN Sonderbeauftragte Merrem kritisiert den Umgang der guatemaltekischen Gesellschaft mit der indianischen Mehrheit des Landes", *Frankfurter Allgemeine Zeitung*, August 10, 2001.

Mincer, J. (1974), *Schooling, Experience and Earnings*, New York, Columbia University Press.

MINEDUC (Ministerio de Educación) (1999), *Memoria de labores* 1996-1999: llevando la educación a los lugares más lejanos, Guatemala.

MINEDUC (2003), *Programa Nacional de Autogestión para el Desarrollo Educativo*, http://www.mineduc.gob.gt/administracion/dependencias/centrales/pronade/pronade.htm, December 2003

MINEDUC (various years), Unidad de Informática, *Anuario estadístico de la educación*, Guatemala, mimeo (booklets for 1991-2000 in printed version, data for 2001 on CD-ROM, preliminary data for 2002 comes directly from the ministry's statistical unit).

MINEDUC and PRONADE (Programa Nacional de Autogestión para el Desarrollo Educativo) (2000a), *Estudio cuasi-experimental de resultados del año 1999*, informe final, Guatemala, mimeo.

MINEDUC and PRONADE (2000b), *Observaciones al informe 'Elementos de análisis de la situación del programa PRONADE y sugerencias para el futuro' de la Misión Técnica Alemana GTZ*, June, Guatemala, mimeo.

MINEDUC and PRONADE (2001), *Manual del COEDUCA*, 2nd edition, Guatemala.

MINEDUC and PRONADE (Programa Nacional de Autogestión para el Desarrollo Educativo) (1999), *Estudio cuasi-experimental de resultados del año 1998*, informe final, Guatemala, mimeo.

MINEDUC and SEGEPLAN (Secretaría General del Consejo Nacional de Planificación Económica) (1980), *Datos estadísticos de la educación primaria rural urbana en Guatemala: situación actual y proyecciones*, Guatemala, mimeo.

Mitchell, B. R. (1998), *International Historical Statistics: The Americas 1750-1993*, London, Macmillian.

Mittak, W. L. (1977), "Guatemala: estudios para la reforestación nacional, fortalecimiento al sector forestal", *Documento de Trabajo* 25, UNDP/FAO, Guatemala, mimeo.

Molketin, G. (2002), *Kriegsursachen und Friedensbedingungen in Guatemala: eine historische Untersuchung über das kriegsursächliche Gewaltgeschehen und die Herausforderungen an den gegenwärtigen Prozess der Friedenskonsolidierung*, Europäische Hochschulschriften Reihe 31, Band 452, Frankfurt am Main, Verlag Peter Lang.

Morales, R. A. (1998), "Determinants of Growth in an Error-Correction Model for El Salvador", *IMF Working Paper* 98/104.

Morán, I. E. and H. A. Valle (2002), "Tres métodos alternativos para la estimación del PIB potencial: una estimación para Guatemala", *Banca Central* (Guatemala), Vol. 11, pp. 97-112.

Müller, D. and M. Zeller (2002), "Land Use Dynamics in the Central Highlands of Vietnam: A Spatial Model Combining Village Survey Data with Satellite Imagery Interpretation", *Agricultural Economics*, Vol. 27, No. 3, pp. 333-354.

Myers, N., R. A. Mittermeier, C. G. Mittermeier et al. (2000), "Biodiversity hotspots for conservation priorities", *Nature*, No. 403, pp. 853-858.

Nakajima, C. (1986), *Subjective equilibrium theory of the farm household*, Amsterdam, Elsevier.

Nations, J. D. and D. Komer (1983), "Rainforests and the Hamburger Society", Environment, Vol. 25, No. 3, pp. 12-20.

Nations, J. D., B. Houseal, I. Ponciano et al. (1989), *Biodiversidad en Guatemala: evaluación de la diversidad biológica y los bosques tropicales*, Washington D.C, Centro para el Desarrollo Internacional y el Medio Ambiente and World Resource Institute.

Nations, J. D., C. J. Rader and I. Q. Neubauer (1999), *Thirteen Ways of Looking at a Tropical Forest: Guatemala's Maya Biosphere Reserve*, Washington D.C., Conservation International.

Nehru, V. and A. Dhareshwar (1993), "A New Database on Physical Capital Stock: Sources, Methodology, and Results", *Revista de Análisis Económico*, Vol. 8, No. 1, pp. 37-59.

Nehru, V. and A. Dhareshwar (1994), "New Estimates of Total Factor Productivity Growth for Developing and Industrial Countries", *World Bank Policy Research Working Paper* 1313.

Nehru, V., E. Swanson and A. Dubey (1995), "A New Database on Human Capital Stock in Developing and Industrial Countries: Sources, Methodology and Results", *Journal of Development Economics*, Vol. 42, No. 2, pp. 379-401.

Nelson, G. and D. Hellerstein (1997), "Do Roads Cause Deforestation? Using Satellite Images in Econometric Analysis of Land Use", *American Journal of Agricultural Economics*, Vol. 79, pp. 80-88.

Nelson, R. and E. Phelps (1966), "Investments in Humans, Technological Diffusion, and Economic Growth", *American Economic Review*, Vol. 56, No. 1-2, pp. 69-75.

O'Hara, S. L, F. A. Street-Perrott and T. P. Burt (1993), "Accelerated Soil Erosion Around a Mexican Highland Lake Caused by Prehispanic Agriculture", *Nature*, Vol. 362, No. 6415, pp. 48-50.

OECD (Organisation for Economic Co-operation and Development) (2001a), *Manual on Productivity Measurement: A Guide to the Measurement of Industry-Level and Aggregate Productivity Growth*, Paris, mimeo.

OECD (2001b), *Measuring Capital: A Manual on the Measurement of Capital Stocks, Consumption of Fixed Capital and Capital Services*, Paris, mimeo.

OAS (Organization of American States) (1991), *República de Guatemala: proyecto de manejo y conservación de los recursos naturales renovables de la Cuenca del Río Chixoy*, Washington D.C., mimeo.

PAFG (Plan de Acción Forestal) (1996), *Plan de Acción Forestal de Guatemala: documento base y perfiles de proyectos*, Guatemala, PAFG/USAID, mimeo.

Pagán, J. A. (2002), "Gender Differences in Labor Market Decisions in Rural Guatemala", *Review of Development Economics*, Vol. 6, No. 3, pp. 428-441.

Papageorgiou, C. (2003), "Distinguishing between the Effects of Primary and Post-Primary Education on Economic Growth", *Review of Development Economics*, Vol. 7, No. 1, pp. 1-22.

Pearce, D. and K. Brown (eds.) (1994), *The Causes of Tropical Deforestation: The Economic and Statistical Analysis of Factors Giving Rise to the Loss of Tropical Forests*, London, University College London Press.

Pendleton, L. H. and E. L. Howe (2002), "Market Integration, Development, and Smallholder Forest Clearance", *Land Economics*, Vol. 78, No. 1, pp. 1-19.

Pesaran, M. H., Y. Shin and R. J. Smith (2001), "Bounds testing approaches to the analysis of level relationships", *Journal of Applied Econometrics*, Vol. 16, pp. 289-326.

Petrakis, P. E. and D. Stamatakis (2002), "Growth and Educational Levels: A Comparative Analysis", *Economics of Education Review*, Vol. 21, pp. 513-521.

Pfaff, A. S. (1997), "What Drives Deforestation in the Brazilian Amazon? Evidence from Satellite and Socio-economic Data", *World Bank Policy Research Working Paper* 1772.

Phillips, J. M. and R. P. Marble (1986), "Farmer Education and Efficiency: a Frontier Production Function Approach", *Economics of Education Review*, Vol. 5, No. 3, pp. 257-264.

Pichón, F. J. (1997), "Colonist Land-Allocation Decisions, Land Use, and Deforestation in the Ecuadorian Amazon Frontier", *Economic Development and Cultural Change*, Vol. 45, pp. 707-744.

Pissarides, C. A. (2000), "Human capital and growth: a synthesis report", Technical Paper 168, OECD Development Centre, Paris.

Plotkin, J. B., M. D. Potts, D. W. Yu et al. (2000), "Predicting species diversity in tropical forests", *Proceedings of the National Academy of Sciences*, Vol. 97, No. 20, pp. 10850-10854.

Prera, M. (1999), *Estimación de una función de producción para Guatemala*, Tesis de Licenciatura en Economía, Facultad de Ciencias Económicas, Universidad Francisco Marroquín, Guatemala.

Pritchett, L. (2001), "Where Has All the Education Gone?" *World Bank Economic Review*, Vol. 15, No. 3, pp. 367-391.

PRONERE (School Survey on Student's Achievement) (2000), *Encuesta del Programa Nacional de Evaluación del Rendimiento Escolar 2000*, Universidad del Valle and Ministerio de Educación, mimeo (the database here is from the Centro de Investigaciones Educativas, Universidad del Valle).

Psacharopoulos, G. and A. M. Arriagada (1986), "The Educational Composition of the Labor Force: An International Comparison" *International Labor Review*, Vol. 125, No. 5, pp. 561-574.

Psacharopoulos, G. and H. A. Patrinos (2002), "Returns to Investment in Education: A Further Update", *World Bank Policy Research Working Paper* 2881.

Renner, S. (2003), *Diversität und Struktur der Avifauna in Bergnebelwäldern von Guatemala: Auswirkungen von Schutzstrategien und deren Evaluierung auf den Erhalt der Primärwälder aus naturschutzbiologischer Sicht*, Ph.D. thesis, Zentrum für Naturschutz, University of Göttingen.

Rodríguez, F. and D. Rodrik (2000), "Trade Policy and Economic Growth: A Skeptic's Guide to the Cross-National Evidence", in B. Bernanke and K. Rogoff (eds.), *NBER Macroeconomics Annual 2000*, Cambridge, MIT Press.

Rodrik, D. (1999), "Where Did All the Growth Go? External Shocks, Social Conflict, and Growth Collapses", *Journal of Economic Growth*, Vol. 4, No. 4, pp. 385-412.

Roldós, J. (1997), "Potential Output Growth in Emerging Market Countries: The Case of Chile", *IMF Working Paper* 97/104.

Romer, P. M. (1990a), "Endogenous Technical Change", *Journal of Political Economy*, Vol. 98, No. 5, pp. S71-S102.

Romer, P. M. (1990b), "Human Capital and Growth: Theory and Evidence", *Carnegie-Rochester Conference Series on Public Policy*, Vol. 32, pp. 251-286.

Rosenfeld, A. (1999), "Oil Exploitation in the Forest", in J. D. Nations, C. J. Rader and I. Q. Neubauer (1999), *Thirteen Ways of Looking at a Tropical Forest: Guatemala's Maya Biosphere Reserve,* Washington D.C., Conservation International, pp. 68-76.

Rozelle, S., J. E. Taylor and A. de Brauw (1999), "Migration, Remittances, and Agricultural Productivity in China", *American Economic Review*, Vol. 89, No. 2, pp. 287-291.

Sader, S. A., D. Hayes, M. Coan et al. (2001), "Forest monitoring of a remote biosphere reserve", *International Journal of Remote Sensing*, Vol. 22, No. 10, pp. 1937-1950.

Sader, S. A., E. B. Martínez, D. E. Irwin et al. (2000), "Estimación de la deforestación en la Reserva Biósfera Maya 1997-1999", in FLACSO (2000), *Nuevas perspectivas de desarrollo sostenible en Petén*, Guatemala, pp. 321-324.

Sagastume, R. (1992), *Informe mapa de la cubierta forestal de la República de Guatemala*, Guatemala, Plan de Acción Forestal, mimeo.

Sakellariou, C. N. (1995), "Human Capital and Industry Wage Structure in Guatemala", *World Bank Policy Research Working Paper* 1445.

Sala-i-Martin, X. (2002), "15 Years of New Growth Economics: What Have We Learnt?" *Discussion Paper* 102-47, Department of Economics, Columbia University.

Scheetz, T. (2000), "Military Expenditures and Guatemala's Peace Process", in J. Brömmelhörster (ed.), *Demystifying the Peace Dividend*, BICC Disarmament and Conversion Studies 1, Baden-Baden, Nomos-Verlagsgesellschaft.

Schubert, R. and S. Dietz (2001), "Environmental Kuznets Curve, Biodiversity and Sustainability", *ZEF Discussion Paper on Development Policy* 40, Center for Development Research, Bonn.

Schultz, T. P. (1988), "Education Investment and Returns", in H. Chenery and T. Srinivasan (eds.), *Handbook of Development Economics*, Amsterdam, Elsevier, pp. 544-630.

Schultz, T. P. (2001), "Women's Roles in the Agricultural Household: Bargaining and Human Capital Investments", in B. L. Gardner and G. C. Rausser (eds.), *Handbook of Agricultural Economics*, Vol. 1a, Amsterdam, Elsevier, pp. 383-456.

Schwartz, N. B. (1987), "Colonization of Northern Guatemala: The Petén", *Journal of Anthropological Research*, Vol. 43, No. 2, pp. 163-183.

Schwartz, N. B. (1990), *Forest Society: A Social History of Petén, Guatemala*, 3rd edition, Philadelphia, University of Pennsylvania Press.

Schwartz, N. B. (1995a), "Colonization, Development and Deforestation in Petén, Northern Guatemala", in M. Painter and W. H. Durham (eds.), *The Social Causes of Environmental Destruction in Latin America*, Ann Arbor, University of Michigan Press, pp. 101-130.

Schwartz, N. B. (1995b), "Reprivatización y privación: sistema tradicional y contemporáneo de tenencia de la tierra en el Petén, Guatemala", *Mesoamerica*, Vol. 29, pp. 215-232.

Schweigert, T. E. (1993), "Commercial Sector Wages and Subsistence Sector Labor Productivity in Guatemalan Agriculture", *World Development*, Vol. 21, No. 1, pp. 81-91.

Schweigert, T. E. (1994) "Penny Capitalism: Efficient but Poor or Inefficient and (Less Than) Second Best?", *World Development*, Vol. 22, No. 5, pp. 721-735.

SEGEPLAN (Secretaría General del Consejo Nacional de Planificación Económica), Unidad de Empleo y Población (1978), *Cuadros estadísticos de población y PEA: censos 1950, 1964 y 1973*, Guatemala, mimeo.

SEGEPLAN and MAGA (Ministerio de Agricultura, Ganadería y Alimentación) (1984), *Recopilación de información comparativa de los censos agropecuarios 1950, 1964 y 1979 y series de superficie, producción y disponibilidad por rubros agrícolas, 1950-1982*, Guatemala, mimeo.

Segovia, A. and J. Lardé (2002), "El funcionamiento económico de Guatemala durante el periodo 1970-2001: cambios registrados y desafíos futuros" in UNDP, World Bank and USAID (eds.), *Desafíos del crecimiento económico en Guatemala*, conference edition, December 9th, Guatemala, mimeo.

Shriar, A. J. (2001), "The Dynamics of Agricultural Intensification and Resource Conservation in the Buffer Zone of the Maya Biosphere Reserve, Petén, Guatemala", *Human Ecology*, Vol. 29, No. 1, pp. 27-48.

Singh, I., L. Squire and J. Strauss (1986), *Agricultural Household Models: Extensions, Applications, and Policy*, Baltimore, John Hopkins University Press.

Sianesi, B. and J. van Reenen (2003), "The returns to education: macroeconomics", *Journal of Economic Surveys*, Vol. 17, No. 2, pp. 157-200.

Solow, R. M. (1956), "A Contribution to the Theory of Economic Growth", *Quarterly Journal of Economics*, Vol. 70, pp. 65-94.

Solow, R. M. (1957), "Technical Change and the Aggregate Production Function", *Review of Economics and Statistics*, Vol. 39, No. 3, pp. 312-320.

Southgate, D. and M. Basterrechea, M. (1993), "Population Growth, Public Policy and Resource Degradation: The Case of Guatemala", *Ambio*, Vol. 21, No. 7, pp. 460-464.

Spielmann, H. O. (1973), "Ursachen, Merkmale und Bedeutung der Bevölkerungsverschiebungen in Guatemala", *Hamburger Geographische Studien* 30, Institut für Geographie und Wirtschaftsgeographie, Universität Hamburg, Verlag Ferdinand Hirt.

Stedmann-Edwards, P. (1998), *Socioeconomic Root Causes of Biodiversity Loss*, Macroeconomics for Sustainable Development Program Office, World Wildlife Fund for Nature, Washington D.C.

Stryker, J. D. (1976), "Population Density, Agricultural Technique, and Land Utilization in a Village Economy", *American Economic Review*, Vol. 66, No. 3, pp. 347-358.

Tax, S. (1953), *Penny Capitalism: A Guatemalan Indian Economy*, Smithsonian Institution, Institute of Social Anthropology, Publication 16, Washington D.C., U.S. Government Printing Office.

Temple, J. R. (2001), "Generalizations that aren't? Evidence on education and growth", *European Economic Review*, Vol. 45, pp. 905-918.

Uemura, M. (1999), *Community Participation in Education: What Do We Know?* Washington D.C., World Bank.

UN Convention on Biological Diversity (1992), http://www.biodiv.org/doc/legal/cbd-en.pdf, November 2002.

UNDP (United Nations Development Programme) (1998), "Guatemala: los contrastes del desarrollo humano", *Informe Nacional de Desarrollo Humano 1998*, Guatemala, Sistema de las Naciones Unidades en Guatemala.

UNDP (1999), "Guatemala: el rostro rural del desarrollo humano", *Informe Nacional de Desarrollo Humano 1999*, Guatemala, Sistema de las Naciones Unidades en Guatemala.

UNDP (2000), "Guatemala: la fuerza incluyente del desarrollo humano", *Informe Nacional de Desarrollo Humano 2000*, Guatemala, Sistema de las Naciones Unidades en Guatemala.

UNDP (2002), "Guatemala: desarrollo humano, mujeres y salud", *Informe Nacional de Desarrollo Humano 2002*, Guatemala, Sistema de las Naciones Unidades en Guatemala.

UNDP (2003a), *Guatemala: una agenda para el desarrollo humano*, Informe Nacional del Desarrollo Humano 2003, Guatemala, Sistema de las Naciones Unidas en Guatemala.

UNDP (2003b), *Human Development Report*, New York, Oxford University Press.

UNEP (United Nations Environment Programme) (2002), *Global Environment Outlook 3*, Geneva.

UNESCO (United Nations Educational, Scientific and Cultural Organization) (1955), *World Survey of Education*, Paris.

UNESCO (1958), *World Survey of Education, Part II: Primary Education.* Paris.

UNESCO (1961), *World Survey of Education, Part III: Secondary Education.* Paris.

UNESCO (1966), *World Survey of Education, Part IV: Higher Education*, Paris.

UNESCO (various years), *Statistical Yearbook*, Paris.

Utting, P. (1993), *Trees, People and Power: Social Dimensions of Deforestation and Forest Protection in Central America*, Geneva, United Nations Research Institute for Social Development and World Wildlife Fund.

Vakis, R. (2002), "Guatemala: Livelihoods, Labor Markets, and Rural Poverty", *Technical Paper* 1, Guatemala Poverty Assessment Program, World Bank, Washington D.C., mimeo.

Valenzuela de Pisano, I. (1996), *Agricultura y bosque en Guatemala: estudio de caso en Petén y Sierra de las Minas*, Guatemala, Universidad Rafael Landívar et al.

Valerio, A. and C. Rojas (2000), *Education Decentralization in Guatemala*, photocopy draft, World Bank, mimeo.

van Soest, D. P., E. H. Bulte, A. Angelsen et al. (2002), "Technological change and tropical deforestation: a perspective at the household level", *Environment and Development Economics*, Vol. 7, pp. 269-280.

Velez, E., E. Schiefelbein and J. Valenzuela (1993), "Factors Affecting Achievement in Primary Schools: A Review of the Literature for Latin America and the Caribbean", *World Bank Human Resources Development and Operations Policy Department Working Paper* 2, Washington D.C.

von Arnsberg, J. (1994), "Economic Parameters of Deforestation", *World Bank Policy Research Working Paper* 1350.

von Thünen, J. H. (1826/1966), *Der isolierte Staat in Beziehung auf Landwirtschaft und Nationalökonomie*, Darmstadt, wissenschaftliche Buchgesellschaft (reprint of the Berlin edition from 1875).

Vosti, S. A., J. Witcover and C. L. Carpentier (2002), "Agricultural Intensification by Smallholders in the Western Brazilian Amazon: From Deforestation to Sustainable Land Use", *Research Report* 130, International Food Policy Research Institute, Washington D.C.

Vosti, S. and T. Reardon (1997), "Poverty-Environment Links in Rural Areas of Developing Countries", in S. Vosti and T. Reardon (eds.), *Sustainability, Growth, and Poverty Alleviation: A Policy and Agroecological Perspective*, Baltimore, John Hopkins University Press, pp. 47-65.

Walker, R., S. Perz, M. Caldas et al. (2002), "Land Use and Land Cover Change in Forest Frontiers: The Role of Households Life Cycles", *International Regional Science Review*, Vol. 25, No. 2, pp. 169-199.

Wilkie, J. W. (ed.) (1993), *Statistical Abstract of Latin America*, UCLA Latin American Center Publications, No. 30, parts 1 and 2, Los Angeles, USA.

World Bank (1995a), *Guatemala: tenencia agraria y manejo de los recursos naturales*, Report No. 14553-GU, Washington D.C., mimeo.

World Bank (1995b), *Guatemala: An Assessment of Poverty*, Report No. 12313-GU, Washington D.C.

World Bank (1995), *Guatemala Basic Education Strategy: Equity and Efficiency in Education*, Report No. 13304-GU, Washington D.C.

World Bank (1996), *Guatemala: Building Peace with Rapid and Equitable Growth*, Country Economic Memorandum, Report No. 15352-GU, Washington D.C.

World Bank (1997), *Guatemala Basic Education Reform Project*, Project Appraisal Document, Report No. PIC703, Washington, D.C.

World Bank (2002), World Development Indicators, CD-ROM, Washington D.C.

World Bank (2003a), *Guatemala: Poverty in Guatemala*, Report No. 24221-GU, Washington D.C.

World Bank (2003b), *Guatemala: Country Economic Memorandum Concept Paper*, Central American Department, Latin American and the Caribbean Region, July 9th, Washington D.C. and Guatemala, mimeo.

World Bank (2003c), World Development Indicators, http://www.worldbank.org/data/wdi2003/index.htm, October 2003.

World Bank et al. (2003), *Household Fuel Use and Fuel Switching in Guatemala*, Joint UNDP/World Bank Energy Sector Management Assistance Programme, Washington D.C., mimeo.

Wößmann, L. (2003), "Specifying human capital", *Journal of Economic Surveys*, Vol. 17, No. 2, pp. 239-270.

WRI (World Resources Institute) (1996), *World resources 1996-1997: a guide to the global environment,* New York, Oxford University Press.

Göttinger Studien zur Entwicklungsökonomik
Göttingen Studies in Development Economics

Herausgegeben von / Edited by Hermann Sautter

Die Bände 1-8 sind über die Vervuert Verlagsgesellschaft (Frankfurt/M.) zu beziehen.

Bd./Vol. 9 Hermann Sautter / Rolf Schinke (eds.): Social Justice in a Market Economy. 2001.

Bd./Vol. 10 Philipp Albert Theodor Kircher: Poverty Reduction Strategies. A comparative study applied to empirical research. 2002.

Bd./Vol. 11 Matthias Blum: Weltmarktintegration, Wachstum und Innovationsverhalten in Schwellenländern. Eine theoretische Diskussion mit einer Fallstudie über »Argentinien 1990-1999". 2003.

Bd./Vol.12 Jan Müller-Scheeßel: Die Privatisierung und Regulierung des Wassersektors. Das Beispiel Buenos Aires/Argentinien. 2003.

Bd./Vol.13 Ludger J. Löning: Economic Growth, Biodiversity Conservation, and the Formation of Human Capital in a Developing Country. 2004.

www.peterlang.de

Druck:
CPI Druckdienstleistungen GmbH
im Auftrag der
Kolibri 360 GmbH
Ferdinand-Jühlke-Str. 7
99095 Erfurt

FSC
www.fsc.org
MIX
Papier | Fördert gute Waldnutzung
FSC® C083411

Kolibri 360 GmbH
Ferdinand-Jühlke-Straße 7
99095 Erfurt, Deutschland
produktsicherheit@kolibri360.de